# PSYCHIATRIC ASPECTS OF MINIMAL BRAIN DYSFUNCTION IN ADULTS

Adult MBD Conference, March 3–4, 1978
Scottsdale, Arizona
Leopold Bellak, M.D., Chairman

# PSYCHIATRIC ASPECTS OF MINIMAL BRAIN DYSFUNCTION IN ADULTS

Edited by

## Leopold Bellak, M.D.

*Clinical Professor of Psychiatry*
*Albert Einstein College of Medicine, and*
*Clinical Professor of Psychology*
*Post-doctoral Program in Psychotherapy*
*New York University*

**GRUNE & STRATTON**
A Subsidiary of Harcourt Brace Jovanovich, Publishers
**New York   San Francisco   London**

*Grune & Stratton, Inc.*
*111 Fifth Avenue*
*New York, New York 10003*

Distributed in the United Kingdom by
*Academic Press, Inc. (London) Ltd.*
*24/28 Oval Road, London NW 1*

Library of Congress Catalog Number 79-2585
International Standard Book Number 0-8089-1192-9

Printed in the United States of America

# Contents

# NEUROPSYCHIATRIC ASPECTS

# THERAPEUTIC ASPECTS

# Contributors

**L. EUGENE ARNOLD, M.Ed., M.D.,** Associate Professor and Director, Division of Child Psychiatry, Ohio State University, Columbus, Ohio

**LEOPOLD BELLAK, M.D.,** Clinical Professor of Psychiatry, Albert Einstein College of Medicine, Bronx, New York, and Clinical Professor of Psychology, Post-doctoral Program in Psychotherapy, New York University, New York, New York

**CHARLES L. BLAIR, B.S.,** M.D. Candidate, University of Connecticut, Storrs, Connecticut

**BARRY L. BORLAND, Ph.D.,** Assistant Professor of Pediatrics, University of Texas Southwestern Medical School, Dallas, Texas

**DENNIS P. CANTWELL, M.D.,** Professor of Psychiatry, Neuropsychiatric Institute, University of California, Los Angeles, California

**STEPHEN M. COHEN, M.D.,** Clinical Assistant Professor of Psychiatry, Medical Center Hospital, University of Vermont, Burlington, Vermont

**JONATHAN O. COLE, M.D.,** Director of Clinical Research, Institute of Research and Rehabilitation, Boston State Hospital, Boston, Massachusetts

**ROBERT K. DAVIES, M.D.,** Associate Professor of Clinical Psychiatry, Yale University, New Haven, Connecticut

**DONALD M. GALLANT, M.D.,** Professor of Psychiatry, Tulane University School of Medicine, New Orleans, Louisiana

**STANLEY I. GREENSPAN, M.D.,** Mental Health Study Center, National Institute of Mental Health, Adelphi, Maryland

**PETER HARTOCOLLIS, Ph.D., M.D.,** Director, C.F. Menninger Memorial Hospital, Topeka, Kansas

**HANS R. HUESSY, M.D., M.S.,** Professor of Psychiatry, University Associates in Psychiatry, Burlington, Vermont

**DONALD KLEIN, M.D.,** Director of Psychiatric Research, New York State Psychiatric Institute, New York, New York

**RUSSELL R. MONROE, M.D.,** Chairman, Department of Psychiatry, University of Maryland, Baltimore, Maryland

**JOHN F. NEIL, M.D.,** Assistant Professor of Psychiatry, University of Pittsburgh, Pittsburgh, Pennsylvania

**PAMELA ROOD, M.Ed.,** Research Associate, University of Vermont, Burlington, Vermont

**GARY J. TUCKER, M.D.,** Professor of Psychiatry, Dartmouth Medical School, Hanover, New Hampshire

**PAUL H. WENDER, M.D.,** Professor of Psychiatry, University of Utah, Salt Lake City, Utah

# Opening Remarks: Becoming Aware of Adult Minimal Brain Dysfunction

Leopold Bellak

The study of minimal brain dysfunction (MBD) in adult psychiatric states is a field barely out of the pioneering stage. Each of the authors represented in these pages has contributed to its early development and each, with the exception of myself, comes to this field after prior experience in child psychiatry.

I became interested in the role of MBD in adults primarily through my patients in private practice, some of whom would tell me about the problems of their dyslexic children. I became convinced that certain aspects were familial by virtue of the fact that dyslexic children and their parents often had some overlapping complaints.

One of the initial things that struck me was that several of these parents had their worst arguments with their spouses while driving in the car. Typically, the driver would get lost and a disagreement would follow. The crux of the disagreement would turn out to be whether a left or a right turn should have been made at some particular junction. I then discovered that problems of orientation and space were common among those who seemed to have difficulty in driving. Some were left-handed. Some had marked problems of impulse control. Others had particularly poor body and self images, and, in fact, at times had difficulty pronouncing certain words (although they were highly intelligent and generally of high achievement). Looking back into their school histories, I found that, indeed, some had had problems with reading and writing.

It was by this means that I first discovered that adults also suffered from dyslexic symptoms and other aspects of MBD. I noticed that their children (several of them had as many as four) had various degrees of dyslexia and other symptoms; some of these children were also found to have petit mal or grand mal seizures. I had occasion to observe several members of certain families—at times as many as four generations—and was duly impressed with the apparent familial nature of this manifestly very variable disorder. Slowly I became aware of a number of psychiatric aspects associated with MBD which I describe in a later chapter of this volume.

Another group that almost independently attracted my attention several years ago comprised schizophrenics who were referred to me for consultation or treatment after a frustrating history of failure to respond to treatment. Some had run away from institutions. Their thought disorders were primarily problems of concreteness rather than over-symbolization or over-ideation. They usually complained that the phenothiazines had made them worse, and I soon found that energizers had a paradoxically stabilizing effect on them; they turned out to have characteristics of MBD, and I described them as a subgroup of the schizophrenic syndrome elsewhere.[1,2]

A third input came to me from a research study of ego functions in schizophrenics, neurotics, and normals, in which factor analysis indicated one group that was primarily characterized by a low stimulus barrier.

It was from these diverse sources that, over the last few years, more definitive notions formed in my mind about the variable syndrome best conceived of as minimal brain dysfunction and the variety of ways in which this syndrome may interact with different kinds of psychiatric problems. I had a chance to study extensively some aspects of MBD in the course of analysis and analytic psychotherapy, and it is particularly on that score that I will report later in these pages.

I found scattered evidence in the literature that others had also become aware of the existence of MBD in adults. It seemed to me, therefore, high time to have a conference on this topic and to present whatever seems to be known or needs to be known to the profession.

Therefore, I approached CIBA-Geigy with the idea of organizing such a meeting. I invited all the contributors of chapters to this book, having known them through their previous work in the field. I regret that the group had to be kept small and that several other outstanding researchers could not also be included. The conference was held in Scottsdale, Arizona, in March, 1978.

It is a pleasure to express my appreciation of the constructive role of CIBA-Geigy and of the pleasant, cooperative and helpful role which, especially, Dr. Alphonso Strollo, Dr. Barry Sachais, Mr. Robert Orsetti and Mr. Richard Mannis played in making this conference possible. I am also grateful to Ms. Lucinda Pitcairn of CIBA-Geigy and to Ms. Marlene Kolbert and Ms. Helen Siegel, who were all helpful with editorial problems.

**REFERENCES**

1. Bellak L: A possible subgroup of the schizophrenic syndrome and implications for treatment. Am J Psychotherapy 30:294–305, 1976
2. Bellak L: Psychiatric states in adults with minimal brain dysfunction. Psychiatric Annals 7:58–74, 1977

Paul H. Wender

# 1

# The Concept of Adult
# Minimal Brain Dysfunction
# (MBD)

In discussing problems of the concept of adult MBD, I would like to address first the problem of the validity of the MBD syndrome in childhood, next describe how I and my co-workers came to the conclusion that the syndrome also exists in adult life, where it is commonly undiagnosed and infrequently treated, and then conclude with the issue of validating the notion of adult MBD.

My current theses, biases, and prejudices concerning this disorder are as follows:

1.  That MBD is a common syndrome of childhood and adulthood;
2.  That the disorder is most probably genetically produced and not produced by brain damage;
3.  That one aspect of the genetically transmitted mechanism is a disorder of monoamine metabolism;
4.  That its response to medication suggests that biochemical remediation is being produced at a relatively early portion of the causal chain and that the nature of response to medication—together with other data—enables us to make some specific inferences about the underlying biochemical deficit.

Let me begin with the matter of nomenclature. There is currently no adequate term for the disorder, and there will be none in the near future. The words "hyperactive" and "hyperkinetic" suggest that excessive motor activity is an intrinsic sign of MBD. It seems that this is not so in that many patients with MBD have normal or even hypoactive motor

1

behavior. Furthermore, hyperactivity, even when present, may disappear with maturation, while many far more troublesome symptoms do not.

"Minimal brain damage" and "minimal cerebral damage" continue to mislead. The fact that a few brain-damaged children manifest signs and symptoms of MBD hardly means that all MBD children's symptoms are the consequence of brain damage, a point that I emphasized in my monograph.[1] DSM-III will probably designate MBD as "attention-deficit disorder." This focuses on a common attribute of the syndrome and suggests that it is pathognomonic; besides our not knowing if this is so, the phrase designates as a criterion an attribute that is extremely difficult to measure. To obviate these difficulties, I have frequently suggested that we "discover" a short-named 18th-century physician who initially described MBD or something like it and let him (or her) achieve eponymic distinction; barring that, it might not be too immoral to invent such a physician.

The first issues I would like to address are the problems of syndromal definition and validation. The signs and symptoms of MBD are not known, and validity presents some thorny epistemologic problems. With regard to signs and symptoms, I *believe* that the following constitute the major attributes of the disorder:

1. Attentional deficit(s). This is the classic "short attention span" that DSM-III has legislated as pathognomonic. That "distractibility" is also characteristic has been denied by Virginia Douglas on the basis of behavioral observations.[2] Many of my adult MBD patients complain specifically of distractibility. Its presence or absence depends on whether we rely on behavioral measures in preadolescents or subjective ones in adults. It is important to mention that short attention span may be masked by perseverative interests or behavior.

2. Motor abnormalities. These include hyperactivity and clumsiness or soft neurologic signs. It seems to many clinicians that most of the symptoms can occur in the presence of normal or diminished motor activity, and it is likewise apparent that some MBD children are very well coordinated.

3. Deficits in impulse control. Those that are salient and troublesome vary as a function of age. Included are impaired sphincter control, low frustration tolerance, and social impulsivity and social transgressions (which include, more or less progressively, and obviously not invariably, destructiveness, stealing, lying, fire setting, sexual "acting out," and lawbreaking).

4. Altered interpersonal relations. It seems that there is a bimodal distribution of MBD children with regard to independence and dependency. Increased independence (i.e., decreased separation anxiety) would seem to be more typical. Additional signs and symptoms in this

category are resistance to socialization by adults, refractoriness to reward and punishment (i.e., obstinacy, negativism, stubbornness, imperviousness), impaired peer relations (bullying or domineering), and obtuseness to the needs of others.

5. Altered emotional reactivity. This is a heterogeneous category and includes such attributes as increased affective ability, hyperreactivity and overexcitability (lack of modulation), irritability and hot-temperedness, dysphoria, sadness, and low self-esteem. Difficult to place in this category and likewise uncertain are anxiety and compulsivity. The latter is reported by some MBD adults to develop in adolescence and may be seen by those dynamically inclined as the consequence of reaction formation to previously manifested disorganization and impulsivity.

6. Cognitive abnormalities. These include hard-to-characterize abnormalities in cognition (variously called dyslogia, sometimes identified as concreteness or lack of ability to abstract) and a nebulous cluster of cognitive—not perceptual—impairments referred to under the phrase "learning disabilities." Whether these latter are qualitative or quantitative abnormalities remains to be determined.

Next, what are the critical attributes, the signs and symptoms necessary for making the diagnosis of MBD? The fact that these are difficult if not impossible to state has provided considerable consternation in both nonmedical and medical circles. This is unfortunate, but MBD is in no more parlous shape than any other psychiatric syndrome. The same comments apply to schizophrenia and the affective disorders. I would like to make the rather startling statement that there may be no critical attributes of MBD; that is, I am asserting that two individuals may have MBD yet have no symptoms in common. Although seemingly radical, this is not even an innovative assertion.

Nosologists recognize the existence of two sorts of categorization: "monothetic" and "polythetic." The monothetic classification is one in which attributes are specified that all members of a class must have to warrant inclusion; a typical example would be the category of mammals, animals with hair that suckle their young. In polythetic categorization, individuals may be included as members of the same class while having a certain number of specified characteristics that any two members need not have in common; a straightforward medical example of this is rheumatic fever. The "major" and "minor" criteria for its diagnosis are shown in Table 1-1. Since diagnosis of rheumatic fever requires the presence of either two major or one major and two minor attributes, one can easily see that two individuals may have the disorder yet share no symptoms; for example, one individual might have carditis and polyarthritis while

**Table 1-1**
Monothetic and Polythetic Types of Classification:
Attributes of Rheumatic Fever

---

*Major manifestations*
  Carditis
  Sydenham's chorea
  Subcutaneous nodules
  Polyarthritis
  Erythema marginatum
*Minor manifestations*
  Clinical
    Previous rheumatic fever or rheumatic heart disease
    Polyarthralgia
    Fever
  Laboratory
    Acute phase reactions: elevated erythrocyte sedimentation rate,
    C-reactive protein, leukocytosis. Prolonged P-R interval. *Plus* supporting
    evidence of preceding streptococcal infection, i.e., increased ASO or
    other strep. antibodies; positive throat culture for group A streptococcus;
    recent scarlet fever

---

another might have Sydenham's chorea and erythema marginatum. The fact that both of these hypothetical individuals do indeed have rheumatic fever is validated by their common sharing of a similar pathophysiologic mechanism.

    In my asserting that MBD is polythetic, I emphasize that I have no supporting evidence. I have based my assertion on treacherous clinical experience. I have been impressed with the clustering of MBD in families, with different manifestations occurring in different members. That is, beginning with a classically hyperactive child, one may find one sib who has severe coordination difficulties and no behavior problems, another who is learning disabled but completely compliant, and so forth. I have also been impressed that different children with different and only slightly overlapping MBD signs and symptoms respond to stimulant therapy. This latter observation is not only impressionistic—like the first—but even if true may be very misleading. I will return to this point below. What I am suggesting is that the situation in MBD is analogous to that seen in schizophrenia, where starting with a hebephrenic, thoroughly disorganized patient, one may find a relative who is paranoid but well organized, another who is "borderline," and yet another who is merely unusually eccentric. One sees a cluster of related but different clinical syndromes sharing a probable genetic etiology.

    What, then, are the techniques by which we may test the validity of the MBD syndrome? The ultimate basis of validation is unity of cause. In medicine, as in the case of rheumatic fever discussed above, the validity of considering a plethora of signs and symptoms to be a manifestation of the same underlying disease could be demonstrated only by another approach, using techniques at a "lower" or "more basic" level of observation. By understanding the immunologic mechanisms that underlie the syndrome of rheumatic fever it was possible to understand how one process could have a variety of outcomes. The underlying process was unitary; the manifestations were not. As of yet, for no "functional" psychiatric syndrome can we appeal to the electron microscopist or the amine chemist to specify underlying causes. This route is barred to us. If it were not, a hypothetical basic scientist might examine the brains of a group of MBD children and find that one subgroup was characterized by low cortical dopamine hydroxylase; the clinician could then inspect this group and see if it had distinct signs and symptoms. The equally hypothetical developmental psychologist might find that another subgroup had been subject to operationally specifiable sensory or affective privation and its symptomatic characteristics specified. Ultimately, we wish to associate certain patterns of behavior with specifiable psychological experiences, neurologic structure, or neurophysiologic or biochemical functioning. Our problem is what to do till the scientist comes.

The traditional psychiatric approach in establishing syndromes has been inductive and clinical. Without the use of statistical techniques, psychiatrists, like other physicians, have reported signs and symptoms that cluster together and that in some often not clearly specific way define the syndrome. If they can find additional clinical features such as history or prognosis that show an association with the cluster of currently observable signs and symptoms, they may feel happier. Additional "clinical features" have been hard to come by. History is unreliable, and prognosis, on which Kraepelin placed so much hope, is not completely dependable even for dementia praecox. In general, clinicians hope that the more precise the characterization of signs and symptoms, the greater the likelihood of not lumping together what should have been split. The difficulty is that the available clinical techniques alone may prove inadequate. The 19th-century physician, without the pathologist, stethoscope, or sphygmomanometer, would be unable to separate congestive failure secondary to repeated infarctions from that due to mitral stenosis or hypertension. Furthermore, although the splitting strategy has paid off in some areas like that of retardation, it has not in others. As in rheumatic fever, "lumping" may at times be a better strategy.

A second technique is to examine biologic (or psychological) correlates of a presumed syndrome. This technique has been employed with regard to the primary affective disorders in which biogenic amine function has been inspected carefully. Ironically, such inspection seems to have been more successful in subdividing primary affective disorder into subgroups than it has been in characterizing primary affective disorders biologically. While the attempt to characterize the disorders has been unsuccessful, recent studies suggest that it may be possible to subdivide them into low- and high-MHPG urinary subtypes and low- and normal-CSF-5HIAA subtypes: The implication is that there are at least two forms of the disorder, characterized by abnormalities in norepinephrine and serotonin metabolism, respectively. I mention this, though tangential, because there are obvious implications for studies of amine metabolism in MBD.

A third technique is to group disorders on the basis of familial association. If similar or identical illnesses tend to occur in relatives and the frequency is related to the closeness of the genetic relationship, we assume not only that the disorder has genetic components but also that the proposed cluster is a valid one. A difficulty is that familial association may be the result of genetic transmission or social learning. As a result, such data cannot explain whether symptoms cluster on the basis of common biologic features or some—to be explained—tendency for recurrent patterns of social learning to occur. Adoption studies not only can determine the relative effects of nature and nurture but also, equally importantly, can help to define the boundaries of the disorder. The adoption studies of schizophrenia not only have documented the role of genetic factors in their etiology but have demonstrated that the disorder occurs along a spectrum and have revealed which pathologic features occur in the spectrum. By studying the adopted-away offspring of hyperactive adults (if one believes they exist) or of former hyperactive children, one could not only determine the role of genetic factors in the etiology of the syndrome but, by inspecting the behavior of the offspring, see what symptoms cluster together. If, using this strategy, one did indeed find that different offspring had different MBD symptoms in isolation or in nonoverlapping clusters, one could document the truth of the statement that MBD is a syndrome with polythetic manifestations.

A fourth validating technique is response to treatment. As mentioned, this can be the most misleading technique because many seemingly different psychiatric syndromes respond to the same drug. Separation anxiety, agoraphobia, and depression, all seemingly distinct syndromes, respond to tricyclic antidepressants. Agitated depressions, manias, and schizophrenic psychoses, again seemingly distinct syndromes, respond to the neuroleptics. Furthermore, this method may be misleading in that two individuals who are symptomatically identical may not respond to the same treatment. In particular, with regard to MBD, attempts to determine predictors of psychostimulant response have been ineffective. There are no distinct clinical features that distinguish responders from nonresponders.

After this massive preamble, what about the validity of the MBD syndrome? Its validity in childhood is supported by clinical observation, some miniscule evidence from biochemical correlates, some adoption study evidence, and the nature of the treatment response. There is little more to say about clinical observation. In regard to biochemical correlates, studies of urinary monoamine metabolites, blood DBH, and platelet serotonin have essentially been negative. There is one tantalizing CSF study. In an examination of six hyperactive children, Shaywitz[3] found that the accumulation of HVA—the principal dopamine metabolite—in the CSF following probenecid treatment was one-half that of controls and that there was no overlap between the two groups. This is of considerable interest for theoretical reasons, a point to which I shall return later.

What supporting evidence for the syndromal notion comes from genetic studies? Using the technique[4] that Kety, Rosenthal, and I employed to piece apart nature and nurture in schizophrenia, "the adoptive parents method," Morrison and Stewart[5] and Cantwell[6] investigated the adopting and natural parents of hyperactive children. They found that parents who adopted hyperactive children were no different from the parents of pediatric controls, but that among the natural parents of hyperactive children there was an increase of alcoholism, sociopathy, and hyperactivity in the biologic fathers and Briquet's syndrome in the biologic mothers. These findings not only suggest a genetic contribution to MBD—at least the existence of a genetic subgroup—that supports the syndrome notion but also have relevance for the notion of adult MBD. Taken together with other family studies linking sociopathy, alcoholism, and Briquet's syndrome (the St. Louis triad), these findings suggest that genetic factors may link hyperactivity and these disorders.

The final support for the validity of the MBD syndrome comes from the treatment response of MBD children. I have repeatedly commented that this response is of twofold interest. First, it is often remarkable in that rather than returning patients to previous levels of functioning it enables them to function more effectively than they have ever done previously. The implication is that a fundamental deficit is being corrected and that the point of intervention is early in the causal chain. The second point is that drugs that are of benefit in the syndrome increase monoaminergic function in general and dopaminergic function in particular. The amphetamines affect all three biogenic amines, although in the doses clinically employed they probably affect catecholamines selectively. Methylphenidate presumably acts by releasing dopamine stores, and pemoline likewise presumably acts as an indirect dopamine agonist. The tricyclic antidepressants—which are not particularly effective—act variously on norepinephrine and serotonin. The conclusion is that dopamine is the critical neurohumor; the implication is that the MBD patient has dopaminergic underactivity. One cause of this might be failure to synthesize and release dopamine. Such decreased dopamine metabolism would be associated with decreased dopamine catabolism. One would anticipate diminished levels of the principal metabolite of dopamine, HVA, in the CSF; hence the relevance of Shaywitz's finding.

One other important point should be made. Rapoport et al. have recently reported[7] that normal children show the same response to D-amphetamine, in terms of behavior, self-ratings, and psychological and psychophysiologic tests as hyperactive children do. This observation could lead to the erroneous conclusion that CNS amine function is the same in normal and MBD children. This is not necessarily so. The fact that stimulant drugs are useful in the treatment of MBD children does not imply that their effect is paradoxical in MBD children or different from their action in normal children. Psychostimulant medication may well increase dopaminergic activity in both groups.

Consider a parallel situation in regard to endocrine function. Thyroid hormone has the same effect in the hypothyroid person as in the euthyroid one. In both cases there appears to be an internal "thermostat" set at an optimal thyroid level and provided with negative feedback mechanisms to maintain that level. Administration of exogenous thyroid hormone to hypothyroid individuals will raise their levels to optimal ones, and as an apparent result there is no feedback inhibition of the production of endogenous thyroid hormone. This contrasts with the situation in which a normal individual is given exogenous thyroid, when the thyroid homeostat recognizes an excessive level of circulating hormone and "turns down" endogenous thyroid production to keep the total level of circulating hormone levels constant.

If an internal neurotransmitter "thermostat" exists, one would anticipate that the increased dopamine turnover produced by psychostimulant medication in MBD children would not be followed by inhibitory feedback decreasing production or decreasing receptor sensitivity; this appears to be the case. In general, such children retain their responsivity to psychostimulant medication. By contrast, continued administration of stimulant medication to the normal child, as to the normal adult, would be expected to result in receptor-induced negative feedback decreasing rates of dopamine function to normal levels (e.g., by decreasing levels of tyrosine hydroxylase). Accordingly, one would expect normal children to become tolerant to the effects of psychostimulant medication and fail to continue to manifest changes similar to those produced by such medication in MBD children.

How did my colleagues and I come to the notion that adult MBD existed? There are data that would suggest the persistence of MBD into adulthood. It would be nice to say that based on these observations it followed a priori that MBD must continue to exist—in some sense—into adult life. That is the way introductions to scientific papers usually proceed. Unfortunately, to say it is true would be a lie. What happened was much simpler; it followed from clinical observation. In talking to the parents of MBD children, I routinely inquire which parent was temperamentally most like the proband when he or she had been a child. A frequent maternal response was, "What do you mean, 'was'? His mother says he was just like that as a boy and he still is that way. He still never finishes anything he starts, fidgets all the time, gets upset easily, does dumb things without thinking, and won't listen." A similar observation had been made by a friend, Dr. Keith McCloskey, who invented a brilliant diagnostic technique for determining which parent is the gene carrier. It does not involve inspection for congenital anomalies, platelet MAO, or factor analysis; one simply asks the child, "Which of your parents has the worse temper?"

Clinically, I had to take notice when several parents of MBD children told me they had taken diet pills, "speed," or their children's medicine and reported that it calmed them down even though they expected it to pep them up. That was an acute treatment response and could not be disregarded; however, a few parents told me they had taken diet pills or amphetamine (Dexedrine) for years—ostensibly for weight control—and had for only that period in their life been able to control distressing psychological symptoms.

The final input came when I began to consult at the community mental health clinics, where I found that there were a fair number of outpatients who had no clear syndromal status but who presented with many signs and symptoms that would be considered diagnostic of hyperactivity if they were younger. Dr. Johnson, Dr. Reinherr, Dr. Wood, and I decided to take the syndrome by the horns, constructed some rating scales—for which I am again partially dependent on the observations of Dr. McCloskey—and conducted a double-blind crossover study of the effects of methylphenidate on this population.[8] Many of them got better. On the basis of this study, we are now conducting a much larger replication, comparing pemoline and placebo in a double-blind parallel study.

The above is a brief account of how we got where we are. We found some people who reportedly used to act like hyperactive children, who currently act the way one might imagine older hyperactive children to act, and who respond to medication the way hyperactive children are supposed to. But what are we doing? What have we found? What is the validity of the notion of the MBD syndrome in adulthood?

To begin with, what do we mean by the phrase "adult minimal dysfunction?" I can see several meanings—the first two descriptive, the third causal: (1) individuals who have MBD problems in childhood continue to have the same symptoms when they become adults; (2) children who have MBD symptoms in childhood are at increased risk for psychiatric symptomatology in adulthood that bears a resemblance to or is thought to derive from MBD in childhood; and (3) the underlying assumed biologic or psychological pathology that exists in childhood continues to exist in adulthood, where it causes the same or different pathology. Note that the first two assertions—which overlap, since I am a second-rate Aristotelian—make no claims with regard to pathogenesis. They are descriptive. Pathogenetically, they might be explained developmentally. It might merely be the case that whatever causes MBD in childhood goes away but that behavior learned on the basis of MBD in childhood persists. For example, an MBD child might develop low self-esteem because of proclivity for displeasing others; the maturing subject might become exceedingly effective at winning friends and influencing people but maintain low self-esteem as the result of ingrained early learning.

What evidence is there for these three assertions? First, MBD symptoms persist. A number of anterospective studies suggest that they do. In a 2–5-year followup study of "hyperactive children," Mendelson et al.[9] noted that approximately three-fourths continued to have difficulties with concentration, overactivity, and impulsivity. A longer anterospective study, 8–10 years, by Huessy et al.[10] indicated that a group of diagnosed—and treated—MBD children were at 20 times the risk of the comparison group for institutionalization as deliquent with psychiatric disorders. Hartocollis[11] and Quitkin and Klein[12] investigated the histories of adults with impulsive character disorders whose symptoms could be seen as very modest modifications of typical childhood MBD. These investigators found an increased frequency of signs and symptoms of MBD in the childhood of these patients.

Information indirectly supporting the second meaning comes from the family studies linking MBD and the "St. Louis triad." The adoption studies cited, by separating out the effects of nature and nurture, suggest that the genetic load associated with MBD in children is somehow related to the development of alcoholism, sociopathy, and Briquet's syndrome in adults: the parents had the same genetic load when they were children and the experience of being an MBD child predisposed them to psychiatric disorder later and/or their genetic load directly fostered this St. Louis complex of adult psychopathology. The relationship of MBD with alcoholism is strengthened by two additional studies. In a study of the adopted-away offspring of alcoholic fathers, Goodwin et al.[13] found an increased frequency of hyperactivity in the childhood of these adult adopt-ees. Likewise, Tarter et al.[14] found a significantly increased frequency of the history of MBD symptoms in childhood in one subgroup of alcoholics.

A third source of validation for the notion of adult MBD would come from a demonstration of similar biologic abnormalities in the childhood and adult forms. The only biologic abnormality reported in children has not been evaluated in adults; our group plans to do so. A comparable underlying biologic abnormality is suggested from the response of puta-tive MBD adults to psychostimulant medication and tricyclic antidepres-sants. In both respects their responses are comparable to those seen in hyperactive children. Psychostimulant medication often produces—as we have reported and as we are continuing to find—a dramatic response in many such individuals. More importantly, many report sedation (which had been reported in normals by Tecce and others), lack of euphoria, and a failure to demonstrate tolerance to the effects of medication. The re-sponse to tricyclic medication also seems to be similar to that seen in MBD children—an immediate response (hours rather than weeks), usu-ally followed by the development of tolerance over a period of several weeks.

I mentioned at the outset that MBD is a common syndrome of childhood and adulthood. Good morbidity risk figures for childhood do not exist. Certainly none are available for adulthood. If, however, MBD is related to the St. Louis triad, we might inquire as to the morbidity risk for those three disorders and arrive at a ballpark figure for adult MBD. The St. Louis group estimates sociopathy to occur in approximately 6 percent of males and Briquet's syndrome in 2 percent of females. Estimates for the lifetime risk of alcoholism are about 5 percent; alcoholism is undoubtedly a final common pathway, and what fraction is related to MBD, is unknown. Summing the figures, discounting a certain fraction of the alcoholics, say 50 percent, and then multiplying by a constant greater than unity to accommodate the spectrum forms of MBD, one arrives at an approximate figure of 5–10 percent. Oddly enough, that is the same order of magnitude cited for childhood MBD.

The above offers some tentative support for the notion of adult MBD. Before discussing where we go from here, I would like to turn to one somewhat tangential issue, the possible association of MBD and schizo-phrenic symptoms in the same individual. This is an observation Dr. Bellak has reported and it is one that has been observed by others. The longitu-dinal study by Mednick and Schulsinger[15] of the offspring of schiz-ophrenic mothers revealed that many of these youngsters were "hy-peractive" in adolescence and that many of these same adolescents subsequently showed schizophrenic symptomatology. Similarly, Robins's followup study[16] revealed that antisocial personality in adolescence was frequently associated with schizophrenia in adulthood. If these observations are true, what should we make of them? I would suggest nothing yet. Neither of these studies links the two syndromes etiologically, since neither takes into account the question of assortative mating. If it is the case that schizophrenics tend to mate with sociopaths on a greater than chance basis and if there is a genetic contribution to both disorders (and adoption studies indicate there is), one might expect mixed hybrid schizophrenic-sociopathic behavior in the offspring. Since sociopathic behavior overlaps some types of MBD behavior, one might expect to see mixed MBD-schizophrenic symptomatology in such people. A study by Rosenthal and I of the mates (in general *not* husbands) of schizophrenic women who put their children up for adoption revealed that one-third of these co-parents were sociopaths. Mednick and Schulsinger are currently inspecting their data; it will be interesting to see if they find that their "hyperactive" preschizophrenic adolescents were the offspring of sociopathic fathers. The issue is clearly not settled. For the time being, one must be cautious in interpreting the coexistence of schizophrenia and MBD symptoms and not assume that they are both manifestations of identical underlying pathology.

The adult MBD hypothesis is not being advanced as one of ultimate or absolute truth but as a working model. On a probabilistic basis, adult MBD is probably a heterogeneous collection of abnormalities. As a working hypothesis, one employs it because of its usefulness. First, it has identified a group of individuals with relatively clearcut signs and symptoms refractory to traditional psychopharmacologic treatments, who respond specifically and often dramatically to psychostimulant medication; this is an observation of considerable clinical utility. Second, it makes specific predictions that can be tested. These predictions relate to its natural history, relationship with other psychiatric disorders, and anticipated errors of metabolism. Our group is planning to test the last using the refined monoamine "shotgun" approach. My colleagues and I have already measured urinary monoamine metabolites, platelet serotonin, and differential response to the stereoisomers of amphetamine having different neurochemical actions in MBD children. We plan to continue such studies in adults and to perform additional ones, such as studies of cerebrospinal fluid, that are difficult, if not impossible, to perform on children.

The best measure of a scientific hypothesis is its ability to make predictions that can be experimentally tested and are subject to disproof. I have mentioned several implicit predictions of the adult MBD hypothesis. In the next few years we should be able to test some of these predictions.

REFERENCES

1. Wender PH: Minimal Brain Dysfunction in Children. New York, John Wiley & Sons, 1971.
2. Douglas VI: Stop, look and listen: The problem of sustained attention and impulse control in hyperactive and normal children. Can J Behav Sci/Rev Can Sci Comp 4:259–282, 1972.
3. Aman MG, Werry JS: The effects of methylphenidate and haloperidol on the heart rate and blood pressure of hyperactive children with special reference to time of action. Psychopharmacologia (Berlin) 43:163–168, 1975.
4. Wender PH, et al: A psychiatric assessment of adoptive parents of schizophrenics. In Rosenthal D, Kety S (eds): The Transmission of Schizophrenia. Oxford, Pergamon Press, 1968, pp. 235–250.
5. Morrison JR, et al: The psychiatric status of the legal families of adopted hyperactive children. Arch Gen Psychiatry 28:888–891, 1973.
6. Cantwell DP: Genetics of hyperactivity. J Child Psychol Psychiatry 16:261–264, 1975.
7. Rapoport JL, et al: Dextroamphetamine: Cognitive and behavioral effects in normal prepubertal boys. Science 199:560–562, 1978.
8. Wood DR, et al: Diagnosis and treatment of minimal brain dysfunction in adults. Arch Gen Psychiatry 33:1453–1460, 1976.
9. Mendelson W, et al: Hyperactive children as adolescents: A followup study. J Nerv Ment Dis 153:273–279, 1971.
10. Huessy HR, et al: Eight to ten year followup of 84 children treated for behavioral disturbance in rural Vermont. Acta Paedopsychiatr 40:230–235, 1974.
11. Hartocollis P: The syndrome of minimal brain dysfunction in young adult patients. Bull Menninger Clin 32:102–114, 1968.
12. Quitkin F, Klein DF: Two behavioral syndromes in young adults related to possible minimal brain dysfunction. J Psychiatr Res 7:131–142, 1969.
13. Goodwin DW, et al: Drinking problems in adopted and nonadopted sons of alcoholics. Arch Gen Psychiatry 31:164–169, 1974.
14. Tarter RE, et al: Differentiation of alcoholics. Arch Gen Psychiatry 34:761–768, 1977.
15. Mednick SA, Schulsinger F, Sarnoff A: Some premorbid characteristics related to breakdown in children with schizophrenic mothers. In Rosenthal D, Kety SS (eds): The Transmission of Schizophrenia. New York, Pergamon, 1968, pp 267–292.
16. Robins N: Deviant Children Grown Up. Baltimore, Williams & Wilkins, 1966.

## DISCUSSION

Q: What dosages did you use in the pemoline-placebo study?

*Dr. Wender:* Comparatively low doses, usually between 37.5 and 75 mg. We used pemoline because we were afraid that giving methylphenidate would be like giving morphine—everybody would feel better. Pemoline apparently makes one feel worse. Thus when some people felt calmer, this suggested that the drug was doing something other than just generally producing euphoria.

*Chairman Bellak:* I personally am not interested in the etiologic pathogenic implications so much as the mere coexistence of MBD and schizophrenia. I believe that's important, regardless of what the causal relationship might be.

*Dr. Arnold:* I have just a couple of brief comments. One is, I wondered whether you intended to equate distractibility with short attention span.

*Dr. Wender:* No, I think both are characteristic, although Virginia Douglas might disagree. What adults tend to report is that they are easily distractible. A typical patient will report "I'm trying to read a book and hear the refrigerator going on, the cat coming in, the garbage pails rattling, and it drives me crazy because I can't keep my mind on the book."

*Dr. Arnold:* I've heard both kinds of complaints—either primary distractibility but ability to finish a job, or no concern about distractibility but just inability to stick with the job. In regard to Briquet's syndrome being implicated here, I've felt for a long time that hyperkinetic children have a lot of physical complaints that nobody ever reports, because their behavior is so much more prominent. In many cases, these physical effects are considered side effects of medication because when you medicate the child his behavior improves, and then you notice that he has somatic complaints that he may have had all along without your noticing.

*Dr. Wender:* That's a very interesting observation, and one that my wife* ran across recently. She's been working with a group that has been studying the Feingold diet. Some data collected in one of these studies indicated a large number of somatic complaints in MBD children prior to treatment—headaches, bellyaches, nonspecificities.

*Dr. Gallant:* You mentioned that increased plasma dopamine beta-hydroxylase activity is definitely not a factor. But Buchsbaum and Rapoport still seem to feel that in those patients with a high percentage of anomalies, there is increased plasma dopamine beta-hydroxylase activity.

*Dr. Wender:* There's a low correlation, as I recall, something like 0.3,

* Esther Wender, M.D.

but you're quite correct. It also correlates with a history of first-trimester bleeding and hyperactivity in the father.

*Dr. Tucker:* You can correlate DBH with almost anything.

*Dr. Wender:* This was a specific study that has been published. They examined high-anomaly and low-anomaly children and found a difference in dopamine beta-hydroxylase. These were comparison groups, but I'm sure that about one-third of them are minimal brain dysfunctions.

*Chairman Bellak:* If a patient was disturbed by the noise of the refrigerator, I would prefer to say she suffers from a low stimulus barrier. That's what Mednick also observes often in children at high risk.

*Dr. Klein:* I was going to speak to that distractibility point. I think there should be a distinction made. Douglas showed that if you gave the children meaningless, noisy distractors, light noise, they did not suffer from low stimulus barriers. They were able to go ahead and do their jobs just as well as anybody else. We're doing a study right now that would seem to indicate that the meaningfulness of the distractors is what makes the difference. We have children exposed to a slide, and around the slide are either meaningless shapes on a blank field or interesting things—little guns, little gallows, things of the sort that a child might be interested in. Under those circumstances we're finding that the meaningful distractors are much more effective at getting the child away from the center of the slide than the meaningless ones on the blank field. We have some pilot data showing that when you treat these hyperactive children with Ritalin, they focus in and can do both.

*Dr. Wender:* Presumably they're different from normal children in this respect, initially.

*Dr. Klein:* Yes, they are. Initially quite different from normal children. I think when you talk about distractors you've got to be careful about that term and ask what's doing the distracting.

# Follow-up and Family Studies

Hans R. Huessy, Stephen M. Cohen,
Charles L. Blair, Pamela Rood

# 2

# Clinical Explorations
# in Adult Minimal Brain Dysfunction

We have known for a long time that the behavior and learning problems associated with MBD bear a relationship to serious adult psychopathology. Hampered by our preconceptions, it did not occur to us to explore whether or not these adults might respond to the same drugs that children with MBD sometimes respond to. Arnold et al.[1] reported one such case in 1972. Huessy had a case in 1960 that he thought was simply unusual and did not even report; in 1974 he began looking for such adults[2,3] and here reports his experiences with pharmacotherapy in over 200 cases. This work is a clinical exploration, a valid undertaking that provides experiences leading to more definitive research, such as that of Cohen et al.,[4] whose excellent records on a much more limited group of patients made possible some important research findings that we will summarize.

We are discussing a disorder that presents in a variety of ways in children and in an even greater variety in adults and, as clearly shown by Rutter,[5] is correlated statistically with two or more contributory factors. There is no simple unitary etiology. Arnold describes this as the hydraulic parfait model.[6]

Using the commonly described symptoms of MBD—impulsivity, emotional overreactivity, short attention span, easy distractibility, poor self-image, and learning problems—Huessy began to look for adult patients suffering from some of these same symptoms as well as having a history suggesting the presence of these symptoms in childhood. Blair collected the following data on the first 64 cases that Huessy treated:[2] Owing to the unreliability of these patients as historians, data were ac-

**Table 2-1**
Sample of Adult MBD Patients

| | |
|---|---|
| Number | 64 |
| Sex: male/female | 32/32 |
| Age range (years) | 18–64 |
| Behavioral history suggesting MBD | 26 |
| Treated with medication | 4 |
| Learning disabilities | 12 |
| Attended special schools | 6 |
| Completed high school | 41 |
| Attended college | 28 |
| Completed college | 8 |
| Attended graduate school | 1 |
| Still attending school | 7 |

cepted only if verified by another source. Table 2-1 gives the basic data.
The high educational achievement is an artifact because many of these
patients were seen at Spring Lake Ranch, a private therapeutic community, and came from a very high socioeconomic background. The sex
distribution is also skewed, possibly because manifestations of MBD in
males, aggressive acts and temper outbursts, are more likely to result in
incarceration, whereas the predominantly dramatic and sexual nature of
female symptoms leads to psychiatric institutionalization. Table 2-2
shows the most commonly encountered symptoms and contains no sur-
prises. Table 2-3 gives the male–female ratio of some of the symptoms.
Here we see the usual male predominance for antisocial behavior; suicidal
gestures, sleep problems, and mood swings are more frequently seen in
women. Table 2-4 shows the numerical distribution of symptoms among
the subjects; as indicated, most of the patients had five or more symp-

**Table 2-2**
Signs and Symptoms of Adult MBD ($n$ = 64)

| | |
|---|---|
| 72%, impulsivity | 31%, suicidal gestures or attempts |
| 70%, depression | 28%, hyperactivity |
| 56%, anxiety | 17%, nervousness |
| 55%, aggressive outbursts | 16%, alcoholism |
| and temper tantrums | 16%, eating problems |
| 44%, drug abuse | 14%, lethargy |
| 41%, emotional overreactivity | 11%, hallucinations/delusions |
| 33%, sleep problems | 9%, somatic concerns |
| 31%, distractibility | 8%, illegitimate pregnancy |
| 31%, mood swings | 6%, daydreaming |
| 31%, antisocial behavior | |

**Table 2-3**
Outstanding Ratios of Male and Female Signs and Symptoms ($n = 64$)

| Male | Female | Signs and Symptoms |
|------|--------|--------------------|
| 16 | 4 | Antisocial behavior |
| 6 | 15 | Sleep problems |
| 3 | 17 | Suicidal gestures or attempts |
| 6 | 14 | Mood swings |

toms. In Huessy's clinical experience even one disabling symptom warrants a trial of medication. Table 2-5 represents Huessy's attempt to develop an MBD symptom list for different ages. The italicized items have been most prominent in his experience. The literature mentions hypoactive patients with MBD;[7] they too must grow up and will be harder to identify. Table 2-6 shows past medical data in Huessy's patients with multiple psychiatric admissions to hospitals and a multitude of psychiatric diagnoses. Again, this is somewhat distorted because so many of these individuals were seen at Spring Lake Ranch, which meant that their disorder had been of major proportions. Are those with MBD at greater risk for the major psychoses?

Table 2-7 presents family history data and is in line with previous reports that there may be a genetic element in MBD. Cohen et al.[8] many years ago collected similar data for psychoneuroses. Only studies of lifetime histories will let us separate MBD from psychoneurosis. The two populations share hysterical personality as well as some other diagnoses. Are we only interchanging labels? How often have we struggled to find an appropriate diagnostic category for an adult with MBD?

Table 2-8 summarizes Huessy's experiences with 142 medication trials in his first 64 adult MBD cases. Imipramine was the first drug used, because of his reluctance to give a "street drug" to an unstable patient population and his positive experiences with it in treating children.[9] There was a 50 percent positive response to all the commonly used drugs, as indicated in the bottom line of Table 2-8, despite the fact that methylphenidate and dextroamphetamine were used only after a tricyclic had

**Table 2-4**
Sign and Symptom Distribution Within 5 Years of Treatment ($n = 64$)

| No. of Subjects | Percentage of Subjects | No. of Signs and Symptoms |
|-----------------|------------------------|---------------------------|
| 16 | 25 | 8–10 |
| 36 | 56 | 5–7 |
| 12 | 19 | 2–4 |

**Table 2-5**
Symptoms of MBD at Different Ages

| Infancy | Preschool | Elementary School | High School | Adults |
|---|---|---|---|---|
| Restlessness | High fevers | Accident prone | Educationally retarded | Overtalkative |
| Irritability | Accident prone | *Short attention span* | Poor attention span | Low stress tolerance |
| Irregularity | "Into" everything | Daydreams (girls) | *Lack of motivation* | Easily distractable |
| *Excessive crying* | Short attention span | Can't sit still (boys) | Unreliable | Impulsive |
| High fevers | *Destructive* | Low frustration tolerance | Aggressive | *Short fuse* |
| Poor eater | Can't sit still | *Overreacts* | *Impulsive* | Explosive |
| *High activity level* | Temper tantrums | *Learning problems* | Overreacts | Sleep problems |
| | Speech problems | Doesn't complete tasks | Struggles with authority | Mood swings |
| | Gets to sleep late, or | Class clown | Delinquent activity (boys) | *Trouble with lasting relationships* |
| | Wakes up very early | Aggressive | Promiscuity (girls) | *Can't relax* |
| | Cruel to animals | Poor peer relations | Mood swings | Stretches the truth |
| | *Aggressive* | Impulsive | Lies | Trouble with groups |
| | Impulsive | Poor self-image | Accident prone | Alcohol abuse |
| | Trouble with groups | | Suicidal gestures | Overly dramatic |
| | Mood swings | | *Poor self-image* | *Poor self-image* |
| | *Fire setting* | | School dropout | Exposes self (males) |
| | Enuresis | | | Poor job performance |
| | Insensitive to pain | | | Frequent arguments or fights |

**Table 2-6**
Past Medical Data ($n = 64$)

| Number | History |
|---|---|
| 51 | One or more admissions to psychiatric hospital (SLR excluded) |
| 34 | Schizophrenia (14 paranoid, 9 chronic) |
| 16 | Depressive disorders (2 manic depressive) |
| 14 | Personality disorders |
| 9 | CNS organicity |
| 9 | Traumatic early histories suggesting brain damage |
| 11 | Allergies |

**Table 2-7**
Family Data ($n = 51$)

| | Primary Relatives | All Relatives |
|---|---|---|
| MBD-associated disorders | 38 | 53 |
| All psychiatric disorders | 59 | 90 |

**Table 2-8**
Responses to Anti-MBD Medications

| | Imipramine (Tofranil) | Amitriptyline (Elavil) | Methylphenidate (Ritalin) | Dextroamphetamine (Dexedrine) | Diphenylhydantoin (Dilantin) | Pemoline (Cylert) | Methamphetamine (Desoxyn) | Total |
|---|---|---|---|---|---|---|---|---|
| No. of trials | 55 | 26 | 28 | 17 | 13 | 2 | 1 | 142 |
| No. of positive responses | 26 | 12 | 13 | 9 | 7 | 0 | 1 | 68 |
| No. of negative responses | 10 | 7 | 6 | 3 | 2 | 1 | 0 | 29 |
| No. of paradoxic negative responses | 1 | 0 | 1 | 0 | 1 | 0 | 0 | 3 |
| No. of "no effect" responses | 21 | 8 | 9 | 5 | 5 | 1 | 0 | 49 |
| No. of responses with pos-neg aspects | 3 | 1 | 1 | 0 | 2 | 0 | 0 | 7 |
| Positive responses (%) | 47.3 | 46.2 | 46.4 | 52.9 | 53.8 | 0 | 100 | 47.9 |

been tried. This is similar to his findings with children. Wender et al. reported using methylphenidate until control is achieved and then switching to pemoline.[10]

Now let us look at the retrospective study of Cohen, a colleague in private practice, and his co-workers.[4] In hearing Huessy describe the symptoms of his MBD population, Cohen realized that he had treated a number of patients who fit that description in addition to having presented themselves with the primary complaint of depression. From his very complete and standardized records, Cohen selected 12 patients who presented with depression and a history of interpersonal aggression and intense affect. He then selected a control group of 12 patients with depression but no history of interpersonal aggression or temper outbursts; finally, he matched the two groups for age, sex, socioeconomic status, and antidepressant medication. As indicated in Table 2-9, the two groups varied considerably in terms of family and childhood histories, patterns of symptoms, and response to treatment. Hyperactivity and distractibility, impulsivity, temper, and aggression, which identified the experimental group, were rare in the control group, and there was *no* childhood history of MBD among the controls. The depressives with MBD responded almost immediately to tricyclic medication, whereas the control group required the usual 2–4 weeks to respond to pharmacotherapy. Cohen's work will be published in greater detail and using a larger group of patients.

Huessy's treatment of more than 200 MBD patients has led to the following observations about their presenting symptoms and treatment responses:

The most common finding among these patients is that they live in the moment. Frustration must be relieved immediately. They have trouble forming long-range goals, and the slightest difficulty may produce a complete change of plans. Whereas drug abusers try to tune out of our world, medication, when effective, helps these patients to tune in. Patients towards the sociopathic end of the spectrum may object to this effect and refuse to continue the treatment despite its success.

A recent study[11] in children indicated that MBD children are different from control children in their ability to judge the passage of time. Control children, when asked to guess when 30 sec had passed, averaged 27 sec; the MBD children averaged more than 40 sec. A similar experiment with adults might turn out to be a comparatively easy diagnostic test.*

Some of Huessy's population have shown an inability to form lasting relationships. Whether certain individuals have such an inability for unknown reasons and have MBD as well or whether the symptoms of MBD make the formation of relationships difficult or impossible remains to be

---

* A recently completed unpublished study by Huessy, Senior and Towne does not support this hypothesis.

**Table 2-9**
Summary of Cohen's Results of Adults with Depression and Aggression

| | Unipolar Depression Plus Aggression | Unipolar Depression Alone | $p \leq$ |
|---|---|---|---|
| Males | 5 | 5 | |
| Females | 7 | 7 | |
| Mean age | 29.8 | 30.2 | |
| **Family history** | | | |
| Violence–aggression | 7/12 (58.3%) | 0/12 (0%) | 0.01 |
| Poor school performance | 6/12 (50.0%) | 1/12 (8.3%) | 0.05 |
| Hyperkinetic relatives | 4/12 (33.3%) | 0/12 (0%) | 0.05 |
| Depression | 7/12 (58.3%) | 7/12 (58.3%) | — |
| Homosexual, anti-social, eccentric | 4/12 (33.3%) | 2/12 (16.7%) | — |
| Alcohol abuse | 9/12 (75%) | 6/12 (50%) | — |
| Psychoses ("nervous breakdown") | 2/12 (16.7%) | 3/12 (25%) | — |
| **Childhood history** | | | |
| Hyperkinetic diagnosis as a child | 0/12 (0%) | 0/12 (0%) | — |
| Inability to sit still, fighting, poor concentration, dropout, failure | 11/12 (91.7%) | 0/12 (0%) | 0.005 |
| **Symptoms–signs in mental status** | | | |
| Hyperactive | 11/12 (91.7%) | 0/12 (0%) | 0.005 |
| Distractible | 11/12 (91.7%) | 5/12 (41.7%) | 0.025 |
| Impulsive | 12/12 (100%) | 1/12 (8.3%) | 0.005 |
| Temper–aggression | 12/12 (100%) | 0/12 (0%) | 0.005 |
| Antisocial | 7/12 (58.3%) | 1/12 (8.3%) | 0.025 |
| Alcohol abuse | 10/12 (83.3%) | 4/12 (33.3%) | 0.025 |
| Mood swings, depression | 12/12 (100%) | 12/12 (100%) | — |
| Insomnia (0–2 hours) | 8/12 (66.7%) | 3/12 (25%) | 0.05 |
| Amitriptyline HCl (100–250 mg) | 8/10 (80%) | 8/12 (66.7%) | — |
| Imipramine HCl (40–200 mg) | 3/10 (30%) | 8/12 (66.7%) | NS |
| Less than 7 days for remission of sx's | 10/10 (100%) | 0%* | 0.005 |
| Sleep induction and initial depression on medicine | 8/10 (80%) | 1/12 (8.3%) | 0.025 |
| BPRS decrease | 19.6 (1 week) | 16.9 (6 weeks) | |

$p$ Values based on Fischer exact probability test.
* Mean, 5.0 weeks; range 1–8 weeks; one patient had no benefit.

25

seen. Huessy posits that there may be some of both. These people resemble what has been called "the borderline syndrome," and even though one can produce some symptomatic improvement with medication it does not alter their ability to relate. The individuals who cannot relate usually suffer from concrete thinking and an inability to see themselves as others see them, and again the control of impulsivity, emotional lability, and other symptoms will not affect this disability. Again, because of Huessy's association with Spring Lake Ranch, these severe cases are overrepresented in his sample.

Marshall[12] several years ago carried on a project in a New York State penal facility with individuals quite similar to the ones under discussion here. In the totally controlled environment of the prison he used intensive behavior modification techniques with some success. Unfortunately, we cannot place any of our patients into such a controlled penal environment. Would early symptom control with medication have prevented some of these adult outcomes? Would the use of medication in these adults have increased their success rate?

Marshall also had many experiences of medication producing effective symptom control in prisoners followed by their refusal to continue on medication once out of prison. This was also the experience of Goldman et al.[13] when they successfully treated a number of sociopathic prisoners with imipramine; not one of them was willing to continue on the medication after the experiment was over. These experiences do not support the prevalent concern about our creating addicts. It appears that abuse is rare and that refusal to take the drugs is our most common problem.

Adult MBD patients present extremely varied symptomatic pictures depending upon the type of population one works with. The population in the study by Cohen et al.[4] was drawn from a private practice, Marshall's[12] population from a prison, and Huessy's patients from a private therapeutic community and some community mental health centers.[2,3] Populations of alcoholics, college students, or military personnel would present other patterns. Although we seldom think of adults as suffering from learning disabilities, we have had two patients who finally passed their high school equivalency tests while on a medication regime. Symptom configurations, motivation for treatment, and the ability to tolerate treatment will differ.

MBD patients are not protected against any other type of mental illness and may even be at higher risk for other adult mental disorders such as schizophrenia. At Spring Lake Ranch, Huessy has seen a number of individuals who met the criteria for both diagnoses and whose functioning was improved when they were treated for both disorders simultaneously.

There are certain adult behavior patterns that have been linked to MBD. The first, as already discussed, is sociopathy. Another is alcoholism; many of these individuals seem to suffer from chronic internal tension, which is effectively relieved by alcohol, but this soon leads to alcohol abuse or loss of self-control. In three of Huessy's cases the pattern of alcoholism was not yet well established, and successful treatment with small doses of tricyclics seemed to reduce alcohol intake markedly. Inability to tolerate stress, frequent among those of all ages with MBD, is a common finding in alcoholics. The percentage of alcoholics or sociopaths whose disorders are MBD related will be an important question for epidemiologic study.

Difficulty in falling asleep and early-morning awakening are common in MBD children. Hauri[14] at the Sleep Laboratory at Dartmouth Medical School had described a group of insomniacs who responded dramatically to 25–50 mg of amitriptyline. Huessy speculates that these may be a subgroup of adults with MBD.

There seems to be a negative interaction between MBD and premenstrual fluid retention. A number of women had severe problems during their premenstrual periods along with a history consistent with childhood MBD; these young women presented to Huessy with a variety of psychiatric diagnoses. Careful histories revealed that their serious difficulties began after puberty and in the early stages of their disorder appeared only during their premenstrual periods. They would overreact, impulsively act out, or look hysterical. The problems created could not always be resolved before the next episode, and the difficulties would snowball. Control of premenstrual fluid retention by the use of a diuretic ended the cycle. Anti-MBD medication was not used. The case histories supported Huessy's previously reported impression that MBD presents differently in females, i.e., the early grade school female is more involved in daydreaming than in the acting out typical of her male counterpart, and serious difficulties may not show up until conflicts with authority begin in early adolescence. Many of the female teenagers that present in emergency rooms with suicidal gestures and apparently acute depressions belong to this group. They do not fit the usual picture of depressive illness because of their rapid mood changes; instead, they seem to represent the hysterical personality associated with MBD.

Finally, poor self-image is a pervasive symptom and not easily altered, even with successful drug therapy. In the suicidal adolescent we must differentiate a poor self-image from a depressive state. These two are continually interchanged in the literature. Klerman,[15] at the annual meeting of the American Psychiatric Association in Toronto, itemized points that Huessy feels separate these patients from true depressives, i.e., there is an obvious precipitating cause, there are no endogenous signs, the episode is representative of a lifetime maladaptive pattern, and the mood is variable. On the assumption that the patient is a depressive, he or she is given a tricyclic, which turns out to be the appropriate drug for the wrong reason and at too high a dosage, producing side effects and termination of drug therapy.

As with children, Huessy was unable to predict which drug will help which individual or at what dosage. The following drugs, reported to be effective in the treatment of children, have been helpful in treating adults: imipramine, amitriptyline, methylphenidate, dextroamphetamine, methamphetamine, chlorprothixene, and diphenylhydantoin. In the more than 200 adult cases seen by Huessy, only 3 have responded to diphenylhydantoin; all 3 had shown an excitatory response to one or more of the other drugs. Today he would try carbamazepine. The dosages of imipramine required were small; an occasional patient could not tolerate even 10 mg of imipramine, finding 5 mg sufficient. This is similar to a case reported by Klein.[16]

The antidepressant effect of tricyclics takes time and may be a counterresponse to the immediate biochemical effect. The benefit for the MBD patient comes from the immediate effect[17] and lasts just as long as the drug is in the system; i.e., we are dealing with symptom control, not curative treatment. The drugs are not interchangeable. The patient who does not respond to imipramine may respond to an amphetamine or vice versa. Two of Huessy's patients require 30 mg/day of amphetamine, an uncomfortably high dose in view of present attitudes toward amphetamines; however, both have been on this dosage for over a year and give no indication that their requirements are increasing.

We look for just as dramatic a response in adults as we have seen in children. We use the same 3-day drug trials, increasing the dosage every 3 days until we decide that that particular drug is not working; then another drug is tried.

As indicated in Table 2-10, Huessy has used dosages of 5–150 mg of imipramine, 50–125 mg of amitriptyline, 15–100 mg of methylphenidate, 10–30 mg of dextroamphetamine, and 100–400 mg of diphenylhydantoin (in this series there was only one trial of methamphetamine, using 10 mg). In other cases, he has used 5–30 mg of methamphetamine gradumets and particularly appreciates its long-acting effect. In addition, 25–100 mg of chlorprothixene has been used successfully in some cases. Further research may alter these dosage ranges. Huessy seldom goes as high as 100 mg with a tricyclic anymore. His experience with multiple drug usage is limited but warrants further exploration. Long-acting drugs or slow release forms of the short-acting drugs are used whenever possible. Some of our poor treatment outcomes in children may be due to the intermittent control seen with methylphenidate and most amphetamine treatment.

With respect to occasional drug usage, some patients with MBD,

**Table 2-10**
Dosage Ranges of Medications Producing Positive Responses

| Drug | Imipramine | Amitriptyline | Methylphenidate | Dextroamphetamine | Diphenylhydantoin | Pemoline | Methamphetamine |
|---|---|---|---|---|---|---|---|
| Dosage range (mg) | 5–150 | 50–125 | 15–100 | 10–30 | 100–400 | — | 10* |

* Only one trial.

perhaps those with milder cases, appear to be able to cope except under unusual stress. In such stress situations their emotional overreactivity and impulsivity produce a snowballing effect, and they get themselves into serious difficulties, very much like the women with premenstrual problems. For these individuals occasional use of medication for a week or two during stressful situations appears to be sufficient. The patients seem capable of deciding this for themselves and do not show any tendency to abuse the medication. Some other patients, again probably those with milder cases of MBD, do not show a deterioration in adjustment until several weeks or months after stopping medication. Apparently their problems progressively mount over this time until medication is again required.

MBD patients seem to share an unusual sensitivity or even bizarreness of reaction to all drugs affecting the nervous system. A female patient vehemently complained that 30 mg of imipramine a day produced a complete suppression of her sexual drive, while a male patient when given a bolus or station dose of 25 mg of amitriptyline went to sleep for 2 hours in the outpatient clinic. A young female complained of sleepiness on 10 mg of imipramine and showed marked improvement in her educational performance on only 5 mg/day. Still another male patient developed insomnia on 40 mg twice a day, which ceased with elimination of the evening dose. Two male patients have even described a short-lived high from 10 mg of imipramine, but only for the first 2 days. Apparently the same drug is producing opposite side effects, a phenomenon Huessy has also seen in children. Could this be a meaningful way for identifying two different groups of MDB patients?

Many of these individuals have a high tolerance for all types of sleeping medications, and some report an excitatory response to barbiturates. A patient of Huessy's reported an occasion when his friends reacted to "speed" with the expected excitatory response while he became calm and accomplished more work in that day than he'd ever done before. Others report periods of improved functioning while on diet pills. Some authors have described the successful use of lithium for extreme emotional lability. Huessy has two such cases but is not prepared to put them in the MBD category.

Various epidemiologic studies indicate that as many as 50 percent of all children may be at risk for MBD. Is this the same group that is developing adult symptomatology? Huessy's epidemiologic studies[18] indicate that there is a group of children who present symptoms in second grade but who improve without treatment and another group who may not present symptoms until the fourth or fifth grade but who seem to have a poorer prognosis. How these two groups relate to adult psychopathology is not known. Perhaps it is the group presenting symptoms in fourth or fifth grade that is most at risk for later adult disorders. The work of Silver et al.,[19] as duplicated by Arnold et al.,[20] indicates that the learning problems so common in these children can be eliminated either through their intervention program or by postponing the teaching of reading by 6 months or a year. How much adult MBD would this prevent? A study by Detre et al.[21] showed that the most common childhood antecedents of male patients presenting in an adult psychiatric outpatient clinic were the behavioral complex of childhood MBD. From a public health point of view these patients are the most important for us to deal with.

As we review our experiences with psychiatric patients with the concept of adult MBD in mind, many of our clinical notions will have to change. For many of these patients, symptom control through the use of medication is not a sufficient treatment, but it is progress. We must learn how to motivate them to consider further treatment, or is it possible to learn social skills 20 years after the time one normally acquires them?

Adults with MBD are known to blame all their troubles on factors beyond their control. Such denial of personal responsibility may be the only way they can live with themselves. Sudden recognition of the reality of one's irresponsible existence following successful drug treatment can be devastating and carries with it a risk of suicide. If for 20 years an individual has blamed others for constant troubles, the sudden realization that the others may be right may be too much. Overreaction and impulsivity produce unpredictable results under stress. Unexpected suicide or suicide attempts are a possibility.

There are many patients who feel medication started a new life for them. As we do for children, we have drugs that ameliorate adult behaviors that are often disabling. Regarding the use of drugs, Huessy stresses that he is giving the patient a tool for greater self-control and relief from impulsive reactions. The medication increases the number of options. The patient decides to what purpose these benefits are used.

This conference marks the beginning of dealing in a new way with a large group of patients who have produced extensive pain not only to themselves but to society. For some, the new treatment has had dramatic positive effects; for many others, it only beckons us to the possibility that previously untreatable conditions may be treatable or perhaps preventable. Would early treatment reduce adult psychopathology?

Seven case vignettes are appended, illustrating the varied presentations.

## APPENDIX: CASE REPORTS

M. H., a 51-year-old married mother and businesswoman, had been seen in a rural mental health clinic for 6 years with a primary diagnosis of depression. On repeated trials of amitriptyline, she would complain of side effects on daily doses greater than 75 mg, remain on 75 mg/day for several months, and then drop out of treatment and stop her medication; 6–12 months later she would present herself for treatment again.

When first seen she was under some unusual pressures, again complained of depression, and was restarted on amitriptyline. In addition, she was given 20 mg methylphenidate b.i.d. for more immediate relief of her symptoms. She called to report that she had accomplished more in the past 2 weeks than in any previous month. Once again she dropped out of treatment, only to return 4 months later, stating that her drinking was out of control, a problem not previously mentioned. She was given Antabuse and did not return for 4½ months. At that time she proudly reported having been abstinent but also that she was feeling badly, having sleeping problems, and was inefficient. It then came out that for 30 years she had been on 15 mg dextroamphetamine spansules, occasionally taking as many as five a day. During this time she had raised six children, developed a successful business, and had slept well. However, in reaction to the increasing public concern over amphetamines, the doctor supplying her medication discontinued it 6 years ago. Her drinking problems began at that time.

On the basis of this information, the author restarted her on 15 mg dextroamphetamine q.d., and she has been doing well since. She is adamant that dextroamphetamine is more beneficial than methylphenidate and that both of these are far superior to tricyclics. However, she does take 25 mg amitriptyline in the evening for improved sleep; without it she has difficulty in falling asleep, is restless once asleep, and develops a headache around 4 p.m. the following day.

J.M., a 20-year-old college student, came to Spring Lake Ranch, a therapeutic community in Cuttingsville, Vt., from a private psychiatric hospital with a diagnosis of schizophrenia. She had experienced progressive maladaption over approximately 5 years. She was obviously very bright and displayed impressive personal warmth, social judgment, and artistic talents. Careful exploration of her past revealed that as a child she was a loner and frequently accused of daydreaming. In adolescence, conflicts with authority figures developed, after which she apparently experienced acute upsets lasting several days and would leave school or stay out all night. Although she would try to resolve the conflicts, her attempts were often interrupted by other upsets, leaving her with mounting unresolved problems. Finally, at the point when her problems seemed continuous, she entered the psychiatric hospital.

At Spring Lake Ranch we were able to document that for 5 days before her periods she was irritable, explosive, and impulsive. We chose to treat her with a diuretic for 6 days before each period, resulting in complete abolition of her episodic upsets. She has since gone on to a successful art apprenticeship.

R.N., a 25-year-old married laborer, appeared at a mental health clinic acutely upset. He reported that during an argument with his wife, he had broken the windshield of his car, adding, "I'm always the loser when I blow up.'' He had been seen repeatedly in the clinic for crises, with five different personality or neurotic diagnoses. His past history revealed that he had major learning problems, left school after the eighth grade, was always a loner, and had lost many jobs because of arguments or fights with his superiors or co-workers. He also frequently argued with his wife and could not play with his children.

He was then placed on 10 mg imipramine b.i.d., and after 2 weeks he returned with his wife to report that he had had no arguments at home or at work, that the quality of his work had improved, and that he had enjoyed his children. However, he then announced that he would not continue with the medication; he was adamant but unable to give an explanation.

J.K. came to Spring Lake Ranch at age 16 years. She had lived in a single girls' residence for 2 years, communicating with her parents only through their respective psychotherapists. She ''blew up,'' screamed, and threatened at the slightest frustration. She improved dramatically on 20 mg imipramine b.i.d., with further improvement on 40 mg. Approximately every 2 months the patient would request that her medication be cut in half, stating that pressures were building up and she needed a rest. Two to three weeks later she would request a return to full dosage. On the lower dosage she displayed less maturity, less efficient work performance, and a slightly quick temper. Her ability to cope with the higher dose increased over time. Gradually she reestablished direct communication with her family. Her temper outbursts ceased completely, and she left the Ranch for a successful independent living situation. Unfortunately, 6 months later she stopped her medications and has returned to manipulating her parents to support her.

S.J., a 26-year-old divorcee with a childhood history of MBD, at age 20 entered the state hospital. She was finally tried on 10 mg methylphenidate each morning, with dramatic improvement. The doctor prescribing her medication moved away, and she had difficulty in obtaining more. When she saw me, she asked for a 2-week supply only, explaining that once her problems were under control she could manage for 6 months to a year without medication. It appears that whenever her life becomes disorganized due to some unusual stress, she experiences difficulty, and her emotional overreaction and impulsivity cause her problems to snowball. At these times, her medication helps her to become stabilized and integrated.

M.M. was a 27-year-old divorced male with a history of being in and out of prison and unable to hold a job. His criminal offenses were all minor and occurred while he was intoxicated. He had received alcohol rehabilitation and other counseling. When he described his history of drug abuse, it came out that amphetamines had a mellowing effect on him while making his friends speed.

Under our treatment he did not respond to tricyclics, and while methamphetamine was beneficial, he became upset when it wore off; 15 mg dextroamphetamine spansules proved most effective. In addition, he takes 250 mg Antabuse daily, not trusting himself to do without it. He has worked steadily this past year. He recently stopped his Antabuse and has been reported as drinking again. He is still working.

C.M. was a 40-year-old married man referred by an orthopedic surgeon because of difficulty in coping with his back problems and his resulting inactivity. As a child he had had reading problems, dropped out of school in the eighth grade, and was a loner. He was always very physically active, and at one time drove a cement truck 12–16 hours a day. He found being confined at home in a back brace frustrating and that it made things very difficult for his family. Stimulant medications seemed to make him worse. He finally responded well to diphenylhydantoin and was able to work in a rehabilitation program to become a project engineer. Gradually diphenylhydantoin lost its effectiveness. Chlorprothixene 25 mg kept him asleep for 1½ days. After being without medication completely because none seemed to help, diphenylhydantoin was restarted and again found to be effective. On this medication he was able to control his weight, which in turn improved his back. He has worked steadily for the last 3 years, except for the winter months when construction jobs close down.

## REFERENCES

1.  Arnold LE, Strobl D, Weisenberg A: Hyperkinetic adult: Study of the "paradoxical" amphetamine response. JAMA 222:693–694, 1972.
2.  Huessy HR, Blair CL: Clinical explorations in the pharmacotherapy of adult MBD. Unpublished research project, University of Vermont, 1974.
3.  Huessy HR: The adult hyperkinetic. Am J Psychiatry 131:724–725, 1974.
4.  Cohen SM, Oliveau D, Huessy HR: Depression, hyperkinesis and violence: A new syndrome? Unpublished manuscript, University of Vermont, 1977.
5.  Rutter M: Protective factors in children's responses to stress and disadvantage. Presentation read at the Third Vermont Conference on the Primary Prevention of Psychopathology, University of Vermont, 1977.
6.  Arnold LE: Minimal brain dysfunction: A hydraulic parfait model. Dis Nerv Syst 4:171–173, 1976.
7.  Waldrop MF, Bell RQ: Minor physical anomalies and inhibited behavior in elementary school girls. J Child Psychol Psychiatry 17:113–122, 1976.
8.  Cohen ME, Badal DW, Kilpatrick A, et al: The high familial prevalence of neurocirculatory asthenia (anxiety neurosis, effort syndrome). Am J Hum Genet 3:126–158, 1951.
9.  Huessy HR, Wright AL: The use of imipramine in children's behavior disorders. Acta Paedopsychiatr 37:194–199, 1970.
10.  Wender PH, Wood DR, Reimherr FW, et al: Diagnosis and treatment of minimal brain dysfunction in adults. Arch Gen Psychiatry 33:1453–1460, 1976.
11.  Capella B, Gentile JR, Juliano DB: Time estimation by hyperactive and normal children. Percept Mot Skills 44:787–790, 1977.
12.  Marshall C: Verbal communication, 1974.
13.  Goldman H, Dinitz S, Lindner LA, et al: Drug treatment of the sociopathic offender. Presentation read at the 140th Annual Meeting of the American Association for the Advancement of Science, San Francisco, 1974.

14. Hauri P: Verbal communication, Dartmouth Medical School, 1975.
15. Neurotic depression is an unclear diagnostic classification. Roche Rep Frontiers Psychiatry February 15, 1978, 3.
16. Klein DF: Verbal communication, Long Island Jewish-Hillside Medical Center, 1975.
17. Schildkraut JJ, et al: Pharmakopsychiatr Neuropsychopharmakol 9:193–202, 1976.
18. Huessy HR, Cohen AH: Hyperkinetic behaviors and learning disabilities followed over seven years. Pediatrics 57:4–10, 1976.
19. Silver AA, Hagin RA, Hersh MF: Reading disability: Teaching through stimulation of deficit perceptual areas. Am J Orthopsychiatry 11:645–674, 1972.
20. Arnold LE, Barnebey N, McManus J, et al: Prevention by specific perceptual remediation for vulnerable first-graders. Arch Gen Psychiatry 34:1279–1294, 1977.
21. Detre TP, Kupfer DJ, Koral J: Relationship of certain childhood "traits" to adult psychiatric disorders. Am J Orthopsychiatry 45:74–80, 1975.

## DISCUSSION

*Chairman Bellak:*   A particularly valuable suggestion seems to me to employ estimate of time as a diagnostic test. Some of Witkin's tests, field dependence, field independence, might also be especially useful for that purpose.

*Dr. Wender:*   We have been using these tests, and we're finding the men do poorly and the women quite well. Explain that.

*Chairman Bellak:*   "Vive la difference" is all I can say for the moment. One other thing—Dr. Huessy mentioned that MBD people seem to suffer from insomnia. It's my impression that they also dream more and have disturbing dreams more often. Certainly, Greenspan also emphasizes that small dosages of drugs are very effective. Among the common denominator that all of us probably will find is that there is absolutely no tendency to abuse these drugs because patients do not experience euphoria. They just start to feel all right.

*Dr. Gallant:*   By the way, we've seen a few patients who have abused the drugs.

*Dr. Wender:*   So have I. It seems to be the bimodal response. In low doses it calms and then high doses have the same effect as "speed."

*Chairman Bellak:*   That's something we'll have to look into. Maybe only on high doses then!

*Dr. Huessy:*   I skipped one little thing. I described the patient that went to sleep on 25 mg of Elavil. I also had one that on 10 mg complained of sedation. We have others that can't sleep if you give an afternoon dose of tricyclic. Whether that is one basis for grouping them, I don't know. We've also seen in children that too high a dose can produce opposite effects in different children; one falls asleep and the other gets more irritable.

*Dr. Gallant:*   Actually, there have been a lot of data put out by Werry and Sprague that show that a dosage high enough to calm behavior will interfere with learning, so your dosage situation is extremely important—it's essential.

*Chairman Bellak:*   As you say, with 10 mg you're sometimes already too high and may get increased irritability instead of improvement.

*Dr. Wender:*   The reason I asked about the amitriptyline is that a young investigator by the name of Barry Garfinkel in Toronto, who's doing a crossover study in children with desmethylimipramine (DMI) and chlorimipramine and methylphenidate, has found that chlorimipramine seems to be reasonably efficacious and DMI is worthless.

Dennis P. Cantwell

# 3

# Minimal Brain Dysfunction in Adults: Evidence From Studies of Psychiatric Illness in the Families of Hyperactive Children

We will review data on the prevalence and types of psychiatric illness in the families of hyperactive children. The implications of these data for theory and practice will be discussed, especially as they relate to the topic of this symposium: minimal brain dysfunction in adults.

## HYPERACTIVITY IN CLOSE RELATIVES

Several detailed family studies have looked at the question of how often the hyperactive child syndrome occurs in close family relatives of probands with the syndrome. I have studied the biologic parents of 50 hyperactive children and compared them with the biologic parents of 50 normal control children.[1] Morrison and Stewart[2] conducted a similar study of the parents of 59 hyperactive and 41 normal control children. In the Cantwell study 16 percent of the fathers, 4 percent of the mothers, 10 percent of the uncles, 12 percent of the male first cousins, 12 percent of all male relatives, and 6.3 percent of all relatives combined were considered to have had the hyperactive child syndrome themselves as children. In the Morrison and Stewart study the comparable figures were 15 percent for fathers, 5 percent for mothers, 12 percent for uncles, 13 percent for all male relatives, and 7.5 percent for all relatives combined.

Welner *et al.*[3] and I,[1] in separate studies, have looked at the prevalence of the hyperactive child syndrome in the siblings of probands with
the disorder. Welner *et al.* found that 26 percent of the brothers and 9
percent of the sisters met the criteria for the hyperactive child syndrome,
while I found that 22 percent of the brothers and 8 percent of the sisters
met the same criteria. I used the DSM III criteria for attentional deficit
disorder *with* hyperactivity to make his diagnosis; I also looked at the
prevalence of a new disorder that is described in DSM III—attentional
deficit disorder *without* hyperactivity. Two percent of the brothers of
hyperactive children met the criteria for attentional deficit disorder without hyperactivity, and 11 percent of the sisters met the same criteria. Thus
24 percent of the brothers of hyperactive children and 19 percent of the
sisters meet the DSM III criteria for attentional disorders. This approximately equal sex ratio suggests that girls manifest the attentional disorder without the attendant symptoms of hyperactivity, while boys for a
variety of reasons—environmental, genetic, or some combination there-
of—manifest symptoms of overactivity in addition to the core attentional
deficit.

In another type of sibling study Safer[4] examined the full- and half-
siblings of 17 index cases with minimal brain dysfunction. Of the 19
full-siblings, 10 were considered likely to manifest minimal brain dysfunction, whereas that diagnosis was given to only 2 of 22 half-siblings. Thus
55 percent of full-siblings were considered likely to manifest the symptoms of hyperactivity (short attention span and impulsive behavior), as
opposed to only 9 percent of half-siblings.

The conclusion to be drawn from all of these studies is that this
particular syndrome, the hyperactive child syndrome, does seem to be a
familial disorder that is transmitted from generation to generation. Increased prevalence rates for the syndrome have been found in the close
family relatives of individuals who have the disorder themselves. The
Safer study, which reports a sixfold greater increase in the syndrome in
full- compared to half-siblings, also suggests a genetic mechanism for this
familial transmission.

## OTHER PSYCHIATRIC DISORDERS IN CLOSE RELATIVES
## OF HYPERACTIVE CHILDREN

A number of investigators, have suggested on the basis of their own
clinical observations and on historical data that there is an increased
prevalence of psychiatric illness in the families of hyperactive children.
Wender[5] felt that the hyperactive children that he saw had parents with
increased prevalence of mixed types of psychopathology, including

schizophrenia, affective disorders, and sociopathy. Satterfield* found that the parents of hyperactive children had a markedly greater incidence of neurosis, antisocial behavior, "nervous breakdown," suicide, attempted suicide, and alcoholism when compared to parents of matched control children. In their original clinical description of 37 hyperactive children in St. Louis, Stewart et al. [6] noted that over half had at least one first- or second-degree relative whose behavior had led to serious legal or employment problems or had required psychiatric treatment. Presumptive psychiatric diagnosis of these relatives included eight with affective disorders, five with alcoholism or other addictive problems, and six with other disorders. Mendelson et al. [7] followed up 83 hyperactive children from St. Louis Children's Hospital into adolescence. At the time of the followup 22 percent of the fathers and 4 percent of the mothers were having significant marital, legal, or employment problems related to heavy drinking. Nearly 25 percent of the fathers, 10 percent of the mothers, and 37 percent of the siblings had behavior or learning problems as a child.

These clinical and historical data have now confirmed by the two systematic family studies of the hyperactive child syndrome Morrison mentioned above. [1,2] In my study most of the parents of children in the control group did not have any psychiatric disorder, whereas half of the parents of hyperactive children met the criteria for some psychiatric diagnosis. The specific differences between the parents of the hyperactive children and the parents of the control group were in a greater prevalence for alcoholism, sociopathy, and hysteria in the parents of hyperactive children: 30 percent of the fathers of hyperactive children were diagnosed as alcoholics, and 16 percent were given a diagnosis of sociopathy; 8 percent of the mothers of hyperactive children were diagnosed as alcoholics, and 16 percent were given a diagnosis of hysteria or proabable hysteria. No other psychiatric disorders were found to have an increased prevalence in these parents.

In the Morrison and Stewart study [2] one-third of the parents of hyperactive children had some psychiatric diagnosis, while over 80 percent of the parents in the control group did not meet the criteria for psychiatric disorder. As in my study [2] the specific differences between the groups were a greater prevalence of alcoholism, sociopathy, and hysteria in the parents of hyperactive children: 20 percent of the fathers of hyperactive children were given a diagnosis of alcoholism, and 5 percent were given a diagnosis of sociopathy; 5 percent of the mothers of hyperactive children were diagnosed as alcoholic, and 10 percent were given a diagnosis of hysteria. In my study the increased prevalence of alcoholism, sociopathy, and hysteria was found to characterize the second- and third-degree relatives also: 20 percent of the male second-degree relatives

---

* Personal Communication.

were given a diagnosis of alcoholism, and 12 percent were given a diagnosis of sociopathy; of the female second-degree relatives, 2 percent were diagnosed as alcoholic and 8 percent were given a diagnosis of hysteria.

The data from the Cantwell sibling study which found increased prevalence of the hyperactive child syndrome in the brothers and sisters of hyperactive children have not yet been completely analyzed. Eventually specific psychiatric diagnoses will be made on the basis of DSM III criteria for all brothers and sisters of hyperactive children. This should allow some tentative conclusions about the familial relationship of hyperactivity with other psychiatric disorders in childhood.

The Welner study did this to some degree but did not make specific psychiatric diagnoses. They did find that in the nonhyperactive brothers of hyperactive children there was an increased amount of depressive *symptoms*. However, the authors did not attempt to make a case for increased prevalence for a depressive *syndrome* or a depressive *disorder*. In the nonhyperactive brothers there was also a lower full scale and verbal IQ as measured by the Wechsler Intelligence Scale for Children (WISC), as well as lower spelling and math achievement as measured by the Wide Range Achievement Test (WRAT). In the nonhyperactive sisters of the hyperactive probands WRAT testing revealed lower reading and spelling achievement scores. This might suggest that the nonhyperactive siblings of hyperactive boys may also suffer from some degree of learning disability, but a much more systematic study will be needed to answer this question definitively.

## RELATIONSHIP BETWEEN HYPERACTIVITY AND OTHER PSYCHIATRIC DISORDERS IN THE PARENTS OF HYPERACTIVE CHILDREN

Combining the data from my study[1] and the Morrison and Stewart study,[2] we find 19 fathers who were considered to have been hyperactive children. All 19 of these were manifesting psychiatric disorders as adults. Twelve were definite alcoholics, two were sociopaths, one had multiple depressive, obsessive, and compulsive symptoms, and four had undiagnosed mental illnesses with excess alcohol intake as a major symptom. There were 6 exhyperactive mothers—2 were definite hysterics as adults, 2 qualified for a diagnosis of hysteria and alcoholism, and 2 manifested affective disorders as adults.

These data suggest that the hyperactive child syndrome is a familial disorder passed from generation to generation and moreover that a familial relationship exists between the hyperactive child syndrome and three adult psychiatric disorders: alcoholism, sociopathy, and hysteria.

The data presented thus far do not explain whether the possible mechanism of transmission of the hyperactive child syndrome is a genetic or an environmental one, nor do they explain whether the familial relationship between the hyperactive child syndrome and the three adult psychiatric disorders is a genetic or environmental one.

## ADOPTION STUDIES

Morrison and Stewart[8] and I[9] used the adoption study method to test the following hypotheses: (1) The hyperactive child syndrome is genetically transmitted from generation to generation. (2) There is a genetic relationship between the hyperactive child syndrome and three psychiatric disorders of adulthood—alcoholism, sociopathy, and hysteria.

To test these hypotheses both groups conducted a systematic psychiatric examination of the nonbiologic parents of adopted hyperactive children. If the nonbiologic parents and their extended families did not show the same increased prevalence of the hyperactive child syndrome and the other psychiatric disorders found in biologic parents of hyperactive children, then a strong argument could be made for a genetic factor upgrading in the syndrome. The data from both of these studies are quite similar. The hyperactive child syndrome was found to a much greater degree in the biologic first- and second-degree relatives of hyperactive children than in the nonbiologic relatives of the adopted children. This syndrome found was not significantly more prevalent in the adoptive relatives than in the relatives of the control group. These data are consistent with the hypothesis that there is a genetic transmission of the hyperactive child syndrome from generation to generation and with the hypothesis that the familial relationship between alcoholism, sociopathy, and hysteria in parents and the hyperactive child syndrome is a genetic one. Systematic psychiatric examination of the adopting parents did not reveal the high prevalence of alcoholism, sociopathy, and hysteria that had been found in the biologic parents, nor was there an increased prevalence of these conditions in the nonbiologic second-degree relatives of adopted hyperactive children.

## IMPLICATIONS AND CONCLUSIONS

The data from the studies reviewed above suggest the following conclusions:

1. There seems to be an increased prevalence of the hyperactive child syndrome in the close relatives of hyperactive probands.

2. There seems to be an increased prevalence of certain other psychiatric disorders in the close relatives of hyperactive probands. The psychiatric disorders found in the parents and close relatives of the hyperactive children are those considered to be in the "antisocial spectrum": alcoholism and sociopathy in males, hysteria and, to a lesser extent, alcoholism in females.

3. The data suggest that the hyperactive child syndrome is a familial disorder that is transmitted from generation to generation. The mechanism of this transmission could be genetic, environmental, or gene-environment interaction.

4. The adoption studies reviewed above suggest that a strong genetic component operates in the genesis of the syndrome. The suggestion is verified to some degree by twin studies.[9]

5. Those psychiatrically ill relatives in the families of hyperactive children gave evidence of being hyperactive in childhood themselves. This suggests that the hyperactive child syndrome may manifest itself in adults as disturbances in the antisocial spectrum: alcoholism, sociopathy, and hysteria.

What are the implications of these data for theory and research? Clearly the hyperactive child syndrome when defined behaviorally is a heterogeneous disorder etiologically. I have presented elsewhere a model suggesting how children with this disorder can be divided into meaningful subgroups by the use of physical and neurologic studies, laboratory studies, natural history studies, treatment studies, and family studies.[10]

The data reviewed here suggest that a family history–positive group (FH+) and a family history–negative group (FH−) may be a meaningful division of an initial group of children presenting with the hyperactive child syndrome. By meaningful division is meant that the children in the FH+ group may differ from the children in the FH− group in terms of treatment, etiology, natural history, etc. Surprisingly, this has not really been done in a systematic fashion. Indirectly one can extract from the literature the suggestion that those hyperactive children with a positive family history of hyperactivity are also characterized by differences in other areas of the six-stage model developed by the author. The FH+ group differs from the FH− group in physical findings in that they have an increased number of minor physical anomalies as described by Rapoport and Quinn[11] and others. The FH+ group also seems to have increased levels of dopamine beta hydroxylase, suggesting that this FH+ group may be a biologically distinct group.

If one starts with an index group of children who meet behavioral criteria for the hyperactive child syndrome (or the attentional deficit disorder with hyperactivity, using DSM III criteria), one can also use family history data to separate those who have a positive family history of disorders in the antisocial spectrum in their parents. If this is done and they are compared to hyperactive children whose families are free of these disorders, there is limited evidence to suggest that the clinical picture may be somewhat different in that those hyperactive children in the antisocial spectrum parent group have more antisocial, aggressive symptoms themselves not only when seen initially but also at followup. This group may also respond more poorly to stimulant medication than the group with a negative family history.[12]

The limited data available suggest that the study of families of hyperactive children should be a fruitful area of research.

## REFERENCES

1. Cantwell DP: Psychiatric illness in the families of hyperactive children. Arch Gen Psychiatry 27:414–417, 1972.
2. Morrison JR, Stewart MA: A family study of the hyperactive child syndrome. Biol Psychiatry 3:189–195, 1971.
3. Welner Z, Welner A, Stewart M, et al: A controlled study of siblings of hyperactive children. J Nerv Ment Dis 165:110–117, 1977.
4. Safer DJ: A familial factor in minimal brain dysfunction. Behav Gent 3:175–187, 1973.
5. Wender PH: Minimal Brain Dysfunction in Children. New York, Wiley-Interscience, 1971.
6. Stewart M, Pitts F, Craig A, et al: The hyperactive child syndrome. Am J Orthopsychiatry 36:861–867, 1966.
7. Mendelson W, Johnson J, Stewart M: Hyperactive children as teenagers: A follow-up study. J Nerv Ment Dis 153:273–279, 1971.
8. Morrison J, Stewart M: The psychiatric status of the legal families of adopted hyperactive children. Arch Gen Psychiatry 28:888–891, 1973.
9. Cantwell DP: Genetic studies of hyperactive children: Psychiatry illness in biologic and adopting parents. In Fieve R, Rosenthal D, Brill H (eds): Genetic Research in Psychiatry. Baltimore, Johns Hopkins Univ, 1974.
10. Cantwell DP: A medical model for research and clinical use with hyperactive children. In Cantwell DP (ed): The Hyperactive Child: Diagnosis, Management, and Current Research. New York, Spectrum, 1975.
11. Rapoport JL, Quinn PO: Multiple minor physical anomalies (stigmata) and elevated plasma DBH: A major biologic subgroup of hyperactive children. Int J Ment Health 4:29–44, 1975.
12. Cantwell DP: Familial-genetic research with hyperactive children. In Cantwell DP (ed): The Hyperactive Child: Diagnosis, Management, and Current Research. New York, Spectrum, 1975.

## DISCUSSION

*Dr. Gallant:*    As I understood it, you said that those children with a family history of hyperkinetic parents did better on stimulants and those with antisocial relatives did worse? Is that right?

*Dr. Cantwell:*    There has not really been a systematic study of this proposition. The problem is that there is an overlap between the groups. There are children who have a family history of both hyperactivity and antisocial parentage. With a disorder described behaviorally, as this particular disorder is, no matter how rigorously you describe it (and the DSM III is an attempt to do that, with operational criteria), the likelihood is that any group of children who meet the fine behavioral picture are still going to be a heterogeneous group. One way to separate out the group might be to take those with a positive family history of hyperactivity and those without and look for differences in, for example, monoamine metabolism, response to treatment, or long-term outcome. To my knowledge no one has done that systematically yet.

*Dr. Huessy:*    Do you have a clinical impression that there is a difference in response to treatment?

*Dr. Cantwell:*    When we looked at our group we did find that children who had a positive family history of hyperactivity in a first-degree relative did show a better response to stimulants, but we haven't done a controlled study and some other factor may explain their response.

*Dr. Gallant:*    Did you have an opportunity to look into those children that might have a family history of sociopathy or alcoholism?

*Dr. Cantwell:*    We haven't done it yet.

*Chairman Bellak:*    It is not only important to have predictive studies, as Dr. Wender suggested, but eventually "postdictive" studies, a term that Gordon Allport coined, I think. Apparently you might make differential postdictions from the presenting picture in children as to whether there is or is not a family history, which might then lead to further separation of the subgroups after the phenotype that we all run into. The third aspect would be to make collateral inferences that if we find *A*, we should increasingly be able to predict collaterally that there should also be *B*, *C*, and *D*. And then we have a fairly well-defined and scientifically acceptable set of hypotheses.

Barry L. Borland

# 4

# Social Adaptation in Men Who Were Hyperactive: A Follow-up Study of Hyperactive Boys and Their Brothers

Signs of unusual behavior have been traced to infancy in many children diagnosed as hyperactive. Symptoms of hyperactivity become increasingly apparent in these children in their preschool and early school years and have adverse effects on their academic performance as well as on their relations with parents, teachers, and peers. Evidence from recent studies shows that symptoms in hyperactive children are reduced in number and severity as they grow older; however, major symptoms of this disorder seem to persist in many hyperactive children through their childhood and adolescent years and into adulthood.

Follow-up studies show that symptoms of hyperactivity decrease in number and intensity by adolescence in many affected children.[1] However, hyperactivity has not been found to be a syndrome that wanes spontaneously and disappears, as was earlier thought. Instead, the relative importance of some symptoms of hyperactivity seems to change, and effects of the persistence of these symptoms on social and emotional development become more apparent in hyperactive children in their teenage years.

Hyperactive children seem to be less active, distractible, impulsive, and excitable in adolescence than in childhood. However, they continue to do poorly in school and to have difficulty in establishing and maintaining satisfactory relations with peers, parents, and other adults.[2,3] These academic and social failures are closely associated with the poor and distorted self-image of many hyperactive children in adolescence. This is particularly true for those children whose symptoms have not been greatly reduced in number or severity since childhood.[4]

Results of long-term follow-up studies of hyperactive children show that symptoms of hyperactivity persist into adulthood in many cases, with important effects on adult social and psychiatric status. Menkes *et al.*[5] studied 14 patients 24 years after they presented to a clinic with symptoms of hyperactivity, learning problems, and "nonbehavioral criteria" for brain dysfunction. They found that 4 of their subjects were psychotic, 3 were hyperactive, and 2 were mentally retarded. Less than half of these subjects were self-supporting in adulthood.

A more recent follow-up study[6] included 20 men who had been referred to a guidance clinic 20–25 years ago and their brothers. Probands in this study conformed to diagnostic criteria for the hyperactive child syndrome on the basis of information in their clinic records. At the time of the follow-up study, half of the probands had fewer than three of the major symptoms of hyperactivity and half had three to seven of those symptoms. Only one of the brothers had as many as three symptoms of hyperactivity. A large majority of the men who were hyperactive had completed high school, and each was steadily employed and self-supporting; however, nearly half of these men had problems of a psychiatric nature, and despite their normal intelligence they had not achieved socioeconomic status equal to that of their brothers or their fathers. Results of that study indicate that social and psychiatric consequences of hyperactivity relate to its presence in childhood as well as to its persistence in adulthood.

This paper is related to that earlier report[6] and examines relations between childhood hyperactivity and measures of adult social adaptation and self-concept by comparing men who were hyperactive in childhood with their unaffected brothers. Specific attention will be given to examining the extent to which measures of social adaptation and self-concept are associated with the persistence of major symptoms of hyperactivity.

## METHODS AND PROCEDURES

This study began with a review of records of boys who were 4–11 years old at the time they were referred to a child guidance clinic between January 1, 1950 and December 1, 1955. These records were complete with regard to family and social history, psychological tests, and behavioral descriptions of the child. From these records men were selected who had the hyperactive child syndrome based on the criteria of Stewart *et al.*[7] and Mendelson *et al.*[1]

These criteria included both overactivity and short attention span and 4 or more of 35 additional symptoms listed by Mendelson et al.[1] shown over at least a 2-year period prior to clinic referral. In addition, these men had scores above 80 on standardized intelligence tests and had no chronic medical or neurologic disease and no orthopedic or special sensory handicaps. Each subject also had at least one living brother who could serve as a control in this study. (For a detailed description of methods see Borland and Heckman.)[6]

Follow-up information was obtained through personal interviews from 20 men who met the criteria for the study and 18 brothers and two brothers-in-law of these men. The interview was structured and patterned after the one used by Robins.[8] Close attention was paid to military, occupational, and marital histories, social affiliations of the probands and brothers, and to probands' feelings about themselves with respect to measures of social adaptation.

Significance of differences between men who were hyperactive and their brothers was determined by Fisher's exact test of probability except in one case where Student's two-tailed test was used. Statistical significance was accepted at $p \leq 0.05$.

## RESULTS

At the time of the follow-up study, the mean age of the proband was 30.4 years; the mean age of the brothers was 28.1 years. Each of the men in this study was steadily employed and self-supporting except for two brothers who were full-time college students. Clinic records of the probands showed they had an average of 8.6 symptoms of hyperactivity 20–25 years ago. At the time of the follow-up study these men had an average of 3.5 symptoms. Half of the probands reported fewer than 3 symptoms in the interview, and only two probands reported as many as 6 symptoms.

More than half the men in this study had entered military service within 2 years after leaving high school (Table 4-1). On the whole, the probands had spent more time in service than their brothers, but the average military rank of the probands was significantly lower than the average rank of the brothers at time of discharge. This difference approached but did not reach statistical significance (considered as $p \leq 0.05$).

Table 4-1 also shows that fully two-thirds of all probands who entered military service had problems with military police, superior officers, or both. Difficulties of the probands in military service did not seem to be closely related to the number of symptoms at time of study.

A greater proportion of probands than brothers had difficulties with

**Table 4-1**
Problems in Military Service

| | Average Rank* | Average Length of Service (years) | Trouble with MPs (No.) | Disciplined by CO (No.) | Court-Martialed (No.) | Demoted in Rank (No.) | Total With Discipline Problems (No.) |
|---|---|---|---|---|---|---|---|
| Probands | | | | | | | |
| 0–2 (n = 6) | 3.50 | 3.33 | 2 | 3 | 1 | 2 | 4 |
| 3–7 (n = 6) | 3.67 | 3.67 | 2 | 3 | 0 | 1 | 4 |
| All probands | 3.58 | 3.50 | 4 | 6 | 1 | 3 | 8 |
| | SD 1.16 | | $\}p = 0.055$ | $\}p = 0.044$ | | | $\}p = 0.025$ |
| Brothers (n = 11) | 4.63 | 3.21 | 0 | 1 | 0 | 0 | 1 |
| | SD 1.36 | | | | | | |
| | $(0.10 > p > 0.07)$ | | | | | | |

* Values were assigned to the pay grades held by the probands and their brothers at the time of discharge from military service. For example, a value of 4 was assigned if the proband was in pay grade E-4 at the time of discharge.

police or commanding officers while in military service, and this difference was significant ($p = 0.007$). Three probands but no brothers were demoted in rank because of those difficulties. Significantly more probands than brothers had problems with their commanding officer ($p = 0.044$) and with the military police ($p = 0.055$). Thus problems in military service were much more frequent in the probands than in the brothers.

Each of the probands and all of the 18 brothers no longer in school were employed at full-time jobs at the time of the study. None of these men had been unemployed for more than 1 month at any one time in the 5 years prior to the follow-up study. Many of the probands but few brothers had made several job changes in the previous 5 years, however. These men usually gave ''better pay'' or ''better working conditions'' as the first reason for their job changes, but job changes also seem to have involved difficulties in interpersonal relations in work situations. As shown in Table 4-2, more probands than brothers either had been dismissed or ''fired'' from a job or had left a job suddenly with no other job to go to. This difference was statistically significant ($p = 0.004$). Most of these eight probands described jobs they had left or were dismissed from as uninteresting and unrewarding. However, each of them also reported conflicts between themselves and work supervisors or co-workers as conditions involved in their sudden departure from previous jobs.

Differences between numbers of probands and brothers who had left a previous job suddenly without another job to go to were marginally significant ($p = 0.055$). However, significantly more probands than brothers had conflicts with supervisors ($p = 0.017$) and co-workers ($p = 0.002$) at their present jobs. Five probands and no brothers had been dismissed or ''fired'' from a previous job, but this difference was not statistically significant ($p > 0.05$).

The large majority of probands who had left the job suddenly, were fired from a previous job, or had difficulties with supervisors or co-workers at the time of the study continued to report three to seven symptoms of hyperactivity. Significantly more probands with three or more symptoms of hyperactivity had left or been fired from a previous job ($p = 0.025$) and reported difficulties with supervisors or co-workers ($p = 0.05$) than did the probands with fewer symptoms. Probands had more problems than their brothers in each aspect of job history examined in this study.

Nearly half (7) of the 15 probands who had married reported disruptions in their marriage that involved separation, divorce, or frequent serious arguments (Table 4-3). Only one of the three probands who had been separated or divorced was unmarried at the time of the study. One-third (5) of the probands reported frequent serious arguments with their wives, and 4 probands had left home for more than 2 or 3 days as a

**Table 4-2**
Problems Related to Work

| | Left Job Without Planning | Fired From Job | Total Who Left or Were Fired | Difficulties With Supervisor | Difficulties With Co-workers |
|---|---|---|---|---|---|
| Probands | | | | | |
| 0–2 symptoms ($n = 10$) | 1 | 1 | 1$\}p = 0.025$ | 0$\}p = 0.05$ | 2$\}p = 0.05$ |
| 3–7 symptoms ($n = 10$) | 5 | 3 | 7 | 5 | 7 |
| All probands ($n = 20$) | 6$\}p = 0.055$ | 4 | 8$\}p = 0.004$ | 5$\}p = 0.017$ | 9$\}p = 0.002$ |
| Brothers ($n = 18$) | 1 | 1 | 1 | 0 | 2 |

**Table 4-3**
Marital Problems

| Probands | Frequent Serious Arguments With Wife | Left Wife Suddenly | Recurrently Unfaithful | Legally Separated | Divorced Previously | Total No. Reporting Problems |
|---|---|---|---|---|---|---|
| 0–2 symptoms ($n = 7$) | 1 | 0 | 1 | 1 | 0 | 1 ⎫ $p = 0.05$ |
| 3–7 symptoms ($n = 8$) | 4 | 4 | 1 | 2 | 2 | 6 ⎭ |
| All probands ($n = 15$) | 5 | 7 | 2 | 3 | 2 | 7 ⎫ $p = 0.05$ |
| Brothers ($n = 15$) | 2 | 0 | 0 | 0 | 0 | 2 ⎭ |

result of these arguments. Arguments between the probands and their wives related to a wide variety of circumstances, including recurrent infidelity in the cases of two probands.

Marital problems of men in this study were concentrated among probands who continued to have three or more symptoms of hyperactivity. Significantly more of these probands than probands with less than three symptoms reported difficulties related to their marriage ($p = 0.05$). Significantly fewer brothers than probands reported these problems ($p = 0.05$).

In general, more probands than brothers reported a lack of friendships and relatively little involvement in social groups outside their family (Table 4-4). Probands did not differ greatly from their brothers with regard to informal social contacts, but significantly more brothers than probands were members of formal social or fraternal groups or organizations ($p = 0.001$). Although men who were hyperactive did not differ greatly from their brothers with regard to having intimate friendships, significantly more probands than brothers felt that they lacked friends ($p = 0.001$), and significantly more brothers than probands had maintained close friendships for more than 2 years ($p = 0.03$).

Among men who were hyperactive 20–25 years ago, those who had fewer than three major symptoms at interview were more likely than others to have close friends, maintain friendships over time, and be involved in informal social groups. Differences in social affiliations of probands with fewer than three major symptoms of hyperactivity and those with three or more symptoms were not statistically significant, however (at $p = 0.05$).

No single symptom of low self-esteem was identified in more than 7 of the 20 men who were hyperactive, and the majority of these symptoms were noted in no more than 25 percent of the probands or 10 percent of the brothers (Table 4-5). All symptoms of low self-esteem were reported by more probands than brothers, but differences in numbers of probands and brothers with these symptoms were not statistically significant (at $p \leq 0.05$). Probands with three or more symptoms of hyperactivity reported more symptoms of low self-esteem than did probands with fewer symptoms, but this difference also was not statistically significant (at $p \leq 0.05$). It seems meaningful, however, that 25 percent or more of men who were hyperactive 20–25 years ago felt that they lacked self-confidence, felt that they were not well liked by their associates, and were unhappy with career progress and their behavior toward their families. It seems meaningful also that one-fourth of these men, but none of the brothers, had three or more symptoms of low self-esteem and that 20 percent felt that they needed help with their emotional problems.

**Table 4-4**
Social Contacts and Affiliations

| | Has Formal Group Membership | Has Informal Social Group Contacts Monthly | Lacks Friends | Lacks Confidential Friends | Lacks Friendships Lasting 2 Years or Longer |
|---|---|---|---|---|---|
| Probands | | | | | |
| 0–2 symptoms ($n = 10$) | 1 | 7 | 3 | 5 | 2 |
| 3–7 symptoms ($n = 10$) | 2 | 4 | 5 | 8 | 6 |
| All probands ($n = 20$) | 3 }$p = 0.001$ | 11 }NS | 8 }$p = 0.01$ | 13 }NS | 8 }$p = 0.03$ |
| Brothers ($n = 20$) | 15 | 16 | 2 | 9 | 18 |

53

**Table 4-5**
Symptoms of Low Self-Esteem

|  | Probands With 0–2 Symptoms ($n = 10$) | Probands With 3–6 Symptoms ($n = 10$) | No. of Brothers |
|---|---|---|---|
| Not well liked by associates | 2 | 3 | 1 |
| Lacks self-confidence | 1 | 4 | 1 |
| Dissatisfied with career progress | 3 | 4 | 4 |
| Unhappy with behavior toward spouse and children | 0 | 4 | 1 |
| Feels life is hopeless | 0 | 3 | 0 |
| Needs help with problems | 0 | 4 | 0 |
| Thought about suicide | 0 | 2 | 0 |
| Total with three or more symptoms | 0 | 5 | 0 |

## DISCUSSION

Men who were hyperactive 20–25 years ago were all steadily employed and self-supporting. Most of them were married and had children, and many of them had spent time in military service. In these respects men who were hyperactive in childhood were, like their brothers, meeting common demands of adult male roles. However, information reported by these men indicates that many of them had difficulties meeting the demands of their adult roles. These difficulties are most apparent when men who were hyperactive and their brothers are compared with respect to problems encountered in military service, work and marital situations, and formal and informal social affiliations.

Problems of probands in life situations examined in this study indicate that many of these men had difficulty in adapting to social situations and in establishing and maintaining satisfactory interpersonal relations. Problems associated with social adaptation of men who were hyperactive 20–25 years ago were predominant in those who continued to report the greatest numbers of symptoms of hyperactivity. Those who had three or more symptoms of hyperactivity at the time of this study constituted a large majority of those men who reported difficulties in marital and work relations. Probands with the greatest numbers of symptoms of hyperactivity at the time of the study also made up the bulk of all men who lacked social affiliations through friendships and informal groups.

Military service seemed to present particular problems for men who were hyperactive in childhood. The combination of a commitment to a specific period of enlistment, strict enforcement of codes of conduct, and overall structure of military life seemed to present a situation in which men who were hyperactive had difficulty. Brothers of these men, however, did not have such difficulty in adapting to military life.

Considering the numbers of probands who had experienced problems in the adult life situations examined in this study, it does not seem surprising that one-fourth of these men had three or more symptoms of low self-esteem, nor does it seem surprising that 25 percent or more of these men felt that they were not liked, lacked self-confidence, were dissatisfied with their career progress, and were unhappy with their behavior toward their wives and children.

Findings of this study pertinent to measures of self-esteem are similar to results of follow-up studies of hyperactive children in adolescence.[2,7] Those studies showed that one-third to one-half of hyperactive children had low self-esteem by adolescence and that children with low self-esteem tended to be those who had shown little or no decrease in symptoms of hyperactivity between childhood and adolescence. In the present study, symptoms of low self-esteem were most apparent in men who continued to have the greatest number of major symptoms of hyperactivity and who also reported the greatest numbers of difficulties associated with their social adaptation.

In general, men who were hyperactive 20–25 years ago but had fewer than three symptoms of hyperactivity at the time of the current interview did not differ significantly from their brothers with respect to problems in social adaptation in life situations examined in this study. The concentration of these problems in men with three or more symptoms of hyperactivity indicates that social adaptation of men who were hyperactive in childhood is closely associated with the persistence of major symptoms of the disorder. Difficulties related to social adaptation in important life situations of men with the greatest number of symptoms of hyperactivity also seem to be closely associated with the development or persistence of symptoms of low self-esteem in these men.

## CONCLUSIONS

Men who were hyperactive 20–25 years ago were functioning in normal adult male roles and fulfilling basic demands of those roles at the time of this study; however, many of these men had experienced difficulties in social adaptation in important adult life situations. These difficulties were most apparent in men who continued to have several symptoms of hyperactivity. Symptoms of low self-esteem also were most apparent in men whose persistent symptoms of hyperactivity were closely associated with difficulties in social adaptation in important life situations.

## REFERENCES

1.  Mendelson W, Johnson N, Stewart M: Hyperactive children as teenagers: A follow-up study. J Nerv Ment Dis 153:272–279, 1971.
2.  Weiss G, Minde K, Werry JS, et al: Studies on the hyperactive child: VIII; Five-year follow-up. Arch Gen Psychiatry 24:409–414, 1971.
3.  Laufer M: Cerebral dysfunction and behavior disorders of adolescents. Am J Orthopsychiatry 32:501–506, 1962.
4.  Stewart M, Mendelson W, Johnson N: Hyperactive children as adolescents: How they see themselves. Child Psychiatry Hum Dev 4:3–11, 1973.
5.  Menkes M, Rowe J, Menkes J: A 25-year follow-up study on the hyperkinetic child with minimal brain dysfunction. Pediatrics 39:393–399, 1967.
6.  Borland B, Heckman H: Hyperactive boys and their brothers: A 25 year follow-up study. Arch Gen Psychiatry 33:669–675, 1976.
7.  Stewart M, Pitts F, Graig A, et al: The hyperactive child syndrome. Am J Orthopsychiatry 36:861–867, 1966.
8.  Robins LN: Deviant Children Grown Up: A Sociological and Psychiatric Study of Sociopathic Personality. Baltimore, Williams & Wilkins, 1966.

## DISCUSSION

*Dr. Gallant:*   Actually, you seem to have a very clean category here in your followup. Menkes did a 25-year follow-up study in 1967, and he found much more severe pathology developing later on in his patient population. He had about four or five schizophrenics or patients with schizoaffective problems.

*Dr. Wender:*   Menkes' study was retrospective and probably involved maximal brain dysfunction. He had to depend on clinical records. And we can assume that the only diagnosed the most severe instances.

*Dr. Gallant:*   Right. Just looking back at Menkes' study and your study, what would be the big differences between your group on followup and his?

*Dr. Borland:*   I think that the major difference between these two study groups is the way they came. Menkes' patients had more antisocial behavior, the antisocial behavior was more apparent at the time they were selected in childhood, they had a lower IQ, in at least two cases, and delinquency beyond just the antisocial behavior.

*Dr. Gallant:*   Generally speaking, then, you would say that the severity of their illness was greater at the time of entrance into the study.

*Dr. Huessy:*   The kinds of presentations that you get with these patients varies tremendously with the setting. If you're working on a program for alcoholics, you'll see quite a different group than if you are, let's say, in a therapeutic community, rural community mental health center, or dealing with a college population. Nobody so far has mentioned the effect of socioeconomics. The higher the socioeconomic status, the less severe the outcome, all other things being equal. Because the family can do so many extra things for these people and keep them out of criminal channels, for example, when they would have gotten in there otherwise; help them, despite the fact that they get kicked out of public school, go on and get an education in a private school and all this kind of thing. I think when we're dealing with large numbers, we have to agree beforehand that we're all dealing with very different groups of patients and be very careful that we don't generalize from one to another.

*Dr. Cole:*   That probably accounts for Laufer's good followup, in that he had relatively rich hyperkinetic children.

*Dr. Klein:*   From Cantwell's data on sibling studies presented before, one might have speculated that the brothers should not have done so well, yet they sound like a pretty solid group.

*Dr. Cantwell:*   I think there are three or four things that make a difference. One, the social-class setting really makes a difference. I see patients essentially in three settings. Our research project is centered in a community mental health center, which has much more of an inner city population; this is where the sibling study was done. Not only are the siblings there more disturbed, but the parents are more disturbed; these are really severely dysfunctional families. I also see children who come to the UCLA clinic, which happens to be in the wealthiest part of town. It's a long distance from the Barrio or the Watts ghetto, and there's not much public transportation in town, so that we don't get those kind of patients. The third group I see are private patients, a large number of whom are faculty children. The UCLA faculty are not paragons of health, but most likely they are not sociopaths or chronic alcoholics, although a lot of the fathers do have dysphoric mood, impulsive behavior, etc. If you get a family study of the type that I and Morrison and Stewart did, with the same kind of population behaviorally but selected from UCLA, I think you would have a considerably different finding. Siblings of the children that I see at UCLA don't have a great deal of difficulty.

The other thing that is interesting, regarding the sisters, and to some degree the brothers, is that they were not brought in as problems, particularly the sisters. They were not mentioned by the parents as being problems. It was only because we saw them specifically, did systematic studies of them, that we found a high incidence of attentional problems and attendant learning disabilities in the sisters. If you mention them to the parents, they will say, "Yes, we've known that for a long time." But the hyperactive brother is so very troublesome that they bring him in. Over time we've found that as a number of these hyperactive boys are treated and are doing relatively well, the parents then begin to turn their attention to the sibling, who is manifesting similar symptoms, but to a minor degree.

*Dr. Wender:* I think it's interesting to look at that in the way family therapists have looked at that same phenomenon. If the identified patient who is bearing all the pathology is removed, the pathology is projected onto someone else. I've noticed the same squeaky wheel phenomenon. As soon as it gets greased, some lesser squeaks become noticeable in the background. I wanted to ask if the probands were different in the number of symptoms they had as adults from the number of symptoms, or severity of illness, when they had been children. Was it the sicker people who were staying sicker, or were there changes?

*Dr. Borland:* The ones with the most symptoms in childhood had the most symptoms in adulthood.

*Dr. Wender:* I wondered if there was a correlation of severity in symptomatology in childhood and adulthood, and how high the correlation was.

*Dr. Borland:* The problems that were most apparent in childhood were most apparent in adulthood also. The major symptoms in childhood were the major symptoms in adulthood. I wasn't really able to measure the severity of these symptoms within the probands.

*Dr. Huessy:* I think again, by the way, that if you get that kind of data retrospectively, by going back to school records and so on, you'll find that even parents many years later will have a tendency to gloss over just how bad things were in elementary school. Later the child became delinquent and the roof caved in and so they think elementary school really wasn't so bad. Then you go to school records and you find a comment saying that the child's behavior was impossible. Retrospectively it would be very hard to get an assessment of how severe things were in childhood.

*Chairman Bellak:* I guess that means we need longitudinal rather than retrospective studies for MBD. What Dr. Borland's study suggests is that about half of hyperactive children, for practical purposes, improve, recover, do not show significant adult psychiatric pathology, and half do. We need to find if the background variables, e.g., the Hollingshead index, may play a role, as they do for everything else from leprosy to schizophrenia. A study by L. Ciompi and C. Mueller recently showed for schizophrenia that longitudinal studies give the clearest affirmative answer to that [Personal Communication], and I found out the same for leprosy when I had to study leprosy to get a license in Hawaii. Among the recurrent themes is that the people who do present problems not only show low self-esteem but feel unliked. And that's understandable enough in view of their pathology. Part of it, if I may speak briefly as a psychoanalyst, is due to the fact that they don't like themselves, that one part of them is very aware of the defective part in them. They dislike themselves and tend to project that. Therapeutically, particularly if you work on object relations, that's extremely important and certainly a recurrent theme. One of my current patients hears voices accusing him of being no good, and that is definitely the voice of his father and of his peers in elementary school where he remembered that he not only didn't do well in reading and writing and arithmetic, but often bumbled around in the gym and was ridiculed for it.

Jonathan O. Cole, Moderator

# 5

# General Discussion

*Dr. Cole:* I found Wender's paper helpful because I think we're dealing with two, or maybe three, kinds of MBD. The kind I am most comfortable with is the hyperkinetic or attentional deficit type—Der Struwelpeter disease, a child who fits specific diagnostic criteria in childhood and fits comparable criteria in adulthood. I think I can understand that type, and it seems to have a clear genetic factor, although this is less evident than I would like. It's probably not always true.

But at least I have a feeling I have an instrument (Wender's) upon which I can assign patients a nice score and I can say, "Aha! When he was a child he describes behaviors that fall in the 95th percentile of all children on this polythetic syndrome complex." I have a number I can refer to, which probably gives me unreasonable illusory feelings of security and cognitive clarity.

On the other hand, the kind of patients Dr. Bellak, Dr. Hartocollis, and others talk about are difficult patients with problems that the psychiatrist would like to refer to the neurologist, but the neurologist always sends them back to the psychiatrist saying they don't fit any known neurologic disease, even though they may have an abnormal EEG, oddball reflexes, and hints of organicity. They are the kind of patients that when I was a resident we always put on Dilantin and, contrary to Dr. Monroe, it never worked. Maybe because we didn't have 80 psychotics at the same time. But there is certainly a group of psychiatric patients who have some kind of neurologic abnormality and are somewhat atypical for their class and who are rather more resistant to the conventional therapies than other people.

The schizophrenic with brain defects is different, I hope, from the grown-up hyperkinetic child, the adult MBD patient. It would be interesting to know. Maybe when Don Klein talks this will be clearer; it seemed to me that his childhood asocial schizophrenic probably is different from the childhood attention-disordered one. I would be surprised if the two syndromes didn't overlap, but it would be nice if they could be clearly distinguished. They may both have problems in central nervous system functioning. It would make me feel cleaner and clearer if we had at least two separate things we could look at somewhat independently for their effect on outcome and treatment response in later life.

The unavoidable involvement of borderline states with MBD doesn't help either way. Borderline states need more diagnostic help than MBD at the moment. Dr. Bellak's MBD seems to be clearer than the current use of borderline states. Even with John Gunderson's help at McLean, I end up feeling that borderlines are impossible patients whom nobody likes. We called them "personality disorders" when I was a resident, whereas nice people had "neurotic characters." They are unstable, wrist-slashing, impulsive, splitting, generally impossible adolescents and postadolescents who wander around McLean and make up about one-third of the population. I would be fascinated to see what would happen if you looked at them carefully for childhood hyperkinetic disorder. There is only a small proportion in which the hyperkinetic distractibility in childhood really jumps out and hits you in the nose, but if you look more carefully you might find more of it.

A paper in the last issue of *The Archives* [*of General Psychiatry*] tried to compare four different criteria for borderline state and found that there was no diagnostic criterion common to all four. It causes you misgivings as you try to apply a diversely conceived concept to MBD.

On the other hand, it would be very nice if this variously defined MBD predicted treatment outcome, which seems to me the most useful thing for any diagnosis or semidiagnosis to achieve. Stimulant drugs seem to be under threat of extinction by the Federal Government. On the basis of my limited, diverse, and bizzare clinical experience, I think that stimulant drugs do, in fact, provide a valuable treatment alternative in some patients, hyperkinetic or not. People I try Cylert on don't like it. I find it less reinforcing to most people than Ritalin, but it would be very nice if we could get clear data.

I have a question for both Dr. Huessy and Dr. Wender. It is widely said that hyperkinetic children respond badly to phenobarbital. I'm intrigued with how they respond to Valium; it seems to me in this day and age most of the MBD adults that you've looked at must be given Valium by somebody. If they were made worse by Valium, this might be a helpful sign.

*Dr. Huessy:* I have lots of patients who've taken Valium, and the response is totally unpredictable. Some have a very bad response, some think it helps, and some feel that 10 mg does absolutely nothing.

*Dr. Wender:* I haven't tabulated the results with my patients, but a lot of these people have taken Valium. Mainly they don't seem to like it; it makes them stupid and doesn't relieve any of their symptoms. They feel dopey, even on small doses, and their anxiety, depression, whatever it is, is not relieved. There are the occasional ones that like it.

*Dr. Cole:* That's interesting. I suspect it's a heterogeneous group anyway. I was intrigued that Dr. Huessy didn't mention a finding by Joseph Stevens that Dilantin was better than placebo in treating high–ego strength irritable neurotics. He found a nice drug-placebo difference with Dilantin in irritable neurotics. Whether irritable neurotics overlap with MBD—one would have to go back and find out.

*Dr. Arnold:* Incidentally, he had the best response in people who had normal EEGs.

*Dr. Cole:* There is a study which I think never got fully published by Bernard Glueck at the Institute of Living in which he claimed that acting-out adolescents with normal EEGs did better on Dilantin than those with abnormal EEGs. At the time I said that was the reason that none of our abnormal EEG patients at the Payne Whitney Clinic in the early 1950s did not respond to Dilantin; we were giving it to the wrong people.

*Dr. Huessy:* In a child study, the three children who responded well to Dilantin all had normal EEGs.

*Dr. Cole:* That's another conundrum that we will wrestle with, I think, at some future date.

*Dr. Monroe:* I think the main point is that the EEG is no measure of what's going on in the central nervous system. That's one of the problems of relying on it as an indicator for the use of Dilantin.

*Dr. Cole:* Dr. Wender commented that MBD adults respond initially to tricyclics, but then the effect wears off. I would like to know what other people find.

*Dr. Wender:* Dr. Huessy and I disagree about this. Judy Rapoport found with children that after 2 years nobody was taking imipramine—it just didn't work.

*Dr. Cole:* Don Klein found the same thing, so there are varying reports of the effectiveness of tricyclics in children and, I gather, in adults. Certainly the couple of Kleinian panic states with agoraphobia that have managed to come my way respond quite dramatically and rapidly to very small doses of tricyclics. My most recent patient, the wife of a pediatrician, was sure she was taking placebo because she felt better in 2 days. Not having this conference in mind and this being 9 months ago, I did not ask her whether she was hyperkinetic as a child. But she was working on her Ph.D. and seemed to have been a well-adjusted person until she began having mood swings.

*Dr. Klein:*    There's a low incidence of hyperkinesis in the childhood of people with panic attacks who respond to imipramine.

*Dr. Cole:*    They may still have something minimally wrong with their brains, which is the problem. Maybe all psychiatric patients have minimal brain dysfunction.

*Dr. Wender:*    Another important sample difference is that all or many of his patients are inpatients who are treatment failures. One of our exclusionary criteria is being institutionalized.

*Dr. Cole:*    I think Dr. Huessy's sample is made up of patients like those who have been around our wards for 2 years until we admit only partial success and try to find someplace else to put them. Spring Lake Ranch, I gather, is a lovely place to send such patients.

*Dr. Wender:*    I call them "chronic polymorphic nonspecifidis."

*Dr. Cole:*    One of the predictions one would make, again trying to discriminate MBD schizophrenics from MBD nonschizophrenics, would be that if MBD schizophrenics are the same as childhood asocial schizophrenics, tricyclics ought to make them worse, remarkably worse. I gather this is not generally true of Dr. Bellak's and Dr. Huessy's "schizo-phrenics." Neither group, I gather, gets worse.

*Dr. Huessy:*    I gather that the tricyclics make a schizophrenic worse at an antidepressant dosage range, and we use, of course, a much smaller dosage against MBD.

*Dr. Gallant:*    It depends on what schizophrenic you're talking about. If you're talking about the asocial schizophrenic, the childhood asocial or the schizoaffective, that's one thing. But we also have what we call a pseudohomogeneous schizophrenic population; they are just flat-out paranoids and flat affects. We ran a dosage tolerance curve on them in 1965 with imipramine, and even on low dosages they showed some increase in agitation. They really became quite explosive with their hallucinations as we went to higher doses.

*Dr. Huessy:*    Our patients were given antipsychotics, as well as tricyclics. They'd be on something like a phenothiazine, and we'd just add a small dose of imipramine.

*Dr. Cole:*    One of the interesting things that could be done would be to determine blood levels in those patients who respond very rapidly to very low doses of tricyclics to determine if they have the Glassman-approved 240-ng combined plasma level or are, in fact, getting better with 10 ng, in which case maybe you're in a different dose–response curve. You do see people with perfectly ordinary depressions who seem to get dramatically better on 25–50 mg of Tofranil and I'm never sure whether it's a placebo or real response.

The addition of Ritalin to antipsychotics in schizophrenics may not be entirely irrational. There was an old psychiatrist at Boston State who ran an aftercare clinic and always gave people Ritalin or Dexedrine on top of their antipsychotics. In fact, he was the largest single user of stimulants in the State of Massachusetts Department of Mental Health, and his patients did not get rehospitalized. I uncovered an ancient study from Iowa in the 1930s before phenothiazines were available in which they gave Dexedrine to schizophrenics and got about a 40 percent improvement. Somewhere in the recent literature there is a low-dose L-Dopa study in Japanese schizophrenics in which they describe improvement. And there may be a subgroup within schizophrenia which, in fact, does better, rather than worse, on stimulants.

*Dr. Wender:* I did a crossover Ritalin/placebo study on chronic schizophrenics stabilized with neuroleptics. They didn't get crazier, and they did get brighter, more energetic, and more outgoing. We didn't run the study long enough to see if they got tolerant to it.

*Dr. Huessy:* They don't get tolerant. I have people that have been taking Ritalin for 10 years who were chronic schizophrenics. Without the stimulant they would be too slow to hold a job, but with Ritalin or Dexedrine they can. The dosage has stayed the same, year in and year out.

*Chairman Bellak:* As a matter of fact it was A. Myerson who established the usefulness of Dexedrine more than anybody else. It was part of his total-push treatment for all psychotics including schizophrenics, and they seemed to have some pretty good results.

*Dr. Gallant:* Another weird thing is that back in the 1960s we took our chronic schizophrenic population, who had at least eight of the World Health Organization criteria, and added magnesium pemoline to their neuroleptic medication. We did a double-blind study of magnesium pemoline plus a neuroleptic versus placebo plus a neuroleptic. We ran a series of organic and learning tests at that time. There was a tendency for the magnesium pemoline schizophrenics to actually increase their attention span and show better learning on repeat testing. The dosage, though, was about 300 mg, our maximum dosage of magnesium pemoline at that time.

*Dr. Klein:* It might be different for chronic cases; after 10 years of schizophrenia, the brain might be different.

*Dr. Cole:* That would be in keeping with Kornetsky's use of 40 mg of Dexedrine at bedtime in chronic schizophrenics to help them sleep.

I think there is a subgroup in these difficult patients who may have MBD or borderline state who are searching for euphoria. With these people I find that on a stimulant they go up and up and up. They get paranoid and they keep throwing drugs down their system with desperate pressure; I don't know whether they're tolerant or whether they're looking for a different end point from everybody else. I suspect it may be some of both.

On the other hand, there are people on stimulants taking the same dose who feel better. I have a distant relative who's been taking a daily dose of 15 mg of Dexedrine for 15 years, and she can't function without it. Whether she had, in fact, paralyzed her feedback system so that when she comes off for 3 months she stays sleepy for the entire time and has become physically dependent on the whole system or whether in fact she was born 15 mg of Dexedrine too low I can't tell. I understand that she was clearly not hyperkinetic as a child.

*Dr. Wender:* I seriously consider the disease of "congenital hypoamphetanemia."

*Dr. Cole:* She's a reasonable candidate, although she did get through college before she lived through a number of adverse life stimuli and reached this state.

*Dr. Huessy:* I think Leon Oettinger has people about 40 years old who were put on amphetamine at age 5 and 6 whose dosage on a per pound basis has stayed exactly the same and they still need it.

*Dr. Cole:* I've talked to Leon and he takes them off medication every now and then to see if they still need it, and they do. So there are people who do better with amphetamine than without. Some of them look like cases of MBD and some don't.

*Chairman Bellak:* Some of the alpine population, in both Austria and Switzerland, habitually take strychnine and arsenic as stimulants and derive a tremendous tolerance, many times the minimal lethal dose, in the course of their life. It's connected with the low iodine intake and poor thyroid functioning. That's where the original iodine deficiency studies were made. This might possibly be related to amphetamine tolerance.

*Dr. Cole:* I'm not sure it concerns MBD, but Gershon and associates have performed a study of Ritalin in elderly people with memory impairment and found that they were underresponsive to stimulants, and when they did respond they became jittery. We're conducting a study of Ritalin versus placebo in a similar population at Boston State, but I do not know the results yet. I hope that they will be favorable because I keep thinking Ritalin is a good drug.

I am intrigued with how much difficulty people have had in proving that Ritalin is better than placebo in outpatients with mild depression. There are two studies by Karl Rickels that are generally positive and show that the people who respond also like coffee. But other attempts to repeat it have not worked well.

A comment on Huessy's paper: The male/female ratio that occurs in MBD seems to shift radically as you get up into adulthood, where there are suddenly a lot more women. I always thought that the sex ratio for MBD was four or five males to one female in child guidance clinics. This leads to the issue that the girls with attentional deficits are not hyperactive and therefore don't get taken to child guidance clinics.

*Dr. Gallant:*   One explanation for that is that when they become adults, the males get sent into the criminal justice system and the females are seen in the clinic, in the medical system.

*Dr. Wender:*   In an outpatient study, we see people who are selected because they're hurting, and children are brought because they're very irksome to others. When you study the parents of hyperactive children, you often find that the fathers are hyperactive, but they never go for treatment themselves. They take their wives and children for treatment but they're quite happy themselves.

*Dr. Cole:*   My memory of data on use of medical services is that women outnumber men about two to one because they don't as often work during the day.

One comment on spectrum disorders. The idea of spectrum disorders seems intellectually terrible; on the other hand, maybe it's a reality. You can imagine diagnoses as points in space with a large cluster of people around and gaps in between. When you're looking for endogenous versus reactive depression, most of the people you see are somewhat both. In the world of reality there is a lot of spread between diagnostic nodes, and spectrum may be a useful concept rather than something to be avoided.

I have a question for Dr. Wender, Dr. Kety, and company. To what extent does assortative mating account for some of the spectrum disorders?

*Dr. Wender:*   Family studies now include investigation of the co-parent. The old studies are worthless, because they start with one parent with something and never ask about the other.

*Dr. Cole:*   I've heard the comment that looking at parents is worthless genetically. You need to look at 87 relatives and do five huge family trees; this is worth 700 studies in which you look only at the parents. I am in no position to comment on the truth or value of that comment. It's obviously a lot easier and more feasible to get information on just the parents.

*Dr. Huessy:*   Dr. Marshall, who works in penal systems, feels that well over half of the inmates of penal systems are grown-up MBDs with the appropriate histories.

*Dr. Cole:*   Everybody will be given Dr. Wender's handy form, asking what you were like between age 6 and 10.

*Dr. Wender:*   I'm getting normative data and I've devised what I egotistically call either the Wender Utah Rating Instrument, which is the WURI, or the Wender Utah Personality Inventory, the WUPI.

*Dr. Cantwell:*  I think I found the same thing as Dr. Huessy and Dr. Monroe when I spent a year at the Maudsley Hospital in London. One of the striking things about their child psychiatry outpatient department is that they don't see hyperactive children. They don't know what that is. The most common outpatient referral is a phobic child, who won't go up and down a lift, as they call it [an elevator] there, or won't go down into the tube [subway] system. The day a phobic child walks into the UCLA outpatient clinic, all the residents have to gather around to see him, because it's probably the last one they're going to see all year long.

What happens, I think, in England is that the hyperactive children get picked up very early by the correctional system because of their special or what they call "approved" school. The approved schools are schools for "delicate" children, which is another one of their terms. But you find that the delicate children are really hyperactive ones. They are not considered "psychiatric" in the British situation, and they get shunted off at a much earlier age. American children get shunted off in adolescence or later into the juvenile justice system.

*Dr. Cole:*  I wonder a little bit about the incidence of hyperkinetic or MBD children in Japan. My only data come from a neurologist named Drew in Indiana who went to the Atomic Bomb Casualty Commission and did neurologic exams on about 3000 Japanese children. He had one child he couldn't do an eye exam on, but the others sat there very properly and were very cooperative with the whole procedure. They weren't running around the room and they weren't disobedient.

*Dr. Bellak:*  There was an international study by the Bloomingdales who found the incidence of MBD in Japan in children lower than anywhere else.

*Dr. Wender:*  I have a very loose, interesting association with that differential response of Oriental babies to alcohol.

*Dr. Cole:*  Dr. Goodwin's idea on the genetic connection with alcoholism is that if you can't tolerate the stuff, you won't ever become a drunk.

*Dr. Huessy:*  A universal observation by all people who have been to China is that they have not seen any hyperkinetic children anywhere. The answer to all the questions they ask is that these children are not someplace else, just out of sight or anything, but they just don't exist.

*Dr. Monroe:*  They do have them in Japan because I've reviewed Nurubiashi's cases, seen the protocols on that and some of the movies. So they exist. I don't know what the rate is. He's operated on 36 children in 10 years. His cases are pretty extreme, but it does occur.

*Dr. Cole:*  My only other comment was what other people said about Dr. Borland's cases, which was that they looked somehow nicer when they grew up than other people's groups, where everybody's in prison, in state hospitals with schizophrenia, or having other terrible problems. I gather that depends on what population you grow up from rather than anything else.

*Dr. Arnold:* I believe that it's psychosocially induced or a combination of the two. It should not be surprising to find a different incidence in a country with so far different a culture and a different racial makeup. In areas where there is a large Oriental population, such as California, we might be able to take a look at Orientals who still have the same genetic makeup but are Americanized in their culture.

In regard to family studies, is it possible that there are still some pockets of polygamy in Utah where you could check out half-siblings with different mothers and the same father?

*Dr. Wender:* With the entire Mormon genealogy, we have data from four million people entered on computers for the National Cancer Institute. There are "weird" pedigrees in which, for example, a man married sisters so that the children are half-siblings by their father and cousins by their mother.

*Dr. Huessy:* There's one other aspect to this Oriental business. We all know that these MBD children do much better in a very well-structured social situation. They can't handle the open classroom. One thing about [mainland] China, certainly, is the congruence of the messages a child gets, whether it comes from parents, the teacher, the neighbor, the television, it's all the same message, whereas in our society all the messages are different. Their life is 100% structured, which is not true for our children. I would suggest that one of the factors that makes MBD is a society with multiple social lifestyles. The more rigid the social system, the better these individuals do.

*Chairman Bellak:* I'd like to agree to that with regard to the Japanese, about whom I know a little. Control plays such an outstanding role in their character formation that that may well have something to do with the lack of the manifest symptoms of MBD. One karate master spent years in the mountains until he was able to catch flies with chopsticks in midair, to give you an idea of the emphasis on control.

# Neuropsychiatric Aspects

Leopold Bellak

# 6

# Psychiatric Aspects of Minimal Brain Dysfunction in Adults: Their Ego Function Assessment

Any concept, particularly a new one, usually evokes two different attitudes. One is to find the new idea altogether unacceptable. The other is to overextend the concept and apply it to practically everything. Historically, in psychiatry, both tendencies have occurred with the introduction of ECT, phenothiazines, community psychiatry, the concept of schizophrenia, psychoanalysis, and many other schools of thought and therapeutic modalities. The same situation prevails with the concept of minimal brain dysfunction (MBD).

## HISTORY AND CONCEPT OF MBD

The establishment of MBD as a well-defined concept in children can be arbitrarily dated from a 1966 conference on MBD at the National Institutes of Health.[1] Prior to 1966 and up to the present time, MBD has been referred to by various terms that, in fact, designate only some of the symptoms and syndromes now subsumed under the definition of MBD—symptoms such as dyslexia and other learning difficulties.

This chapter utilizes and synthesizes, with permission of the respective publishers, previously published material by the author (Bellak L: Psychiatric states in adults with minimal brain dysfunction. Psychiatr Ann 7:575–589, 1977; Bellak L: A possible subgroup of the schizophrenic syndrome and implications for treatment. Am J Psychotherapy 30:194–205, 1976) with new observations on this subject.

Orton[2] and Strauss and Lehtinan[3] were among the pioneers of MBD in the United States. Early recognition of childhood MBD is suggested by Cantwell,[4] who cites the colorful and well-known German children's story *Der Struwelpeter*. This is a tale written over a century ago by a physician concerning the adventures of an unruly lad who would not cut his hair or his nails, who engaged in all sorts of mischief, and displayed frequent temper outbursts.[5] As far back as 1940, in the psychiatry department of the Massachusetts General Hospital, under the chairmanship of Stanley Cobb and under the supervision of F. L. Wells, one of the pioneers of clinical psychology in the United States, we were taught to examine all children for left-right dominance, verbal and performance IQs were compared, and special note was taken of mirror writing, letter reversals, and speech difficulties, including stuttering.

Though MBD in children has been written about for many years, most systematically by Wender,[6] and discussed under different names and in different contexts, this syndrome only very recently provoked real interest in regard to its role in psychiatric disorders of adults.

The relationship between MBD in children and the same symptoms in adults has been largely overlooked because they are most obvious in childhood and indeed decrease or disappear in some by age 12 years owing to neurologic maturation. It is my impression, however, that even more often they persist into adulthood. People learn to compensate for these difficulties, masking them (when not in school no one holds them to account), or they are not aware that problems such as constantly getting lost when driving are related to difficulties with spatial orientation, as part of a minimal neurologic dysfunction.

The most sophisticated concept and model of MBD (also only in relation to children) has probably been formulated by Arnold.[7] A Venn diagram shows the overlap of MBD, behavior disorders, and learning disorders (Fig. 6-1). The hydraulic parfait model illustrates the concept of symptom production by additive accumulation of pathologies from various etiologies (Figs. 6-2 and 6-3); this implies a psychophysiologic disorder. It also implies a multidimensional spectrum of etiologies that could be important for treatment plans in individual cases.

The many and diverse manifestations of MBD have certainly led to the abuse of the concept, especially in some school systems, but probably also to unwarranted skepticism concerning its existence and usefulness. In this context, it may be useful to compare MBD to the aphasic syndrome. In its sensory and motor form, and in many variations on those two in degree and kind, aphasia represents a similar problem of apparent vagueness, yet it is a well-established concept in medicine.

In discussing MBD in relation to adult psychiatric patients, it must again be stated that MBD is a multifaceted disorder that interacts subtly and in quite variable ways in different people according to the psychody-

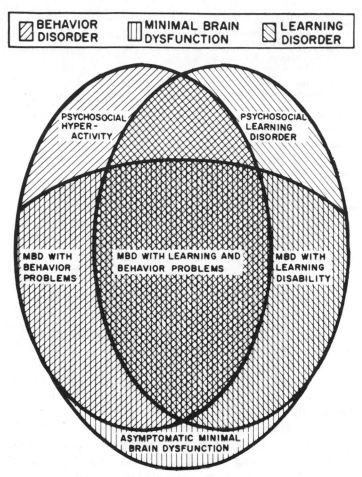

Fig. 6-1. Relationship of minimal brain dysfunction to hyperactivity and learning disorders showing overlap and fact that MBD does not account for all hyperactivity and learning problems. [Reprinted with permission from Diseases of the Nervous System (Arnold E: MBD: A hydraulic parfait model. 37:171–173, 1976).]

namic and structural aspects of their personalities. It does exist, however, as a syndrome that plays an important part in psychiatric disorders of adults. Cognitive functioning—including the registration, storing, and retrieval of experiences—is, of course, affected by any dysfunction in any of the organs involving sense perception. The person with MBD suffers such distortions not only in the initial perception of experiences but also in their subsequent recording and recall. Thus the effects of MBD on adult personality development cannot be disregarded by anyone searching for the experiential factors generally considered basic for psychiatric disorders.

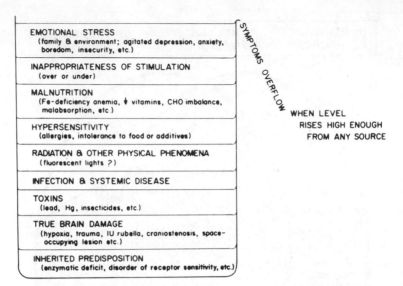

EMOTIONAL STRESS
(family & environment; agitated depression, anxiety,
boredom, insecurity, etc.)

INAPPROPRIATENESS OF STIMULATION
(over or under)

MALNUTRITION
(Fe-deficiency anemia, ↓ vitamins, CHO imbalance,
malabsorption, etc.)

HYPERSENSITIVITY
(allergies, intolerance to food or additives)

RADIATION & OTHER PHYSICAL PHENOMENA
(fluorescent lights ?)

INFECTION & SYSTEMIC DISEASE

TOXINS
(lead, Hg, insecticides, etc.)

TRUE BRAIN DAMAGE
(hypoxia, trauma, IU rubella, craniostenosis, space-
occupying lesion etc.)

INHERITED PREDISPOSITION
(enzymatic deficit, disorder of receptor sensitivity, etc.)

SYMPTOMS OVERFLOW

WHEN LEVEL
RISES HIGH ENOUGH
FROM ANY SOURCE

Fig. 6-2.   Hydraulic parfait model of minimal brain dysfunction. When the level of total pathology rises high enough from *any* combination of layers, behavior and learning disorder symptoms spill over. [Reprinted with permission from Diseases of the Nervous System (Arnold E: MBD: A hydraulic parfait model. 37:171–173, 1976).]

One of the earliest studies was performed by Cantwell,[4] who hypothesized that hyperactive children grew into hyperactive adults. To test the theory, he conducted a systematic psychiatric examination of the parents of 50 hyperactive children and the parents of 50 matched control children. The parents of the hyperactive children had an increased incidence of alcoholism, sociopathy, and hysteria, and Cantwell judged 10 percent of these parents to have been hyperactive children themselves.

Studies by Borland and Heckman[8] support Cantwell's findings. They suggest that many emotional problems result from the persistence of symptoms of hyperactivity into adult life; they believe that most social and psychiatric consequences of the disorder relate to its presence in both childhood and adulthood.

In the Borland and Heckman study, hyperactive children and their brothers were followed up 25 years after the initial contact. MBD symptoms had been considerably reduced in the patients. Nevertheless, half of the probands had psychiatric problems that affected their socioeconomic status, despite normal intelligence and education. They frequently changed jobs; to them, work was a means of avoiding feelings of restlessness.

A number of longitudinal and adoption studies suggest that MBD

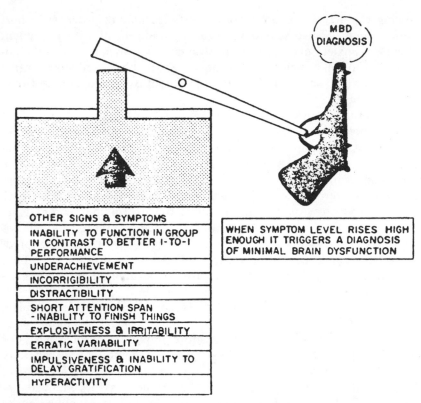

OTHER SIGNS & SYMPTOMS

INABILITY TO FUNCTION IN GROUP
IN CONTRAST TO BETTER I-TO-I
PERFORMANCE

UNDERACHIEVEMENT

INCORRIGIBILITY

DISTRACTIBILITY

SHORT ATTENTION SPAN
- INABILITY TO FINISH THINGS

EXPLOSIVENESS & IRRITABILITY

ERRATIC VARIABILITY

IMPULSIVENESS & INABILITY TO
DELAY GRATIFICATION

HYPERACTIVITY

WHEN SYMPTOM LEVEL RISES HIGH
ENOUGH IT TRIGGERS A DIAGNOSIS
OF MINIMAL BRAIN DYSFUNCTION

Fig. 6-3.   Hydraulic parfait concept of relationship between MBD symptoms and diagnosis. Sufficient symptoms in sufficient quantity produce enough pressure to "trigger" a diagnosis. [Reprinted with permission from Diseases of the Nervous System (Arnold E: MBD: A hydraulic parfait model. 37:171–173, 1976).]

persists into adult life, where its existence is camouflaged by the application of a variety of diagnostic labels. To test the hypothesis that MBD persisted into adulthood, Wood et al.[9] identified 15 putative MBD adults on the basis of MBD-like complaints, self-descriptions of MBD characteristics in childhood, etc. Of the 15, 11 were then given a double-blind trial of methylphenidate hydrochloride, and 8 of them showed a significant response to it. Other stimulants or tricyclic antidepressants were also tried, and 8 of the 15 showed a good response and 2 a moderately favorable response. The authors of this study concluded that MBD does persist into adult life, with the signs and symptoms lessening or disappearing in the third and fourth decades of life rather than in the teens.

Mann and Greenspan have offered suggestions for the identification and treatment of adult brain dysfunction.[10] Their 20 patients each had the following characteristics: a history of early learning disorder with short attention span, diffuse severe symptoms in adulthood with prominent elements of anxiety and depression, dramatic improvement with the administration of imipramine, and a mental status characterized by rapid speech and many shifts of subject (but without overt indicators of psychotic thinking).

According to Hartocollis,[11] evidence of "soft neurologic signs" is often overlooked in adolescent and young-adult psychiatric patients. Reporting on such a group whose difficulties were not obviously organic but who had responded poorly to treatment, he noticed that there was often an unevenness in psychologic test performance—for example, a discrepancy between verbal and performance IQ scores. He found that these patients had a history of frustration, failure to perform up to parental and school expectations, poor results from psychiatric treatment, and evidence of organicity—but the evidence had been overlooked or ignored. Such persons can learn to function with much less frustration once these neurologic signs are recognized and a properly structured environment is provided, Hartocollis notes.

Many of these authors believe that the concept of MBD may explain a group of adult impulse disorders; the pharmacologic techniques useful in treating MBD in childhood therefore provide a rational basis for treating psychiatric patients who have poorly understood and generally treatment-unresponsive symptoms. Adults treated with small amounts of methylphenidate, pemoline, and tricyclic antidepressants showed improvement. Both the low doses of drugs and the patients' rapid response to medication were comparable to experience with the use of these agents in children.

In summary, it may be said that a number of authors who have investigated the possibility of MBD occurring in adults have concluded that it is an etiologic factor in some of the most common and least understood psychiatric disorders.

## DEFINING MBD IN TERMS OF EGO FUNCTIONS

MBD needs to be operationally defined in adults as well as in children, and it can be so defined by the *systematic assessment of crucial ego functions*.

This is a technique of assessment I have previously described for schizophrenia (another slippery concept!). In a way analogous to Arnold's concept of MBD, I described schizophrenia as a multifactorial psychobiologic syndrome of different causes and pathogeneses, sharing as a final common pathway severe but variable disturbances of the functions of the ego.[12] I have therefore found it useful to study schizophrenics in terms of their ego-function disturbances.

A number of other investigators have also found ego-function assessment useful for their particular work. One study by Milkman and Frosch[13] used ego-function assessment to differentiate the personalities of amphetamine and heroin addicts (see bar diagram, Fig. 6-4). Sharp and Bellak[14] found it useful in their assessment of analytic patients (Fig. 6-5), as did Ciompi et al.[15] (Fig. 6-6). In a pilot study of the effect of imipramine in schizophrenics with MBD (Bellak, Conte, & Fielding, Albert Einstein College of Medicine, 1976–1977, unpublished), ego-function assessment was used in evaluating changes or their lack (Fig. 6-7).

An analogous ego-function assessment of MBD may prove helpful in clarifying the concept and systematizing the descriptions of the syndrome. Assessment of the 12 crucial ego functions can be made in an operational, statistically valid, and reliable way.

Although the ego-function concept is part of a set of psychoanalytic propositions and is most useful within the entire matrix of psychoanalytic theory, it can also be used simply as a systematic mental-status examination by clinicians not psychoanalytically trained or inclined. Ego-function assessment may also be used as a research tool to investigate various psychiatric syndromes (Personal Communications: Henry Kravitz, M.D.; Peter Hartocollis, M.D., Ph.D.; and others) and to evaluate drug effects.[16] It is also useful in evaluating the effects of psychotherapy and psychoanalysis.[14,15] (In this last capacity, ego-function assessment has an additional advantage: each function can be defined in such a way that independent observers, using a 13-point rating scale, can reach satisfactory statistical agreement.)

Ego functions and their components are indicated in Table 6-1. The functions can be graphed as in Fig. 6-5, which plots not only the patient's current ego functioning but characteristic optimal and minimal functioning as well. Plotting such curves permits the physician to see at a glance the amount of discrepancy in ego functioning between periods of minimal stress and periods of maximal stress. At the same time, it enables the physician to pinpoint the specific ego functions that exhibit the greatest degree of vicissitude.

I would like to comment briefly on each of the ego functions listed in Table 6-1—not in the logical order indicated in the Table but rather in a descending order of importance insofar as they play a role in most cases of MBD in adults.*

---

* A research project is now under way to study the role of MBD in a subgroup of the schizophrenic syndrome; one goal of the project is to study the ego-function assessment of schizophrenics who have MBD in contrast to those who do not.

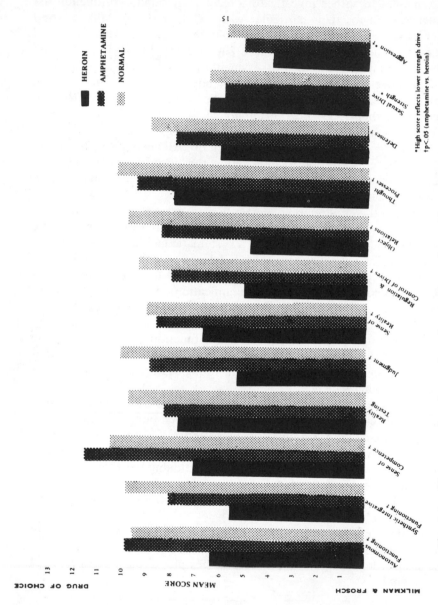

Fig. 6-4. Mean ego function ratings for amphetamine subjects, heroin subjects, and normals in the abstinent condition, with ratings for sexual and aggressive drive strengths. Reprinted with permission from John Wiley & Sons (Milkman and Frosch[13]).

80

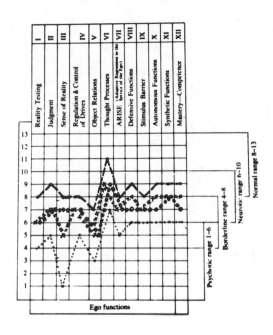

Fig. 6-5. Patient A—ego function assessment at onset of analysis. Highest level (-----), characteristic level (×××××), current level (ooooo), lowest level (·····). [Reprinted with permission from John Wiley & Sons (Bellak, Hurvich, and Gediman: Ego Function in Schizophrenics, Neurotics, and Normals).]

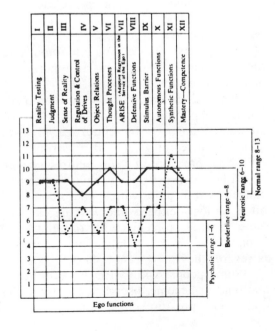

Fig. 6-6. Ego function profiles of a psychoanalytic patient at first evaluation (·····) (mean 4.2 points) and approximately 1 year later (——) (mean 5.2 points). [Reprinted with permission from Ciompi et al.[16]]

81

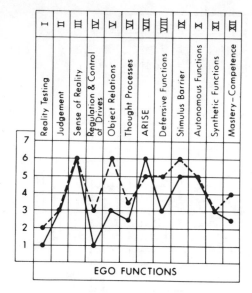

Fig. 6-7. Ego function profiles of a schizophrenic patient with coexistent MBD before (——) and after (-----) treatment with imipramine (tofranil). [Reprinted with permission from The Journal of Nervous and Mental Disorders (Bellak et al.[17]).]

## Autonomous Functions

These are concerned with the basic perceptual and motor functions. We speak of primary autonomous functions, involving concentration, attention, memory, learning, perception, and motoric behavior, and secondary autonomous functions, which involve special skills, works, interests, and hobbies.

Motor disturbances in autonomous functioning typically present themselves in such symptoms as hyperkinesis, synkinesis, lack of coordination, and motor overflow.

Hyperkinesis may be apparent in infancy. Symptoms include restlessness and other problems that will usually bring the child to the attention of a teacher by school age. Many of these pertain to language—difficulty in learning to read or write. A neurologic examination may reveal the presence of "soft neurologic signs."

Adult with MBD may have the same cognitive disturbances, evidenced by difficulties with spatial relationships. They may, for example, often get lost—either while walking or while driving. They are likely to have general problems with orientation. Verbal expression may be impaired—if it is only mildly impaired, they may stutter; if the impairment is severe, they may seem aphasic.

Some people with MBD have difficulties with overall functioning and tend to become disorganized, especially when required to perform under time pressure or sensory overload (Personal Communications:

**Table 6-1**

Ego Functions and Their Components*

| Ego Function | Components | Ego Function | Components |
|---|---|---|---|
| 1. Reality testing | Distinction between inner and outer stimuli<br>Accuracy of perception<br>Reflective awareness and inner reality testing | 7. Adaptive regression in the service of the ego | Regressive relaxation of cognitive acuity<br>New configurations |
| 2. Judgment | Anticipation of consequences<br>Manifestation of this anticipation in behavior<br>Emotional appropriateness of this anticipation | 8. Defensive functioning | Weakness or obtrusiveness of defenses<br>Success and failure of defenses |
| 3. Sense of reality and sense of self | Extent of derealization<br>Extent of depersonalization<br>Self-identity and self-esteem<br>Clarity of boundaries between self and world | 9. Stimulus barrier | Threshold for stimuli<br>Effectiveness of management of excessive stimulus input |
| 4. Regulation and control of drives, affects, and impulses | Directness of impulse expression<br>Effectiveness of delay mechanisms | 10. Autonomous functioning | Degree of freedom from impairment of primary autonomy apparatuses<br>Degree of freedom from impairment of secondary autonomy |
| 5. Object relations | Degree and kind of relatedness<br>Primitiveness (narcissistic, attachment, or symbiotic-object choices)<br>Degree to which others are perceived independently of oneself<br>Object constancy | 11. Synthetic-integrative functioning | Degree of reconciliation of incongruities<br>Degree of active relating together of events |
| 6. Thought processes | Memory, concentration, and attention<br>Ability to conceptualize<br>Primary-secondary process | 12. Mastery-competence | Competence (how well the subject actually performs in relation to his existing capacity to interact with and actively master and affect environment)<br>The subjective role (subject's feeling of competence with respect to actively mastering and affecting environment)<br>The degree of discrepancy between the other two components (i.e., between actual competence and sense of competence) |

* Reprinted with permission from Psychiatric Annals (Bellak L: Psychiatric states in adults with MBD. 7:58–76, 1976).

H. Kravitz, M.D.; P. Hartocollis, M.D., PH.D.; and others). A teenage student with MBD, for instance, may have difficulty passing examinations under time pressure but be capable of performance commensurate with high intelligence if the time pressure is removed. In some adult patients with MBD, I have observed an increase in anxiety approaching catastrophic levels when they have been subjected to inordinate internal or external pressure.

Such people respond poorly to any kind of overload—time pressure, excessive light or noise, or excessive social contact. The result often is disorganization, with possible disturbances in attention and the reversion of thinking from the abstract to the concrete, and may also involve problems of impulse control.

It is important here to keep in mind what I have pointed out elsewhere[12]—that ego functions interrelate with each other and that a disturbance in one is likely to have an effect on the functioning of others. In this respect, the ego functions interrelate with each other like the subfunctions of intelligence on the WAIS (Wechsler Adult Intelligence Scale).[12] Nevertheless, they still vary enough to merit separate consideration.

Catastrophic reactions of people with MBD should not be mistaken for schizophrenia, although at times this condition may coexist with the schizophrenic syndrome.

It is important to help such patients to develop a lifestyle that avoids all kinds of overload. Psychotherapy may be helpful to avoid internal overload by psychodynamic conflicts. In crisis situations, drugs may be indicated, typically imipramine or methylphenidate, at times mixed with diazepam, sodium diphenylhydantoin, or both.

### Regulation and Control of Drives

As I have noted, an outstanding characteristic of the child with MBD is a profound disturbance in the regulation and control of drives and impulses. The persistence of this characteristic into adolescence and adulthood has now been documented by several investigators.[4] Emotional outbursts—including assaultive behavior, restlessness, and inability to hold jobs—are typical manifestations of MBD in the adult. There is suggestive evidence that a high percentage of the people with alcoholism, drug addiction, and other social problems are minimally brain damaged.[4]

People with MBD have a tendency to *act out* on a neurotic or psychotic level. They act—instead of verbalizing—because verbalization was impaired or failed to develop properly in childhood.[17,18]

Many of these patients engage in violent activities to get rid of their tensions or, at other times, use drugs to give them some relief. Marijuana is most common among those used. Overworking and hypomanic-type activity are other aspects of their behavior. Their impulsivity often impairs their judgment. Related to this lack of regulation and control of drives is a tremendous need for constant stimulation; otherwise they suffer feelings of emptiness and depersonalization.

One patient of mine, a highly gifted artist, frequently developed "pie in the sky" projects in which it was a close race between his losing interest or their failing. He literally would be with a different woman every day, initially expecting that each one would be "the woman" of his life. Psychotherapy had much to do with teaching him self-observation and self-reporting, making him aware of his constant stimulus hunger and constant overideation. It sensitized him to "signal awareness" when he was about to act-out and to reinforce, as much as possible, impulse control. Sometimes it is helpful to permit or encourage the development of obsessive-compulsive controls as a defense against impulse breakthrough.

### Stimulus Barrier

A low stimulus barrier was noted in 25 percent of the schizophrenics in our original ego-function study.[12] Although the patients in this study were not examined neurologically, subsequent clinical experience has revealed that adults with MDB, both schizophrenic and nonschizophrenic, are easily overloaded by visual and auditory stimuli.

The same phenomenon as low stimulus barrier has been described by Mednick and Schulsinger as a high arousal pattern on the galvanic skin response.[19] The question of whether or not patients who demonstrate a high arousal pattern also show other signs of MBD warrants future investigation. It is widely agreed that people who demonstrate a low stimulus barrier or high arousal pattern also exhibit a great deal of stimulus hunger.[20]

Stimulus barrier is of clinical importance in only a relatively small percentage of patients, but when it is important, particularly as a low stimulus barrier, it may play a major role in their psychopathology. Their response to the result of the low stimulus barrier may be variable. On the one hand, they may show extreme restlessness and the need for a great deal of stimulus input, such as loud music, "psychedelic" effects, and stimulation by drugs. In these instances, their external stimuli may help to counteract flooding by internal stimuli. This might be similar to the case of a typical adolescent who drowns out his troubles with loud rock music.

Usually, however, a low stimulus barrier will manifest itself in great sensitivity to noise, to lights, to too active a social scene, or to an overload of tasks or time pressure. Under such circumstances, this type of person complains of headaches, actual migraines, and disorganization, which may resemble a thought disorder. Overload is the key word to explain what ails these people, and therapy may have to be concerned with helping them to avoid the overload by treating them with drugs that will increase the stimulus barrier. Diphenylhydantoin (Dilantin) is at times useful, and a wide variety of other anxiolytic and tranquilizing drugs may be of help.

## Thought Processes

Verbalization plays a crucial role in the development of most children after they reach the age of about 30 months. When there is MBD, however, development of language skills is delayed. As Greenacre[18] has noted, the child who has difficulty in learning is likely to develop motoric acting-out in lieu of verbal communication. Problems with verbalization appear to be related to difficulties with thinking; typically, the person with MBD is more at home with concrete than with abstract thought. Sequential thinking is often impaired—perhaps leading to a very specific difficulty, such as the inability of a highly intelligent adolescent to enumerate the months of the year. The adult schizophrenic with MBD shows not excessive symbolization and overinclusion but rather concreteness of thinking.

In turn, concrete thinking is related to problems in perceptual organization. This phenomenon was originally demonstrated by Goldstein,[21] as part of the development of Gestalt psychology, in his study of perceptual deficits of German soldiers with head wounds in World War I.

Sometimes, a patient is referred to me as a schizophrenic because of a thought disorder. It occasionally turns out that it is primarily a matter of concrete thinking or disorganized thinking under the impact of anxiety and other pressures in a person suffering from MBD. In that case, psychotherapy designed to decrease the anxiety and the internal pressure is very helpful. The patient also has to be taught how to go about problem solving and learning to speak slowly. Syllable reversals often play an obvious role in this disturbance. Pressured thought, for all practical purposes, is identical with overideation, occurs and is experienced as unpleasant by the patient, and interferes with tasks. Imipramine or methylphenidate can slow this process down. Patients can be taught "signal awareness," i.e., be made conscious of factors that disturb them enough to start them off on disordered thought processes.

Some patients suffering from very concrete thinking actually have to be taught self-observation, inner reality testing.

## Sense of Reality and Sense of Self

Problems with spatial orientation are a hallmark of the adult with MBD. They continue to be evidenced with difficulties in distinguishing left from right and are also apparent in situations where the adult is required to have a sense of direction—for example, in order to read a map or to navigate while driving. The child with MBD has difficulties vis-à-vis spatial orientation that lead to problems in the establishment of clear boundaries for himself. Failure to establish clear boundaries, in turn, has an effect on object relations, leading to insufficient individuation and a poorly defined self-image. Freeman et al.[22] consider this phenomenon to be the basic factor in the development of schizophrenia. Typically, both children and adults with MBD feel perplexed, and others suffer from the uncomfortable sensation of being lost, which may at times produce high levels of anxiety. Adults with MBD have poorly defined body images as part of their self-images, and the interactions of this with the other symptoms that arise from impairments in their autonomous functions often makes them clumsy.

Because problems of self-boundaries are involved and there exists a lack of healthy introjects, these patients complain of a feeling of emptiness, as described for borderline patients, especially by Kernberg[23] and by Kohut.[24] In terms of object relations, a disorder of this ego function leads especially to symbiotic relationships. Feelings of depersonalization are frequent and occur as complications in the process of psychotherapy. These patients usually respond well to diazepam, while phenothiazines tend to increase their feelings of unreality. Dreams are especially informative about self-representations and disturbances in the self-image. For instance, one patient usually dreamt of herself as a tiny little black spot encased in a plastic cube. Another patient dreamt of herself as an open and empty refrigerator, suggesting both how cold and empty she felt and how little she had to give.

In schizophrenics with marked disturbances of body boundaries, a technique originally described by May et al.,[25] body ego technique, may be useful. They not only engage the patient in rhythmic exercise, as many others have done, but also in systematic interchanges of touching of the body and the floor and other people to increase a feeling of differentiation of proprioception as distinguished from the perception of nonself.

## Object Relations

Secondary to the problems arising from poorly defined self-boundaries are object relations that are often of a symbiotic nature. Individuation–separation is incomplete on a neurologic cognitive basis, and this is then manifested psychodynamically. Since MBD children are often the subject of ridicule, they frequently become asocial or suspicious of others as they grow older. Their impatience, labile moods, and inability to concentrate further impair their ability to relate to others.

It is my guess that a large percentage of patients widely described as suffering from borderline conditions, especially because of their object relations difficulties, suffer from the latter because of developmental problems related to MBD. Since children with MBD often feel clumsy because of their motor problems and stupid because of their dyslexia and other learning difficulties, and since they are only too often made to feel inferior by peers, teachers, and parents, they have further reason for secondarily developing poor object relations. When these patients are "schizophrenic," they predominantly suffer from delusions and hallucinations of people laughing at them and considering them foolish.

People with difficulties in object relations on the basis of having MBD are examples par excellence of the "porcupine dilemma."[26] On a cold winter day some porcupines decided to move together to give each other some warmth, only to find that they stung each other with their quills. They moved apart again, and were cold. They moved back and forth until they found the optimal distance at which they gave each other some warmth without hurting each other.

People with MBD are like porcupines with a particularly strong need for warmth and, at the same time, extremely sensitive skin and long, sharp quills. The net result is that they are people who suffer from labile object relations, moving back and forth. Among other things, their relations are interfered with by explosive disruptions of regulation and control of drives and inhibited by their fear of their own perceived potential loss of regulation and control of drives. One young schizophrenic, for instance, was primarily asocial because he felt easily ridiculed and was afraid that his rage might burst out as it had once on a single occasion. He therefore preferred to live in isolation, creating a self-imposed prison.

### Mastery and Competence

MBD adults often exhibit lack of self-confidence. This is developed as they become aware of the disturbances of autonomous functions, such as speech, writing, and fine motor coordination (i.e., the use of a needle, hammer, pen, pencil) as well as their difficulty in performing many functions requiring gross coordination, such as athletic activities.

Failure in school often plays a role in the development of a lack of confidence, and even very intelligent people often carry with them the feeling of being inadequate physically and mentally. On the other hand, some develop successful defenses: in Alfred Adler's terms, they "overcompensate." In one patient, it led to hypomanic overactivity, with its own resulting pitfalls. In addition, the patient exhibited a constant need for clowning in order to feel accepted.

### The Synthetic-Integrative Function

By definition, this function is concerned with the synthesis and integration of conflicting emotions, drives, and thoughts so that smooth intellectual performance, appropriate emotion, and coordinated motor activity become possible. MBD patients have a difficult task in this regard, in view of their difficulties with impulse control. Clinically, their problems produce symptoms that are often resistant even to lengthy and skillful psychoanalysis. There seems to be more integrative work that needs to be done than the cerebral integrative-synthetic capacity of the MBD adult permits.

The most colorful example of a lack of synthetic-integrative ego function predates Freud. Pierre Janet (whose term "psychasthenia" is as close as any to the concept of ego weakness in psychoanalytic terms) told the story of the French lady who went to market with the typical net bag, which she stuffed with cabbages, beets, long bread, carrots, and some fruits. As she went along, some of the carrots fell out. She stuffed the carrots back in, and some oranges fell out. In short, her net bag did not have sufficient "synthetic capacity," and many a patient suffers from similar problems. This holds true especially in the course of some therapies: note the patient who typically loses one symptom only to develop another—because basically he or she doesn't seem to possess enough synthetic-integrative capacity to permit smooth ego functioning. These patients also have to be taught not to overload and to organize carefully, and drugs may have to be administered at specific periods. This function, for instance, may be typically interfered with premenstrually as a result of water retention (which also lowers the stimulus barrier) and the accompanying endocrine changes. It may be useful for the patient to take both diuretics and minor tranquilizers routinely 3 or 4 days before menstruation is expected.

Psychotherapy, of course, can reduce conflicts that dynamically interfere with integration and synthesis.

### Adaptive Regression

This ego function is a complex one to discuss in relation to MBD because of the lowered external and internal stimulus barriers. A person who is suffering from MBD is flooded by internal and external stimuli from the psyche and the environment. In a gifted person with enough synthetic-integrative function, this low stimulus barrier may lead to substantial artistic and scientific creativity. Such people are more "open" to unconscious and preconscious ideation.

Historical examples of such people probably include Michelangelo, da Vinci, Newton, and Einstein. In the absence of talent, intelligence, and sufficient integrative function, it leads instead to pseudoart, as exemplified by schizophrenic productions or amateurish efforts. In some, obsessive defenses minimize adaptive regression in the service of the ego. In the fortunate, other good ego functions lead to creative Gestalt formations in artistic and scientific fields.

The relationship between poor ego function generally, such as in schizophrenics, and creativity possibly finds some support in Heston's finding[27] that the families of schizophrenics have not only a high incidence of schizophrenia but also a high incidence of creative people. My own practice includes a considerable number of people with MBD who are creative as business people, artists, scientists, etc.

### Defenses

Because of the major problem of impulse control, the defenses are often too weak to deal with the conflicts existing among drives, superego, and reality. In extreme cases, this may result in psychotic phenomena. In less severe cases, it probably accounts for some of the anxiety phenomena that seem resistant to psychotherapeutic intervention, as in some neurotics in whom the diagnosis of MBD has usually been missed.

It will be interesting to investigate my hunch that nightmares are experienced more frequently and with greater intensity by people suffering from MBD than by "normals."

Some persons with weak defenses (in the sense that they function inadequately) become excessively rigid; weak defenses thus undoubtedly account for some obsessive traits. As in obsessive-compulsives without MBD, there may be fluctuation from obsessiveness to impulse breakthrough.

Some gifted people with MBD may develop a whole complex character structure as a defense against various aspects of MBD.

One patient of mine, who had suffered from a severe learning disability and had little formal education, nevertheless is today highly successful as a businessman and is the president of several corporations. He can, for the most part, think only in concrete terms and prepares himself for complicated corporate conferences by developing many concrete scenarios. "If A says such and such, and B replies with such and such, what will I say?" His thinking is very similar to the way some people work out complex chess moves in a game. In addition to this particular type of thought process, he has learned to overcome his once vicious lack of impulse control by a particularly rigid moral code. As a child, he had damaged several other students severely in fights but started to sublimate early by training a great variety of animals. One of his most fascinating attempts along this line was the building of a giant aquarium, 12 feet long, 6 feet high, and 3 feet deep, that he stocked with a variety of vicious fighting fish. In order to keep these voracious piranhas and other fighting fish from devouring each other immediately, he overstuffed the tank with goldfish and other ready bait and was extremely proud when he eventually had a dozen killer fish living in peace with each other most of the time. He controls his acquisitive needs rigidly by means of his own personal code of honor, which is not necessarily always consistent with what we would consider a publicly acceptable one but to which, on his own terms, he remains faithful.

### Judgment

Judgment may often be poor in adults with MBD, even though reality-testing functions are intact. This is because sound judgment is based not only on an accurate perception of reality but also on the ability to regulate the expression of internal drives and impulses so as to meet the demands imposed by reality. In people with MBD, difficulties with the latter may result in defects in judgment that in turn may typically lead to ill-conceived, violent, or criminal acts. At times, a life history may be characterized by spectacular failures as a result of judgment impaired by impulsiveness—apparently due to MBD. The criminal behavior that can stem from MBD-associated impairments of judgment should be given more attention by those interested in the problems of forensic psychiatry.

Judgment in people with MBD is, of course, most often interfered with by their problems with impulse control. Acting out is typical for them.[17] Their need for quick gratification is their main problem in this area. Otherwise, even if they are psychotic, judgment is usually not especially impaired.

### Reality Testing

This ego function is only sometimes affected by excessive drive and impulse push. At times, impulses that are subjectively overwhelming are projected onto external objects, which the MBD adult then reacts to inappropriately, since the impulses are experienced as outside forces rather than recognized as drives originating within the self.

The adult with MBD may attempt to exert control over factors in the external environment—including people—in a paranoid fashion. In some schizophrenics with MBD, reality testing is only minimally impaired. Because of this, and because of their low impulse control, they are often the patients who go AWOL from hospitals. I would, in fact, go so far as to say that I would consider MBD immediately in any schizophrenic patient who goes AWOL or shows sociopathic tendencies and good organizational ability, e.g., causes trouble on the ward, even though this is accompanied by delusions and hallucinations.

## MBD IN RELATION TO ADULT CLINICAL STATES: SOME HIGHLIGHTS AND NOSOLOGIC PERSPECTIVES

MBD may be present in a group of people who must be considered psychiatrically normal. Such seemed to be the case in relatives of patients I had occasion to interview. Undoubtedly the interaction of a relatively mild organic disorder in a person with unimpaired or even better-than-average intelligence, as well as fortunate experiential factors, account for the existence of this group.

MBD may play a role in the format of a variety of psychiatric conditions and may influence the specific nature of each. In persons suffering from anxiety (psychodynamically understandable as a response to experiential factors but occurring in subjects who also have MBD), the anxiety often seems more extreme and less amenable to psychotherapeutic intervention than would have been expected from their life histories. This holds true especially where free-floating anxiety, acute anxiety attacks, and panic states are concerned.

*In hysteria* combined with MBD, the problem of self-boundaries may be expressed as a more serious disturbance of object relations than one would otherwise expect.

*Claustrophobic symptoms* may be related to problems with object relations: the fear of being engulfed or smothered may be related to a symbiotic merging on the basis of cognitive developmental problems of MBD.

*Depressives* often attempt to decrease the stimulus input in order to avoid overload and disorganization. Bellak and Berneman[28] have suggested a theory to account for the depressive and manic features, as well as the facile transition from one to another, in terms of a utilization of different defense mechanisms to deal with stimulus overload, stimulus hunger, and a low stimulus barrier.* Thus complete withdrawal and

---

* There is no conceptual reason why experiential factors would not sometimes trigger biochemical changes; at other times, pathologic metabolic changes could in turn produce psychologic changes in patients so predisposed.

avoidance are seen as an attempt to deal with excessive external stimuli; the increased stimulus hunger of the hypomanic, resulting in a flooding with stimuli, may be seen as an attempt to drown out internal conflicts. The latter phenomenon is exemplified not only by the manic and hypomanic but also by the seeking of "psychedelic" and other stimulation by adolescents who might otherwise suffer depressions or feelings of depersonalization.

The possible role of MBD in delinquent and criminal behavior has been described by Cantwell,[4] among others.

In patients suffering from the borderline syndrome, MBD often makes a major contribution to poor organization of the self-image. A distorted and primitive self-image will often persist in these patients despite extensive psychotherapy—clearly expressed, for example, in dreams of their being small, helpless, isolated, or swallowed up. Symbiotic relations frequently persist in this group as a result of their continuing problems with self-boundaries, even when there do not seem to be sufficient experiential data to account for them.

## SCHIZOPHRENIA AND MBD

Several authors have referred to the relationship between MBD and schizophrenia, and some have described the interaction of MBD in schizophrenics. Tucker et al.[29] found a strong but not exclusive relationship between neurologic impairment and thought disorder as well as between neurologic impairments and schizophrenia. Rochford et al.[30] found that patients with affective disorders did not have neurologic abnormalities, while those diagnosed as schizophrenic or having personality disorders and neuroses did. Furthermore, schizophrenics had a greater percentage of impairments. Moreover, patients with neurologic abnormalities exhibited various kinds of poor social judgment and behavior as well as such symptoms as blocking and distractibility. Their results "support the hypothesis that diffuse CNS dysfunction adversely affects the individual's personality development."

Quitkin et al.[31] suggest the existence of a subgroup of schizophrenics characterized by "soft neurologic signs." They found that patients diagnosed as "schizophrenic with premorbid associability," as well as those with "emotionally unstable character disorders," exhibited neurologic impairments not found in the rest of the patients. Therefore the authors consider CNS impairment a criterion for syndrome validity.

There is suggestive evidence that persons with childhood MBD may be predisposed to schizophrenia as adolescents and adults. Handford[32] hypothesizes that individuals who experience brain hypoxia prenatally, perinatally, or immediately after birth will be at risk for MBD in childhood and for schizophrenia as adults, possibly resulting from damage to the dopaminergic pathways.

Fish et al.[33] have analyzed early developmental profiles to identify infants vulnerable to schizophrenia. In one pilot study at a baby clinic, 16 infants from families with a high incidence of social and psychiatric disorders were examined periodically from the age of 1 month, and predictions of schizophrenia were made on the basis of an uneven neurologic development. The children were given psychologic examinations at 9–10 years of age, and those originally diagnosed as vulnerable to schizophrenia had significantly higher incidence of disorder than the others. In a study by Fish and Hagin,[34] the visual-motor development of ten infants whose mothers were schizophrenic was measured from birth to 2 years of age. Psychologic evaluation after 10 years revealed a relationship between poor neurologic integration in childhood and later emotional impairment. Both Handford and Fish favor early therapeutic intervention for children at risk and for their families.

Neurologic findings in identical twins discordant for schizophrenia were discussed by Mosher et al.[35] In this study, some very suggestive evidence was found for a relationship between "soft neurologic signs" and schizophrenia. Huessy's findings[36,37] in adult schizophrenics whom he considered hyperkinetic further support this hypothesis.

Powerful although inadvertent support comes indirectly from a study reported by Rosenthal et al. at the National Institutes of Mental Health, in collaboration with a Jerusalem-based group, in which 50 children of schizophrenic parents and 50 controls were examined neurologically in great detail. According to a summary by Mosher and Feinsilver,[38] each group was divided at the median to form subgroups composed of high and low scorers. Comparison of the two high-scoring subgroups revealed that the index group had significantly higher scores than the controls. No significant differences were found between the two low-scoring subgroups. However, when the subjects were divided into those above and those below age 11 years, the younger index group had higher neuropathology scores than the older group. These findings suggested that certain abnormal neuropathologic traits detectable at younger ages may disappear, decrease, or be masked as puberty approaches. The authors concluded that these outward signs of an apparently inherited predisposition to schizophrenia tend to disappear at puberty. Since the general opinion is that maturation at least decreases the manifestations of MBD, it seems very likely that we are dealing with the role of MBD played in the offspring of some schizophrenic parents. It is my unsupported theory that these particular "schizophrenic" parents also suffered from MBD.

Handford's hypothesis that infants with brain hypoxia are at risk for

MBD in childhood and schizophrenia in adulthood, mentioned above, is similar to my own convictions about the pathogenesis of psychosis in the presence of MBD. Many years ago I began to suspect neurologic findings in some schizophrenics. There were histories of unexplained bouts of high fever in infancy that led me to wonder whether or not such occurrences could have resulted in cortical damage and, subsequently, the psychiatric syndromes I was encountering.[39]

Many years later, a confluence of data from a factor-analytic study with clinical data[12] again brought the question of schizophrenia with MBD to my attention. Members of one factor-analytic group of schizophrenics were characterized not only by the signs and symptoms of schizophrenia but also by impulsiveness, a history of having low stimulus barriers, escape from psychiatric institutions, sociopathy, a paucity of hallucinations, and a variety of MBD phenomena.[40]

The hypothesis that I first published in 1949[39]—namely, that the schizophrenic syndrome consists of many etiologic and pathogenic groups—is finally finding increased support. One such subgroup, I believe, is composed of schizophrenics with MBD. While the cause of the MBD may be attributed to prenatal, perinatal, or postnatal factors, I continue to be impressed with the frequency of familial occurrence of the dysfunction—appearing in various degrees of neurologic and psychiatric disturbance, including at times the absence of any major problems. Undoubtedly, the interaction of MBD and experiential factors plays a role in the spectrum of many psychiatric disturbances.

Could MBD being a genetic disorder be the reason that there have been an increasing number of reports indicating a genetic origin for schizophrenia? If so, schizophrenia might well be the epiphenomenon of MBD in these cases. A reexamination of the incidence of familial MBD, as well as of the presence of MBD in patients diagnosed as schizophrenic in high-risk groups and patients identified in genetic studies, may help to clarify this question.

So far the research on schizophrenics with MBD has not included neurologic studies of other members of the schizophrenic's family. It is my clinical impression, however, that familial genetic factors play a very large role in MBD. If there are data indicating a genetic transmission of "schizophrenia," they may well be based on cases of familial MBD in which the manifestation of the schizophrenic syndrome is secondary to MBD.* It is hoped that investigations with genetic data will reexamine the

---

* This, of course, is part and parcel of my "multiple-factor psychosomatic theory of schizophrenia"[39]—namely, that a multiplicity of etiologic factors (including organic ones) may cause a weakening of the ego functions, which in turn may lead to the clinical psychiatric picture of schizophrenia.

subjects to see if this hypothesis can be substantiated. I believe that a search should be made for MBD in relatives of the neurologically implicated schizophrenic children described by Goldfarb.[41]

The phenotype of schizophrenia as a function of MBD can be understood in terms of the severe affliction of body image and self-image due to problems in spatial cognition. Linguistic and conceptual problems further complicate maturation, as seen in dyslexias. Impulse control is impaired cortically, especially since the low stimulus barrier leads to easy overloading and "overflow," not only strictly neurologically but also emotionally. The low stimulus barrier also interferes with the organization of thought and language. These phenomena in turn cause secondary emotional problems, especially during the school years.

The diagnostic differentiation of this subgroup can be accomplished with a careful personal history and family history concerning MBD and neurologic and neuropsychologic testing. Such persons are also likely to show more impulse disorders and often schizoaffective features as well as a low stimulus barrier (noises on the ward will often make them violent and disorganized).

Aside from the neuropsychologic and clinical symptoms, this group is diagnostically characterized by a poor response to phenothiazines alone. Therapeutically, imipramine (at times combined with diphenylhydantoin and diazepam) is often useful. Psychotherapy must include education concerning MBD and should deal with the primary and secondary cognitive and emotional aspects of MBD as well as other problems, such as feeling "stupid," "awkward," or "crazy."

Prognosis depends, in part, on the severity of the MBD.[38] A research team at Albert Einstein College of Medicine, Bronx Municipal Hospital Center, is currently exploring the propositions concerning such a subgroup of schizophrenia with MBD in a pilot study. In this study all patients of average intelligence admitted with the diagnosis of schizophrenia or schizoaffective disorders between ages 16 and 60 years are specifically asked for a personal history and family history of any kind of symptoms that could be related to past or present MBD. If a significant number of items are found to be present, the patient is administered a special version of ego-function assessment, is also examined for 21 "soft neurologic signs," and then undergoes a battery of neuropsychologic tests specially selected for this project. The patient is evaluated on the NOSIE (nurse's observational scale for inpatient evaluation) before and after 1 week on medication and on the symptom checklist. If all these investigations support the coexistence of MBD with the schizophrenic syndrome and if the patient has been responding poorly to phenothiazines, he is given imipramine (25 mg t.i.d.).

From the small sample studied so far, our impressions are, of course, still quite unreliable. Tentatively, it seems as if approximately 10 percent of schizophrenics examined may indeed have coexistent MBD. Some may be fitted better by the diagnosis of schizoaffective disorder than schizophrenia. They certainly all have behavioral problems on the ward, including escaping. One patient who had previously taken amphetamine on his own and felt much calmer with it did worse with the imipramine (for reasons unknown), and another patient with florid symptoms did not respond to either phenothiazines or imipramine. It may well be, especially with schizoaffective patients with MBD, that they may need imipramine and haloperidol combined to control their symptoms. The pilot study is planned as the forerunner of an extensive, controlled, double-blind study of patients suffering from schizophrenia with MBD, using a drug crossover design.

## TREATMENT OF PSYCHIATRIC STATES WITH CONCURRENT MBD

Whether MBD is etiologic, pathogenic, or merely coexistent with the patient's psychiatric state, it merits special consideration by itself in terms of treatment plans. Thus any of the psychiatric states in which MBD may also be present require the standard form of treatment with consideration given to two factors—MBD as a contributor to the particular disorder and the treatment of MBD as necessary and possible in coordination with other treatment needed.

When MBD is present at all, it is vital that the patient be acquainted with the nature of this dysfunction. Usually the patient will be quite unaware of having MBD. The practitioner then has an educational task to perform—namely, to explain to the patient that the problems in spatial orientation, the manner in which senses are easily overloaded by stimuli, and motor-sensory problems have an understandable explanation. It is crucial to find and discuss with the patient the secondary effects that the MBD symptoms have had. For instance, one patient felt stupid because he had to repeat the first grade. He had been ridiculed by others for being clumsy in physical education and had been made fun of for mirror-writing. In addition, he had always been puzzled and frightened by occasional excessive emotional outbursts.

In neurotic states, the presence of MBD may account for more anxiety than is expected on the basis of experiential data. If psychodynamic working through does not lead to sufficient success, it is vital that the patients learn signal awareness—namely, that they become aware of the fact that certain circumstances, like overloading, may produce panic-like situations beyond all reasonableness. Many problems of object relations have to be understood in terms of the influence of MBD. Under certain circumstances, patients may have the need to distance or isolate themselves. Small amounts of imipramine in neurotics have been found useful by Wood et al.,[9] Mann and Greenspan,[10] and myself.

Depressed patients, especially manic-depressive patients, may find it necessary to regulate input and output predicated on a lower stimulus barrier in MBD cases. In such an instance, imipramine is much more promptly effective in treating such MBD symptoms as agitation than in treating depressive ones. Within 1–2 hours of medication definite symptom relief can be experienced.

Borderline patients generally have definite problems with self-boundaries and with symbiotic object relations, and their personal histories are likely to indicate that these problems occur at a frequency far higher than one would normally expect. Depersonalization may occur more frequently. In addition to drug treatment, education about the symptoms and signs of MBD and treatment of the many psychogenic features are possible. It is important to increase the awareness of these patients to their MBD symptoms and teach them how to cope with them. Administering imipramine, possibly with the addition of diazepam (rather than the phenothiazines) for their anxiety, is advisable.

In schizophrenics, and sometimes in patients with schizoaffective disorders, the problems of impulse control, depersonalization, and agitation are outstanding. Medication with imipramine—and the exclusion of phenothiazines—is especially critical. In the case of severe disturbances of self-boundaries it is useful to employ exercises to establish self-boundaries, as in the body-ego technique of May et al.[25]

Such patients with MBD are particularly likely to be difficult management problems, and they often escape from psychiatric hospitals—not because their reality testing and thought processes are significantly disturbed but because their impulsiveness and restlessness make it difficult for them to remain on the ward. Imipramine may effectively quiet them.

In disturbed patients with MBD and serious psychiatric states, trials with varying doses of Ritalin (methylphenidate), Amphetamine and also Lithium and Dilantin (diphenylhydantoin), separately or two of them combined, may have to be tried. As a general rule, it is best to start with very small doses (e.g. 5 mg. Ritalin twice a day) as many patients with MBD are also easily overloaded by drugs. One can then increase the dosage if the smaller ones do not seem to be effective. In women, Dilantin is especially often useful premenstrually, to avoid outbursts.

## PREVENTION AND COUNSELING

Genetic counseling may be considered for adult MBD patients in their childbearing years in view of the familial aspects encountered in many MBD patients. Parents who have MBD should be told that their children may be overresponsive to stimuli and may be hyperkinetic, etc. The parents should be advised to keep stimulation of the children to a reasonable minimum, and to make plans for special training in language development and possibly in physical education, as well as for individual instruction as needed in the primary grades. The parents should be instructed to be alert for the appearance of other symptoms of MBD as they occur.

Special training of the child may be useful as a preventive measure. Training in eye-hand coordination, special visual-auditory instruction, and other general measures to help the child deal with MBD should help the child respond better to the educational process and avoid emotional problems that otherwise could develop secondary to the social aspects of MBD symptoms.

## REFERENCES

1. Clement S: MBD in Children: Terminology and Identification. Phase One of a Three-Phase Project. U.S. Dept. of Health, Education & Welfare. NINDB Monograph 3 (PHSPR 1415), 1966.
2. Orton S T: Reading, Writing and Speech Problems in Children. New York, Norton, 1937.
3. Strauss A A, Lehtinan L: Psychopathology and Education of the Brain-injured Child, Vol 1. New York, Grune & Stratton, 1947.
4. Cantwell D P: Psychiatric illness in the families of hyperactive children. Arch Gen Psychiatry 27:414–417, 1972.
5. Hoffman H: Der Struwelpeter: Oder lustige Geschichten und drollige Bilder. Leipzig, Insel, 1845.
6. Wender P H: MBD in Children. New York, John Wiley & Sons, 1971.
7. Arnold L E: MBD: A hydraulic parfait model. Dis Nerv Syst 37:171–173, 1976.
8. Borland B L, Heckman H C: Hyperactive boys and their brothers: A 25-year follow-up study. Arch Gen Psychiatry 33:663–675, 1976.
9. Wood D, Reinherr F, Wender P, et al: Diagnosis and treatment of MBD in adults. Arch Gen Psychiatry 33:1453–1460, 1976.
10. Mann H B, Greenspan S I: The identification and treatment of adult brain dysfunction. Am J Psychiatry 133:1013–1017, 1976.
11. Hartocollis P: The syndrome of MBD in young adult patients. Bull Menninger Clin 32:102–114, 1968.

12.  Bellak L, Hurvich M, Gediman H: Ego Functions in Schizophrenics, Neu-
     rotics, and Normals: A Systematic Study of Conceptual, Diagnostic, and
     Therapeutic Aspects. New York, John Wiley & Sons, 1973.
13.  Milkman H, Frosch W A: The drug of choice. J Psychedelic Drugs 9:11–24,
     1977.
14.  Sharp V, Bellak L: Ego function assessment of the psychoanalytic process.
     Psychoanal Q 47:52–72, 1978.
15.  Ciompi L, Ague C, Dauwalder J P: L'objectivation chargements psycho-
     dynamiques: Experiences avec une version simplifiée des ''ego strength
     rating scales'' de Bellak et al. Read before the 10th International Congress of
     Psychotherapy, Paris, July 4–10, 1976.
16.  Bellak L, Chassan J, Gediman H, et al: Ego function assessment of analytic
     psychotherapy combined with drug therapy. J Nerv Ment Dis 157:465–469,
     1973.
17.  Bellak L: The concept of acting out: Theoretical consideration. In Acting
     Out—Theoretical and Clinical Aspects. New York, Grune & Stratton, 1965.
18.  Greenacre P: General problems of acting out. Psychoanal Q 19:455–467,
     1950.
19.  Mednick S A, Schulsinger F: Some premorbid characteristics related to
     breakdown in children with schizophrenic mothers. In Rosenthal D, Kety S
     S (eds), The Transmission of Schizophrenia. New York, Pergamon, 1968.
20.  Ludwig A M: Sensory overload and psychopathology. Dis Nerv Syst
     36:357–360, 1975.
21.  Goldstein K: The Organism. New York, American Books, 1939.
22.  Freeman T, Cameron J, McGhie A: Chronic Schizophrenia. New York,
     International Universities, 1958.
23.  Kernberg O: Borderline Conditions and Pathological Narcissism. New York,
     Aronson, 1975.
24.  Kohut H: The Analysis of the Self: A Systematic Approach to the Psy-
     choanalytic Treatment of Narcissistic Personality Disorders. New York,
     International Universities, 1971.
25.  May P, Wexler M, Sackar J, et al: Non-verbal techniques in the re-
     establishment of body image and self identity: A preliminary report.
     Psychiatr Res Rep 16:68–82, 1963.
26.  Bellak L: The Porcupine Dilemma. New York, Citadel, 1970.
27.  Heston L L: The genetics of schizophrenia and schizoid disease. Science
     167:249–256, 1970.
28.  Bellak L, Berneman R: A systematic view of depression. Am J Psychother
     25:385–393, 1971.
29.  Tucker G, Campion E, Silberfarb P M: Sensorimotor functions and cognitive
     disturbances in psychiatric patients. Am J Psychiatry 132:17–21, 1975.
30.  Rochford J M, Detre T, Tucker G J, et al: Neuropsychological impairments
     in functional psychiatric diseases. Arch Gen Psychiatry 22:114–119, 1970.
31.  Quitkin F, Rifkin A, Klein D: Neurologic soft signs in schizophrenia and
     character disorders. Arch Gen Psychiatry 33:845–847, 1976.
32.  Handford H A: Brain hypoxia, MBD and schizophrenia. Am J Psychiatry
     132:192–194, 1975.

33. Fish B, Shapiro T, Halpern F, et al: The prediction of schizophrenia in infancy: III. A ten-year follow-up report of neurological and psychological development. Am J Psychiatry 121:768–775, 1965.
34. Fish B, Hagin R: Visual-motor disorders in infants at risk for schizophrenia. Arch Gen Psychiatry 27:594–598, 1972.
35. Mosher L R, Pollin W, Stabenau J R: Identical twins discordant for schizophrenia. Neurologic findings. Arch Gen Psychiatry 24:422–430, 1971.
36. Huessy H R: The adult hyperkinetic. Am J Psychiatry 131:724–725, 1974.
37. Huessy H R, Cohen A H: Hyperkinetic behaviors and learning disabilities followed over 7 years. Pediatrics 57:4–10, 1976.
38. Mosher L R, Feinsilver D: Current studies on schizophrenia. Int J Psychiatry 2:21–22, 1973.
39. Bellak L: A multiple-factor psychosomatic theory of schizophrenia. Psychiatr Q 23:738–755, 1949.
40. Bellak L: A possible subgroup of the schizophrenic syndrome and implications for treatment. Am J Psychother 30:194–205, 1976.
41. Goldfarb W: Childhood Schizophrenia. Cambridge, Mass, Harvard Univ, 1961.

Peter Hartocollis

# 7

# Minimal Brain Dysfunction in Young Adults

Adopted from child psychiatry, the concept of minimal brain dysfunction has recently found application in adult cases with diverse psycho-pathologic manifestations, schizophrenia and borderline disorders in particular, but also in much milder cases, including conceivably some that escape psychiatric attention. Admittedly, the concept is as problematic as when applied to children, and perhaps even more so, since it depends partly on historical data, information that dates back to childhood and that may or may not be reliable or even retrievable.

## THE SYNDROME AND ITS DIAGNOSIS

Underlining the minimal brain dysfunction concept or syndrome is a hypothesis of organicity. It is supported by the frequent finding of equivocal neurologic signs such as skull asymmetry, spina bifida occulta, strabismus, crossed laterality, atypical tendon reflexes, and various other anomalies of ectodermal origin. Very important in this connection is the testimony of neuropsychologists, who have tried to develop batteries of tests sensitive to organic brain impairment of any degree on the basis of the performance of subjects with known cerebral lesions. Such is the Halstead-Reitan battery of neuropsychological tests and its various modifications, one of which we have had the opportunity to use extensively at the Menninger Foundation.

Even though minimal brain dysfunction implies organicity, it would be erroneous to invoke the concept whenever brain damage is suspected behind an emotional or characterologic disorder. The diagnosis should conform with the requirements of the syndrome of minimal brain dysfunction as it presents itself in childhood and, as with any legitimate syndrome, should obligatorily include all or most of its essential features: (1) specific behavioral or adaptational manifestations, actual as well as historical; (2) perceptual-cognitive irregularities; (3) emotional lability; and (4) soft neurologic signs.*

Presumptive as it is by definition, the diagnosis of minimal brain dysfunction needs to be established according to certain guidelines. Even in the absence of a known history of brain injury the possibility cannot be ruled out. Therefore, the degree of brain dysfunction as measured by special procedures such as the Halstead-Reitan test battery should not exceed a certain degree of recognition; in other words, it should not be too obvious or too handicapping for the individual. Where one should draw the line is difficult to decide; of course, trauma is not the only possible cause of brain dysfunction, even though it is the easiest to detect. Whatever the cause or causes may be, they must have been operative since birth—even before birth—or since early childhood. An array of such presumptive causes has been described by Wender,[1] who has also proposed a broader biochemical theory of minimal brain dysfunction, and by others.[2,3]

Minimal brain dysfunction should be also differentiated from mental retardation, with which it shares similar elements, in particular an impairment in general adaptation and an onset of clinical manifestations before mental maturity, specifically before the 17th year of life. Like minimal brain dysfunction, mental retardation is not an etiologic entity. It can be attributed to a variety of factors, some of which are as presumptive as the ones involved in minimal brain dysfunction, and some of which may be the same in both conditions. By definition, however, minimal brain dysfunction cannot be diagnosed in the presence of mental retardation, since it would no longer be minimal. In fact, minimal brain dysfunction is characterized by at least an average intellectual endowment, even though such an endowment is impaired in a number of crucial respects.

Minimal brain dysfunction is a contributory factor or possibly a specific determinant of personality development and psychiatric illness in young adults. It presumably interacts with one or another personality type or disorder, which might or might not have developed without its presence. The least one can say about the pathogenicity of MBD is that it

---

* The presence of an abnormal EEG may be significant but not conclusive evidence in support of the syndrome not so much because minimal brain dysfunction does not involve a detectable physiologic disturbance but because of limitations in the current application of EEG.

precipitates the development of some major psychiatric disorder at some point beyond childhood. During preadolescence and early adolescence, the social maladjustment that characterizes children with the syndrome of MBD becomes more pronounced, turning often into antisocial behavior. The postadolescent development of the MBD child is less certain, with some children tending to "outgrow" their difficulties in practically all spheres. As Wender[1] states, "It is a widely held belief among child psychiatrists that the MBD syndrome first improves and later disappears as a child grows older" (p. 75). Such a favorable development, however, is not likely to occur until the individual grows well beyond adolescence or young adult age.[4]

Symptoms of minimal brain dysfunction in young adults are usually overlooked by diagnosticians because they are interwoven in the clinical picture of the case or, when noticed, interpreted as manifestations of a particular emotional or personality disorder rather than as part of a developmental condition originating in childhood. Any one of the symptoms or signs that make up the MBD syndrome may be an expectable element of any given psychiatric condition other than MBD, while any one of the same symptoms or signs—for example, learning difficulties, easy to diagnose in a school-age child but as easy to overlook in a nonacademic environment—may be present in an otherwise normal individual. After reviewing the small but suggestive literature of MBD in adults, Bellak[5] concluded that childhood MBD not only persists in later years, but that "it is an etiologic factor in some of the most common and least understood psychiatric disorders" (p. 578). According to one such study,[6] in a 25-year followup of hyperactive children, half of them had emotional problems that interfered with their socioeconomic status and social adaptation in general.

In my own earlier study of young adult psychiatric inpatients,[7] a sizable group had a childhood history suggesting strongly the presence of MBD in childhood; the syndrome could be detected in the current psychiatric picture, which varied diagnostically but included predominantly borderline disorders. Also remarkable, indeed intriguing, was the fact that a larger group of patients, suspected initially but not confirmed by the results of neuropsychological testing as suffering from minimal brain dysfunction, had some borderline personality disorder. In the same study, I found that so long as it remained unrecognized, the presence of MBD in patients carrying one of the major psychiatric diagnoses made for a distorted prognosis and unrealistic treatment plan. More recently, Mann and Greenspan[8] reported similar findings in addition to claiming dramatic improvement of the overall condition of MBD patients with the administration of imipramine.

An alert clinician can tentatively recognize a young adult patient with

MBD from the unevenness of performance and attitudes and the paradoxical impression such unevenness creates. One is struck by discrepancies in ego functioning, namely, a difficulty in using abstract concepts in spite of normal or even superior verbal ability, sufficient memory but short attention span, or excellent muscular coordination in one or two skills with virtual incompetence in most others. A blend of good will and obstinacy makes the exercise of authority with such patients very frustrating, splitting parents or hospital staff members into "bad" and "good guys" who accuse each other of being either "too harsh" or "spoiling" the individual in question. Early history as recalled by parents is reminiscent of the current difficulties of both patient and treaters. Thus childhood problems are often recalled as caused by stressful circumstances or unfair treatment by adults and peers rather than by the patient's own inability to cope with pressures and relationships involving mutual expectations and compliance to any set of standards. The use of denial and rationalization is characteristic of such recollections on the part of both parents and patients. Characteristic is also the impression of parents, often substantiated by teachers' reports, that the patient had a much higher potential as a child than was indicated by his or her actual performance. Finally, something that may alert a clinician to suspect the presence of minimal brain dysfunction is an increased frustration in efforts to establish a therapeutic alliance, a stubborn resistance to treatment, or a sense of fluidity in the doctor-patient relationship that leaves one feeling helpless and angry.

## RELATED PSYCHOPATHOLOGY

The presence of contrasts or paradoxes in MBD, including the development of a negative therapeutic reaction for those individuals already in treatment, is a phenomenon strikingly similar to that found in borderline personality disorders. In addition, borderline patients and individuals with minimal brain dysfunction share a very labile affective disposition, notably a readiness for anger and temper tantrums, which have a common base in low frustration tolerance. Irritability and restlessness, characteristic of patients with minimal brain dysfunction—giving rise to hyperkinetic behavior in childhood—correspond to the complaint of free-floating anxiety common with borderline patients. Borderline patients and individuals with minimal brain dysfunction share a low self-esteem and a defective sense of identity, which create vague dissatisfaction with oneself and the world, a sense of emptiness, loneliness, or narcissistic hurt—painful experiences that may lead to impulsive self-destructive action and are often diagnosed as depression or anhedonia. In common with borderline individuals, MBD patients tend to blame others for their discontent and failures, ready to perceive themselves as victims of injustice, neglect, or abandonment. To the extent that borderline elements are present, object relationships of MBD patients are fragile or very sensitive, subject to paranoid ideation and emotional remonstrations.

Both minimal brain dysfunction and borderline personality organization are controversial psychiatric entities that refer to children or young adults with largely overlapping phenomenology. The finding that imipramine, ordinarily used in the treatment of psychotic depression, is beneficial to patients with minimal brain dysfunction[5,8] seems to provide circumstantial support to the hypothesis of common identity between minimal brain dysfunction and at least some of the borderline personality disorders. As Klein has noted,[9] "A significant drug-placebo difference in favor of imipramine, but not for chlorpromazine, was shown with regard to global improvement of pseudo-neurotic schizophrenics [otherwise known as borderline], associated with distinct mood elevation and decrease in clinging indecision" (p. 369). Likewise, Bellak[5] has found that schizophrenics with MBD respond more favorably to imipramine than to phenothiazines. Could Bellak's schizophrenics be really borderline patients with a manic-depressive propensity? Stone's[10] contention that borderline patients "appear to have a strong genetic loading . . . inclined toward the manic-depressive end of the phenotypic spectrum" (p. 358) may be of interest in this connection.

As already noted, minimal brain dysfunction has been also linked to schizophrenia. The suggestion has been made that MBD in childhood predisposes to the development of schizophrenia in adolescence and young adulthood. More specifically, it has been postulated that MBD is a contributory factor in determining one group among the schizophrenias.[11-13] Other studies are suggestive of a familial origin for both disorders, raising the question of whether or not the familial predisposition is not one and the same for both schizophrenia and MBD when the two coincide.[14]

The quality of a person's ego defenses and integrity or stability of internal self-object boundaries that psychological testing with projective techniques may reveal are crucial psychodynamic factors in the process of differential diagnosis, which may be secured on the basis of the presence or absence of miscellaneous and generally mild congenital neuroskeletal abnormalities and neuropsychological test findings of irregularities in perceptual-cognitive performance. As pointed out above, a history of learning difficulties in childhood, more than any allegation about hyperkinesis, is a crucial although not adequate criterion of minimal brain dysfunction in young adults.

It is conceivable that minimal brain dysfunction may be present in neurotic as well as fairly well-adjusted individuals. Anecdotal evidence has been cited by Bellak.[5] An otherwise superior native endowment under optimal environmental conditions may enable one to escape serious emotional disturbance, faulty personality development, or social maladjustment in later life. The contention, however, that persons with MBD are likely to have parents who suffer from the same disorder would make the hypothesis of optimal early environment for otherwise normal adult individuals with MBD difficult to maintain.

## AN ILLUSTRATIVE CASE

Brian S. was first admitted to our hospital when 16 years old. The presenting problems were school failure, aggressive sexuality, and antisocial behavior. Brian's mother was a chronic alcoholic and his father a man who spent a great deal of time away from home pursuing his business and allegedly women. He described himself as "intolerant of incompetence."

During her pregnancy with the patient, Brian's mother received treatment for thyroid deficiency and anemia caused by periodic vaginal bleeding and was subject to more than occasional mood changes. Delivery was 7 weeks premature. The baby was placed in an incubator for 2–3 days and remained jaundiced for a month. Attempts to breastfeed him were unsuccessful. He was "colicky" for the first 3 months and would not give up the bottle, the mother feeding him in her own bed until the birth of a second child 2 years later. The boy spoke his first words at 15 months but did not manage full sentences until he was 3 years old. Although he began walking at 15 months, he was more clumsy than other children of his age, and his poor coordination and awkwardness in general continued throughout childhood. The mother recalled that when he was 4 years old other children "picked on him" to an unusual extent. His first grade teacher thought that he was retarded, but the parents had always believed that he had considerable intellectual potential. Psychometric testing during the second grade indicated that he was on the "bright side." At fourth grade the parents arranged for remedial reading lessons with a private tutor for a tendency to transpose syllables within words. Brian completed 1 year of high school and dropped out in his second year, just prior to admission to this hospital.

Brian's behavior had always had an aggressive quality in and out of home. At age 8 or 10 he began to bully other children, particularly his siblings. He could never stand to lose a game, he would break any rules in order to win, and when he could not win he frequently spoiled the game for other children in some aggressive fashion. He was never able to be part of a large group of peers, yet he managed to have one close friend, usually a quiet, acquiescent boy, for whom he would become the leader, domineering him. He worked regularly during out-of-school hours, and in his paper-delivering job he became supervisor for 26 other boys. When his mother threatened to divorce the father and the parents briefly separated, he ran away from home;

later he led two other boys in a robbery. He was caught writing bad checks. His 15-year-old sister complained that he attempted to rape her. Finally, he was asked to leave school, and he took a job in a bookstore. There he stole some merchandise. On the suspicion that his 14-year-old brother had reported him to the police, he assaulted him and injured him severely, at which point the father, with help from the police, hospitalized him in his home town and then transferred him to this hospital.

Brian described himself as having always been restless, reluctant to go to sleep at night, and hating to get up in the morning. For several years he experienced violent headaches, nervous stomach, and shaking of hands. Except for mild hand tremor, physical and neurologic examinations, including laboratory tests, were within normal limits. On psychological examination he was found to be uncomfortable with his height and length of arms and legs, hyperalert, suspicious, and frightened as if expecting to be assaulted. He used projection, externalization, and counterphobic defenses, being at times on the verge of complete disregard of reality. He had great difficulty organizing his experiences into a logical pattern and was reluctant to engage in verbal tasks. He gave inappropriate responses to unstructured stimuli, showing a preoccupation with oral-aggressive fantasies. His total IQ was 108 (verbal, 102; performance, 115). He perceived people as distant, inconsistent, and changeable. He continually set up situations for displaying a defiant attitude toward authority figures, testing their seriousness of purpose and degree of control over him.

Results of neuropsychological testing (Halstead-Reitan battery) were summarized as follows: "This is a subject with some mild impairment of adaptive capacities. . . . He displays a mild ideational dyspraxia; possible mild body dysgnosia; mixed hand dominance, mixed foot dominance, and strong left ocular dominance; some impairment in verbal compared to performance groups of subtests, etc. His average impairment rating is 1.75, with 66.7% of the ratings in the impaired range, a score compatible with mild-to-moderate cerebral dysfunction. The pattern is inconsistent with focal structural damage in either of the hemispheres, and suggests [instead] a diffuse distribution of dysfunction. There are inconsistencies in the adaptive level measured by these tests. For example, abstraction capacity, psychomotor problem-solving capacity and perceptual skills are all in the normal-to-nearly-normal range, while there are scattered signs of specific language difficulties, spatial relations, dysgnosias, dyspraxias, and deficiencies in working memory."

During the first few weeks of hospitalization, Brian engaged frequently in threatening behavior, as if to test the ability of the hospital to control him. He appeared tense and frightened, and in a defiant way he often refused to take medication or to comply with requests until confronted with firm insistence. When irritated he would go to his room and throw objects around. He was placed on chlorpromazine 400 mg daily and was started in group psychotherapy. During the summer he enrolled in high school courses, but his attendance was inconsistent. Nine months after admission, during the Christmas holidays, when both his hospital physician and group therapist were absent, he became quite depressed and superficially scratched his arm with a broken glass. A month later he went AWOL but returned voluntarily shortly afterwards.

Two years after his admission a review conference note indicates that Brian had made some gains in being able to control his behavior, but his reflectiveness and involvement in the treatment program remained marginal. While in many ways he was more compliant to the expectations of the living environment, he continued to provoke by silence, being very mistrustful and defensive despite obvious involvement with treatment personnel. Two years later he was transferred to Day Hospital. He obtained the equivalent of high school diploma and began employment with a service station, then enrolled for a course at the local university. While sometimes unpredictable and explosive in social relationships, he remained for the most part isolated, except for acquaintances from work or patients he knew in the hospital.

About 4 years later and 8 years since his admission to this hospital, he had a violent argument with his girlfriend, beat her up, and then attempted suicide. He was readmitted to our hospital, where he appeared anxious but declined medication. After 6 weeks of uneven behavior, he was transferred back to Day Hospital and encouraged to seek employment. A few months later, his therapist concluded that Brian was using treatment as a way to avoid responsibility for his sociopathic actions and advised him to seek treatment in another hospital setting. Brian informed the therapist that he would return instead to his family, and to that effect he made arrangements with his probation officer to leave the state. Thirteen years since he first came to this hospital, Brian was once more brought to our attention because of a legal suit on the part of a young woman who contended that the hospital had discharged the patient "prematurely" to the effect that he had kidnapped her and threatened her with physical violence. Brian S. was now a young adult 29 years old.

## TREATMENT CONSIDERATIONS

Even though long and intensive, treatment of young adult patients with minimal brain dysfunction in our hospital has produced generally disappointing results. Some have improved, but it is difficult to tell what makes for the difference. What helps seems to be an individual, private thing.

Obviously, treatment should be geared to the major psychopathology diagnosed in the case, borderline, schizophrenic, or other. Regardless of the method of treatment used with patients whose diagnosis includes MBD, however, they and their relatives should be made aware of the entire clinical picture. Presumptive as it may be, the diagnosis of minimal brain dysfunction provides the patient and his treaters with a guideline of functions that can be improved with remedial learning and acceptance as part of one's native structure. Characteristically, patients and their relatives seem to be unaware of any symptoms or signs of MBD, and those symptoms that they know about they prefer to attribute to a personality or psychotic disorder. Such an understanding tends to foster a climate of denial and to bias treatment. A patient who labors under the effects of a pervasive, even though not so easily observable or objectively verifiable organic deficit, can best be helped if he recognizes and accepts limitations.

Yet to suggest that a patient and family should be advised of the presence of minimal brain dysfunction is not meant to imply that it would make things easier for anyone concerned, at least initially. The diagnosis and handling of MBD is indeed bound to increase rather than ease the problems of doctor and patient alike, to begin with because the diagnosis is by nature presumptive and therefore easy to minimize or disregard. Resistance to accepting it and doing something about it is also generated by the fact that the patient and those who deal with the patient socially or professionally find it difficult to orient their attitudes and treatment to the requirements of the diagnosis. Patients should be helped to recognize cognitive and physical limitations, not in order to excuse them, but so as to become more objective about them and apply themselves to a treatment plan that requires remedial learning and better emotional adaptation. Patients should be impressed with the treaters' determination not to allow them to deny their difficulties in exchange for their help, love, and respect.

## REFERENCES

1. Wender P H: Minimal Brain Dysfunction in Children. New York, Wiley-Interscience, 1971.
2. Omenn G S: Genetic approaches to the syndrome of minimal brain dysfunction. Ann NY Acad Sci 205:212–222, 1973.
3. Pontius A A: General discussion. Ann NY Acad Sci 205:61–64, 1973.
4. Wood D, Reinherr F, Wender P H, et al: Diagnosis and treatment of MBD in adults. Arch Gen Psychiatry 33:1453–1460, 1976.
5. Bellak L: Psychiatric states in adults with minimal brain dysfunction. Psychiatr Ann 7:454–457, 1977.
6. Borland B L, Heckman H C: Hyperactive boys and their brothers: A 25-year follow-up study. Arch Gen Psychiatry 33:669–675, 1976.
7. Hartocollis P: The syndrome of minimal brain dysfunction in young adult patients. Bull Menninger Clin 32:102–114, 1968.
8. Mann H B, Greenspan S I: The identification in treatment of adult brain dysfunction. Am J Psychiatry 133:1013–1017, 1976.
9. Klein D F: Psychopharmacological treatment and delineation of borderline disorders. In Hartocollis P (ed), Borderline Personality Disorders. New York: International Universities, 1977, pp 365–383.
10. Stone M H: The borderline syndrome: Evolution of the term, genetic aspects, and prognosis. Am J Psychother 31:345–365, 1977.

11.  Quitkin F, Klein D R: Two behavioral syndromes in young adults related to possible minimal brain dysfunction. Gen Psychiatr Res 7:131–142, 1969.
12.  Quitkin F, Rifkin A, Klein D R: Neurologic soft signs in schizophrenia and character disorders. Arch Gen Psychiatry 33:845–847, 1976.
13.  Bellak L: A possible subgroup of the schizophrenic syndrome, and implications for treatment. Am J Psychother 30:194–205, 1976.
14.  Mosher L R, Feinsilver D: Current studies on schizophrenia. Int J Psychiatry 2:21–22, 1973.

## DISCUSSION

*Chairman Bellak:*   I wonder how many of the patients considered borderline in the general psychiatric literature, including those of Kohut and Kernberg, happen to be MBD patients. Of course, there may be a good reason for this, since we know that MBD patients have problems with spatial orientation, therefore problems in individuation and separation, and may well present with typical, psychodynamically speaking, borderline problems. Your presentation reminded me again of how many patients in the last three decades I probably misdiagnosed by failing to make the diagnosis of MBD in connection with the symptom picture. About your question of how some people with MBD could fall within a normal range of the spectrum, as I suggest: In the first place, Dr. Borland's data suggest that about half of the probands turn out all right, and, presumably, they too had parents that suffered from MBD. The other thing is that I suspect some lucky people manage, by virtue of their sensitivity to internal stimuli, to become creative instead of presenting psychopathology. I am reminded that Heston has reported that some relatives of schizophrenics have a particularly high incidence of creativity.

Russell R. Monroe

# 8

# Epileptoid Mechanism in Episodic Dyscontrol of Aggressive Criminals*

Episodic dyscontrol is defined as an abrupt single act or short series of acts with a common intention carried through to completion with either relief of tension or gratification of a specific need. I have described it as a subgroup of episodic behavioral disorders that include any precipitously appearing maladaptive behavior interrupting the lifestyle and life flow of the individual.[1] The behavior during episodic dyscontrol is out of character for the individual and out of context for the situation. The act, accompanied by intense dysphoric affects, results in a behavioral response unmodified by reflective delay. Thus it can be said there is a short circuit between the stimulus and the act, without the hindsight and foresight of reflective delay. The acts then are usually destructive to self or to others.

I have postulated that the mechanism behind such dyscontrol acts could be predominantly neurophysiologic (limbic seizural activity) or psychodynamic (hysterically determined) and have pointed out that in a clinical setting most individuals fell along a continuum between these two polar extremes. At the extreme of limbic seizural activity there was a true short circuit between the stimulus and the action due to functional blocking of connecting neurons. Such behavior tended to be brutish and uncoordinated with little symbolic meaning (primary dyscontrol). At the

* Supported by NIMH Grant MH 21035 and the Maryland Psychiatric Research Center.

extreme of hysterical dyscontrol, although the acts might be equally explosive, there was either conscious or unconscious premeditation (secondary dyscontrol). I have further postulated that when the epileptoid (limbic seizure) mechanism predominated, the dyscontrol acts were likely to be stereotyped, with no or spurious environmental precipitation, and accompanied by partial amnesia rather than the complete amnesia characteristic of the hysterical end of the continuum.

I have noted[1] that in childhood the sex ratio of episodic dyscontrol seemed to be three males to one female, while in adulthood this ratio appeared to be reversed. Further examination of the clinical data suggested that adult males showing dyscontrol behavior probably were relegated to the criminal justice system, while adult females entered the mental health system. I also postulated that focal limbic seizures were relatively common because of the sensitivity and unusually low seizural threshold of this area. Thus perinatal complications, infantile convulsions, central nervous system insults, either injuries or infections, and metabolic imbalances could influence this limbic susceptibility. Furthermore, many individuals with episodic dyscontrol also reported autonomic dysfunctions (suggesting seizural spread to the hypothalamic area), leading to innumerable, transitory physical complaints and dysfunctions. Thus it seemed possible that individuals with epileptoid episodic dyscontrol were not only likely to have committed antisocial acts but also may well have had bizarre and frequent illnesses and unexplained physical complaints. Interestingly, when the basic mechanisms approach the epileptoid pole, there appears to be frequent hysterical elaboration of the symptoms. It is therefore not surprising that such individuals in adulthood are diagnosed as antisocial personalities or as suffering from Briquet disorder (somatization disorder).

It is pertinent that the dyscontrol syndrome be considered as at least one subgroup of the adult version of the minimal brain dysfunction of childhood because parents of children diagnosed as showing minimal brain dysfunction have a high prevalence of antisocial behavior (in males) or Briquet disorder (in females).[2]

## EXPERIMENTAL DESIGN

This is a report on one aspect of a study of 93 recidivist aggressors detailed elsewhere.[3] These criminals were incarcerated at Patuxent Institution in Maryland on indeterminate sentences as "defective delinquents." A defective delinquent was defined legally as "an individual who, by the demonstration of persistent aggravated antisocial or criminal behavior, evidences a propensity towards criminal activity, and who is found to have either such intellectual deficiency or emotional unbalance, or both, as to clearly demonstrate an actual danger to society so as to require such confinement and treatment, when appropriate, as may make it reasonably safe for society to terminate the confinement and treatment." Practically speaking these individuals had been incarcerated most of their adult lives and, in fact, much of their childhoods and had demonstrated, on repeated releases from incarceration, that they could not continue living outside a prison without immediately reverting to their antisocial behavior.

The data, which were collected by a number of individuals representing different disciplines and diverse viewpoints, were recorded in such a way that they could be utilized for statistical analysis. The data collected were the following:

1. Neurologist. A neurologic examination and history including the following categories, described in detail elsewhere:[4] neurologic history—birth data, head injury, epilepsy suspect, central nervous system insult such as infections or drug abuse; neurologic examination—including congenital stigmata, hyperacusis, photophobia, apraxia, asymmetries of motor strength, gross coordination and balance, and proprioceptive sensation.
2. Psychiatrist. A mental status and psychiatric history as recorded on the current and past psychiatric scales of Endicott and Spitzer (CAPPS), with an addenda including dyscontrol behavior;[3] a mood and affect scale.
3. Therapist. A rating by the group therapy leader, a member of the staff of the Patuxent Institution not associated with the research study.
4. Self-rating of dyscontrol behavior (Monroe dyscontrol scale), which included the following 18 items rated never, rarely, sometimes, or frequently:

    1. I have acted on a whim or impulse.
    2. I have had sudden changes in my moods.
    3. I have had the experience of feeling confused even in a familiar place.
    4. I do not feel totally responsible for what I do.
    5. I have lost control of myself even though I did not want to.
    6. I have been surprised by my actions.
    7. I have lost control of myself and hurt other people.
    8. My speech has been slurred.
    9. I have had "blackouts."
    10. I have become wild and uncontrollable after one or two drinks.
    11. I have become so angry that I smashed things.
    12. I have frightened other people with my temper.
    13. I have "come to" without knowing where I was or how I got there.
    14. I have had indescribable frightening feelings.
    15. I have been so tense I would like to scream.
    16. I have had the impulse to kill myself.
    17. I have been angry enough to kill somebody.
    18. I have physically attacked and hurt another person.

5. EEG computer analyses. Number of theta (3–7 Hz) waves exceeding −3 dB amplitude in 5-min prehyperventilation, 5-min hyperventilation, and 5-min posthyperventilation periods; drug-activated record.[3]
6. Psychologist. A battery of psychologic tests to measure CNS integration, cognitive control, and personality characteristics. These data are reported elsewhere.[3]

The psychiatrist and the neurologist made separate global estimations of the possibility for an epileptoid mechanism behind the individual's behavior, utilizing entirely different data sources. That is, the neurologist based her estimation on the neurologic history and examination, while the psychiatrists made their global estimation of an epileptoid mechanism on the basis of the current and past psychiatric scales (CAPPS), particularly the addenda devoted to dyscontrol characteristics.*

The neurologist's evaluation of estimated epileptoid mechanisms was based on the following criteria: (1) episodic dizziness, lightheadedness, blurred vision, and headaches; (2) "déjà vu" or "jamais vu;" (3) perceptual size, space, shape, or time distortions; (4) absentmindedness or forgetfulness; (5) unexplained dropping of objects or unexplained falling; and (6) episodic enuresis.

The psychiatrists based their global estimation of an epileptoid mechanism on histories of (1) prodromal affects or prodromal autonomic symptoms; (2) lack of premeditation; (3) no delay between stimulus and response; (4) minimal symbolism in the act; (5) minimal secondary gains; (6) primitive direct expression of affects; (7) confusions during the act; (8) uncoordinated or brutish motor behavior; (9) tension relief rather than precise need gratification; (10) sense of compelling force to action; (11) remorse or concern for behavior; and (12) partial but not complete amnesia for act.

## RESULTS

Table 8-1 shows the many common behavioral correlations between the neurologist's and the psychiatrist's global estimations of an epileptoid mechanism. So many common correlates are surprising when one considers the divergence in the data base. Also, the correlation coefficients, all significant at the 0.05 level and beyond, are more impressive when one considers that in most instances they do not represent a total score on a measuring instrument but individual items. A number of these correlations are congruent with the concept of an adult version of minimal brain dysfunction. This congruency is evidenced by the history of central ner-

---

* The neurologist on this study was Dr. Barbara Hulfish, Assistant Professor of Psychiatry (Neurology), Dept. of Psychiatry, University of Maryland School of Medicine. Psychiatrists included not only the author but also John R. Lion, M.D. and George U. Balis, M.D., both Professors of Psychiatry, Dept. of Psychiatry, University of Maryland School of Medicine.

**Table 8-1**

Significant ($p \leq 0.05$) Product-Moment Correlations Common to Both Psychiatrist's and Neurologist's Global Estimation of an Epileptoid Mechanism ($n = 93$)

| Data Source | Variable | Coefficients | |
| | | Neurologist | Psychiatrist |
| --- | --- | --- | --- |
| Global estimate | | | |
| Neurologist | Epilepsy suspect | 1.00 | 0.26 |
| Psychiatrist | Episodic estimated epileptoid mechanism | 0.26 | 1.00 |
| Neurologic | Head injury | 0.33 | 0.22 |
| evaluation | Short fuse | 0.30 | 0.21 |
| | Hyperacusis* | 0.18 | 0.17 |
| | Neurologic scale | 0.35 | 0.40 |
| EEG | High theta count | 0.22 | 0.19 |
| Psychiatric | Anger | 0.24 | 0.34 |
| history | Violence | 0.26 | 0.27 |
| | Impulsivity | 0.32 | 0.34 |
| | Antisocial traits in childhood | 0.20 | 0.20 |
| | Poor effort to improve one self | 0.20 | 0.21 |
| | Sullen/pouts | 0.22 | 0.20 |
| | Superficial and excessive involvement | 0.22 | 0.40 |
| | Aimless | 0.18 | 0.20 |
| | Total time of institutionalization | 0.19 | 0.21 |
| Mental status | Grandiosity | 0.29 | 0.20 |
| | Less impairment of daily activities | 0.19 | 0.21 |
| Dyscontrol | Self-rated dyscontrol | 0.34 | 0.34 |
| behavior | symptoms | | |
| | Lack of premeditation* | 0.23 | 0.51 |
| | Lack of personal discomfort regarding act† | 0.19 | 0.25 |
| Mood-affect | Intensity of emotions | 0.20 | 0.20 |
| scales | Impulsiveness | 0.24 | 0.23 |
| Group therapist | Excessive motor | 0.22 | 0.34 |
| ratings | activity | | |
| Psychomotor | Holtzman: movement | −0.20 | −0.23 |
| data | MMPI: hypomania scale | 0.24 | 0.27 |

\* Entered into psychiatrist's or neurologist's estimation of an epileptoid mechanism.
† Contrary to prediction.

vous system "insult" and soft neurologic signs, in the neurologic part of these data, and the angry, violent, impulsive, antisocial traits, as well as the superficial interpersonal involvement, the aimlessness, intense emotions, and excessive motor activity, in the psychiatric history and mental status examination.

In Table 8-2 the behavioral correlations unique to the psychiatrist's global estimation of an epileptoid mechanism are listed, exhibiting further collaboration of symptoms suggestive of an adult version of the minimal brain dysfunction, including emotional fluctuations and overactivity, histrionic behavior, and poor school performance.

Table 8-3 lists the correlations unique to the neurologist's global estimation of an epileptoid mechanism suggesting further evidence of minimal brain dysfunction in terms of the lack of inhibition and nonacceptance by group therapy members.

Several correlations lend further support to the epileptoid mechanism; for example, in Table 8-1 such factors as "short fuse" and hyperacusis and in Table 8-2 such factors as photophobia, amnesia, fugue, and dissociative states.

As mentioned above, the concept of a limbic system seizure that spreads to the hypothalamus resulting in physiologic imbalances seems to be supported by such correlations with physiologic disorders, hypochondriasis, insomnia, poor physical health, and prodromal autonomic features; this along with the correlation with histrionic character traits suggests the possibility that a number of individuals with an epileptoid limbic mechanism may manifest Briquet disorder.

The high correlation with theta counts and the total neurologic scale reveals the potency of a neuropsychiatric evaluation in identifying these individuals. Further evaluation of our data indicates that the historical aspects of our neurologic scale are as potent as the total scale (Table 8-4). Therefore when examining for soft neurologic signs the neurologic examination itself may be less important than a careful history that elicits possible damage to the central nervous system. Also, as yet unsystematized data suggest a strong genetic component for this epileptoid mechanism. It is proposed that the standard psychiatric history include the following data that are not usually reported:

1.  Family history of impulsivity, sociopathy, alcoholism, and hysteria.
2.  Perinatal complications.
3.  Infantile convulsions.
4.  Childhood hyperactivity, distractibility, short attention span.
5.  School behavior problems.
6.  Learning disabilities.

**Table 8-2**

Significant ($p \leq 0.05$) Product-Moment Correlations Unique to Psychiatrist's Global Estimation of an Epileptoid Mechanism ($n = 93$)

| Data Source | Variable | Coefficient |
|---|---|---|
| Neurologic evaluation | Birth data | 0.28 |
| | Photophobia | 0.22 |
| | Hypersensitivity to touch | 0.20 |
| | Good coordination* | 0.18 |
| Psychiatric history | Overreact emotionally | 0.19 |
| | Histrionic | 0.31 |
| | Stubborn | 0.27 |
| | Fluctuation of feelings | 0.20 |
| | Lack of responsibility | 0.20 |
| | Degree of psychopathology | 0.38 |
| | Lower-school grade achievement | 0.18 |
| | Poor overall academic performance | 0.25 |
| | Poor adolescent sexual adjustment | 0.20 |
| | Poor adult heterosexual adjustment | 0.21 |
| | Poor physical health | 0.27 |
| | Amnesia, fugue, dissociative state | 0.22 |
| | Hypochondriasis | 0.26 |
| | Insomnia | 0.18 |
| | Agitation | 0.20 |
| Mental status | Psychophysiologic | 0.21 |
| | Anxiety | 0.18 |
| | Lack of guilt* | 0.22 |
| | Antisocial acts | 0.17 |
| Dyscontrol behavior | Primary/secondary dyscontrol ratio | 0.24 |
| | Number of impulsive acts | 0.20 |
| | Severity of impulsive acts | 0.21 |
| | Aggression during act | 0.19 |
| | Lack of secondary gains to behavior† | 0.23 |
| | Prodromal anger | 0.23 |
| | Prodromal autonomic† | 0.22 |
| Mood-affect scales | Wide range of feelings | 0.18 |
| | Emotional lability | 0.25 |
| Prison adjustment | Frequent rule infractions | 0.23 |
| Group therapist ratings | More physical hostility | 0.27 |
| | Negativistic behavior | 0.19 |
| | More verbal hostility to group members | 0.25 |
| | More verbal hostility to therapist | 0.20 |
| Psychometric data | Holtzman location | 0.19 |

* Contrary to prediction.

† Entered into psychiatrist's estimation of an epileptoid mechanism.

**Table 8-3**

Significant ($p \leq 0.05$) Product-Moment Correlations Unique to Neurologist's
Global Estimation of an Epileptoid Mechanism ($n = 93$)

| Data Source | Variable | Coefficient |
|---|---|---|
| Neurologic evaluation | Repetitive dreams* | 0.23 |
|  | Neurologic stigmata | 0.18 |
| Psychiatric history | Lack of inhibition | 0.26 |
|  | Passive-aggressive | 0.20 |
|  | Lack of ideas of reference | 0.22 |
|  | Outpatient treatment | 0.18 |
|  | Previous incarcerations | 0.26 |
| Mental status | Lack of suicide–self-mutilation† | 0.21 |
| Dyscontrol behavior | Unconscious premeditation | 0.24 |
| Group therapist ratings | Negativistic thinking | 0.26 |
|  | Nonacceptance by group members | 0.21 |
| Psychometric data | No. of positives on Canter-BIP (Bender) | 0.18 |
|  | BIP difference score (Bender) | 0.19 |
|  | Holtzman: reaction time | −0.20 |
|  | Holtzman: color | −0.20 |
|  | Holtzman: integration | −0.19 |
|  | Holtzman: human | −0.25 |
|  | Holtzman: anxiety | −0.23 |
|  | Holtzman: barrier | −0.27 |
|  | Matching familiar figures: reaction time | −0.22 |
|  | Auditory discrimination task: error, noise | 0.25 |
|  | Hand test: modified acting-out | 0.26 |

* Entered into neurologist's estimation of an epileptoid mechanism.
† Contrary to prediction.

7.  CNS infection.
8.  Toxic metabolic insult.
9.  CNS trauma.
10.  Risk taking, accident prone.
11.  Adolescent impulsiveness and acting-out.
12.  Adult dyscontrol.
13.  Formes frustes of epilepsy.
14.  Confusional psychotic reactions.
15.  Criminal behavior.
16.  Vicarious response to drugs of abuse and/or prescribed drugs.

**Table 8-4**

Product-Moment Correlational Comparisons from the Neurologic Scale, the Neurologic History Subscale (I), and the Neurologic Examination Subscale (II)

| Data Source | Variable* | Correlation Coefficients ($n = 93$, $p \leq 0.05$) | | |
| --- | --- | --- | --- | --- |
| | | Neurologic Scale | Neurologic History Subscale I | Neurologic Exam Subscale II |
| Dyscontrol behavior | Episodic estimated epileptoid mechanism | 0.40 | 0.38 | 0.25 |
| | Primary/secondary dyscontrol ratio | | 0.19 | |
| | Self-rated dyscontrol symptoms | 0.31 | 0.24 | 0.24 |
| | Lack of premeditation | 0.18 | 0.19 | |
| | Specificity of affect | 0.18 | | |
| | No. of antisocial or impulsive acts | | 0.19 | |
| | Fear-panic affect during act | | | 0.19 |
| | Prodromal motor restlessness | | | 0.19 |
| | Prodromal anger | 0.20 | | |
| | Prodromal autonomic | 0.17 | | |
| EEG | High theta counts | 0.21 | 0.28 | 0.25 |
| | Clinical rating of chloralose-activated theta waves | 0.33 | 0.26 | 0.21 |
| | Spike slow | 0.22 | | |
| | Behavior | | | −0.20† |
| Psychiatric history | Overreact emotionally | 0.27 | 0.34 | 0.23 |
| | Anger | 0.31 | 0.34 | |
| | Violence | 0.28 | 0.20 | 0.28 |
| | Impulsivity | 0.39 | 0.34 | 0.19 |
| | Poor judgement | 0.27 | 0.23 | 0.20 |
| | Self-defeating behavior | 0.20 | | |
| | Fluctuation of feelings | 0.21 | | |
| | Lack of responsibility | 0.22 | 0.24 | |
| | Grandiosity | 0.24 | | 0.27 |
| | Overall severity | 0.19 | | |

121

**Table 8-4** (continued)

| Data Source | Variable* | Correlation Coefficients ($n = 93, p \leq 0.05$) | | |
| --- | --- | --- | --- | --- |
| | | Neurologic Scale | Neurologic History Subscale I | Neurologic Exam Subscale II |
| | Stubborn | | 0.17 | |
| | Lack of inhibition | | 0.24 | |
| | Poor adaption to stress | | 0.22 | |
| | Sensitive | | 0.17 | |
| | Superficial/excessive involvement | | 0.24 | |
| | Degree of psychopathology | 0.18 | 0.20 | |
| | Neurotic traits of childhood | 0.31 | 0.18 | |
| | Antisocial traits in childhood | 0.21 | 0.22 | 0.27 |
| | Poor adolescent friendship pattern | 0.23 | | |
| | Outpatient treatments | 0.17 | 0.20 | 0.17 |
| | Poor efforts to improve | 0.17 | | |
| | Poor physical health | 0.17 | | |
| | Amnesia, fugue, dissociative state | 0.22 | | 0.20 |
| | Hypochrondriasis | 0.17 | 0.23 | |
| | Depression | | 0.19 | |
| | Suicidal thoughts | | 0.19 | |
| | Phobias | | 0.23 | |
| | Agitation | | 0.20 | |
| | Total time of incarceration | | | 0.20 |
| | Decline in occupational status or responsibility | | | 0.19† |
| Mental status | Psychophysiologic reactions | 0.18 | | 0.20 |
| | Grandiosity | 0.27 | 0.32 | |
| | Belligerence-negativism | 0.26 | 0.23 | 0.18 |
| | Anxiety | | 0.19 | |

| | Subscale I | Neurologic scale | Subscale II |
|---|---|---|---|
| **Mood-affect** | | | |
| Lack of fatigue-inertia | 0.17 | | |
| Level of tension | 0.19 | | |
| Emotional lability | 0.25 | 0.21 | 0.18 |
| Impulsiveness | 0.27 | 0.20 | 0.22 |
| Vigor-activity | | 0.18 | |
| Number of feelings | | 0.26 | |
| Emotionally responsive | | 0.21 | |
| **Group therapist ratings** | | | |
| Good participation | 0.25 | | 0.25 |
| (Volitability) range of emotional responses | 0.34 | | 0.34 |
| Verbal hostility to therapist | 0.23 | | 0.26 |
| Excessive motor activity | | 0.26 | |
| **Prison adjustment** | | | |
| Frequent rule infractions | 0.21 | | 0.24 |
| **Psychometric data** | | | |
| MMPI paranoia scale | | 0.21 | −0.18† |
| WAIS digit span | | | |
| WAIS verbal IQ | | 0.19 | |
| WAIS similarities | | 0.24 | |
| Canter-Bender: no. of positives | 0.18 | | |
| Canter-Bender: class | 0.19 | | |
| Holtzman: FD, form definitiveness | 0.18 | 0.20 | |
| Holtzman: A, animal | 0.17 | | |
| Holtzman: At, anatomy | 0.21 | | |
| Holtzman: Ab, abstract | −0.18 | | 0.25 |
| Holtzman: L, location | | 0.24 | −0.18 |
| Time estimation task | | 0.22 | |

* A Fisher $r$ to $z$ transformation was used to determine whether, for each criterion variable, the variance accounted for by its relationship with subscale I was significantly greater or less than the variance accounted for by its relationship to subscale II or to the neurologic scale as a whole. (Hays WL: Statistics for Psychologists. New York, Holt, Rinehart & Winston, 1965, pp. 529–535.)

† Subscale I = neurologic scale < subscale II. All those without asterisks: subscale I = neurologic scale = subscale I; subscale I = neurologic scale > subscale II.

Electroencephalographic data, particularly generalized paroxysmal theta activity with drug activation in prehyperventilation, hyperventilation, and posthyperventilation, seem to reflect the central nervous system instability that correlates with a global estimation of an epileptoid mechanism. Data reported elsewhere also indicate the significance of random spiking for this behavioral syndrome,[4] but very few of our subjects had evidence for focal temporal lobe abnormalities.

## CONCLUSION

Symptoms suggesting a limbic epileptoid mechanism in aggressive criminals correlate with behavioral symptoms, many of which are thought to be characteristic of either the childhood or the adulthood minimal brain dysfunction syndrome. There is a correlation as well with a history of CNS insult and soft neurologic signs. The concept of an epileptoid dyscontrol syndrome should be explored as the mechanism behind a subgroup of the minimal brain dysfunction syndromes both in childhood and adulthood.

## REFERENCES

1. Monroe RR: Episodic Behavioral Disorders. Cambridge, Mass., Harvard Univ, 1970.
2. Cantwell DP: Psychiatric illness in the families of hyperactive children. Arch Gen Psychiatry 27:414–417, 1972.
3. Monroe RR (ed): Brain Dysfunction in Aggressive Criminals. Lexington, Mass., D. C. Heath and Company, 1978.
4. Monroe RR, Hulfish B, Balis GU, et al: Neurologic findings in recidivist aggressors. In Shagass C, Gershon S, Friedhoff AH, (eds), Psychopathology and Brain Dysfunction. New York, Raven, 1977.

## DISCUSSION

*Dr. Huessy:*   I'm beginning to feel that there is an undue proportion of MBD patients with reports of unusually high fevers in childhood. They'll say that at one time they had the measles and a temperature of 106°F, 105.5°F. I always thought these people were autonomically overreactive, and I wonder if you or anybody else had found this.

*Dr. Bellak:*   We reported that in a paper in 1948 on schizophrenia.

*Dr. Monroe:* Our neurologists questioned for that intensively. The CAPPS scale, which we selected because it focuses on episodic symptoms, does not cover that. Interestingly, it doesn't focus on hyperkinesis in childhood, so we missed that because we weren't anticipating that kind of data.

*Dr. Cole:* Dick Jenkins at Iowa a long time ago classified delinquents as socialized and unsocialized. I'm inferring that most of these antisocial MBD people are not members of the "mafia," who go around functioning effectively in group activities, but are, in fact, what Jenkins would call unsocialized delinquents, or what I used to call sick psychopaths when I was in the Army, that is, people who commit violent acts with very little secondary gain, with very little knowledge of how to get away with it.

*Dr. Davies:* They're the ones that serve the time voluntarily.

*Dr. Monroe:* Of our four groups, the one that showed the neurologic signs we call the epileptoid group—that's the high EEG abnormalities, the high dyscontrol symptom. We had another group with high dyscontrol symptoms and no EEG abnormalities, which we called the hysteroid group. They were the ones that were amnestic for their behavior. They got all the side effects from the drugs and complained about it. There was another group that had EEG abnormalities but no dyscontrol symptoms. These showed up as socially inept, irresponsible, poor in judgment, aimless, poor in interpersonal relationships, alcohol abusing—the old inadequate psychopath. They were not particularly impulsive but just completely socially inept. And the fourth group, the ones that showed no dyscontrol symptoms and no abnormal EEG, which would have been a normal population if a nonprison group, they were what we think were the pure psychopath. The only thing they showed was that they were better at abstract thinking and functioned better than all the rest. But remember, this is a group that had been incarcerated year and year after year, and repeatedly, for repeated offenses; they were hardly a normal group.

*Dr. Hartocollis:* Did you test for cerebral dominance?

*Dr. Monroe:* We did not. We tested for hands. I think that Yeudall's data on left and right hemispheres is very interesting, and we are analyzing whatever data on left-right phenomena we have, and we're collecting such data from now on.

Gary J. Tucker

# 9

# Sensorimotor Disturbances in Psychotics

It has often been noted that when psychological testing is used to evaluate the central nervous system, schizophrenics frequently cannot be differentiated from organic patients, especially with regard to sensorimotor disturbances. This has led to the interpretation that the specific tests are not sensitive enough to differentiate schizophrenics from organics; it is seldom considered that perhaps the deficits noted in the schizophrenic patients are neuropathologic components of the schizophrenic process.[1] It has been characteristic of psychiatric theorizing to look primarily at the environment of the patient rather than at the "equipment" with which the patient functions.

If one looks at evidence for sensorimotor disturbances in the major psychotic diagnostic categories one is impressed by the substantial data for its presence in schizophrenic patients and, to a lesser extent, in major affective disorders.[2] It is also interesting that if one examines the recent category as defined from genetic studies, that of the schizophrenic "spectrum disorders," the entities within these spectrum disturbances also have a high incidence of sensorimotor disturbances.

It will review the concept of sensorimotor disturbances, particularly soft signs, and discuss their implications. The various studies describing soft signs in all psychotic diagnostic categories will be discussed and an attempt made to determine if these soft signs have any implications in themselves. Other issues to be examined are the changes in these signs over time, their prognostic significance, and their relationship to age, sex, and other demographic variables.

## NEUROLOGIC "SOFT SIGNS"

"Soft" neurologic signs are usually defined as signs indicative of nonlocalizing or diffuse dysfunctions, as opposed to "hard" neurologic signs, which have anatomic localizing value or indicate specific lesions. Table 9-1 represents a partial listing of the number of soft signs that have been cited as indicating diffuse cerebral lesions.[2-8] As one can see, these signs range from low IQ levels, e.g., mental retardation, to abnormal EEGs to various movement disorders. The wide array of signs available for study and the almost idiosyncratic selection by investigators have led to some difficulty in interpretation and correlation of the various studies that have been done. This has also led to the possible overlooking of specific replicable abnormalities in these studies that could lend increasing support to central nervous system involvement in these psychopathologic entities. For example, there are increasing numbers of studies that note lowered achievement and IQ levels and decreased social development in schizophrenic patients, as well as the many studies that have found various EEG abnormalities; almost all of these studies have

**Table 9-1**
Typical Soft Signs Used in Various Studies[1,3,6-8,12,17]

| |
| --- |
| Stereognosis |
| Graphesthesia |
| Bilateral simultaneous stimulation |
| Coordination, balance, gait |
| Sensory (light touch, position, vibration, pain, slow extinction, or poor lateralization) |
| Synkinesis |
| Choreoathetosis |
| Dystonia |
| Tremor, tics |
| Speech disturbances |
| Adventitious motor overflow |
| Motor impersistence |
| Auditory visual integration |
| Vestibular dysfunctions (decreased or increased responses) |
| Cranial nerve disorders that are nonlocalizing |
| Diffuse EEG abnormalities |
| Decreased or increased reflexes |
| Hoffman's sign |
| Poor clonus |
| Mental retardation |
| Memory disturbances |
| Nonlocalizing indicators of cerebral dysfunction on various psychological tests |

used varied critiera, thus diminishing their total force.[2] Regardless of this diversity, the total array and fairly consistent occurrence of soft signs in studies of schizophrenic patients, and to some extent other diagnostic categories, lend some interest and importance to this area.

The quality of soft signs, in their being indicative of diffuse dysfunctions, rather than localizing, is in itself of some interest. Most of these signs are evident only upon active testing or upon the request of the experimenter that the person perform some various functions, whereas the more localizing neurologic signs are often evident at rest, e.g., paralysis, atrophy, etc. The fact that soft signs are indicative of functional disturbances is similar or analogous to the various behavioral disturbances that come to psychiatric attention; most psychiatric deficits are not evident unless the person is asked to function or perform.

## STUDIES OF SOFT SIGNS

Neurologic studies of adult schizophrenic patients have shown varied results, but if the criteria of soft or minor neurologic signs (nonlocalizing) are used in contrast to hard or major signs (localizing), there is evidence of neurologic dysfunction in adult schizophrenia. Pollin et al.[5] and Hertzig and Birch[6] performed detailed neurologic examinations on adolescent and adult schizophrenic patients and found more soft neurologic signs in these patients than one would have expected by chance. Increased soft neurologic signs in schizophrenic patients have also been found by Kennard,[9] Larson,[10] and Rochford et al.[4]

Rochford et al.[4] studied 65 hospitalized patients for the presence of the following soft signs: motor impersistence, stereognosis, graphesthesia, extinction to bilateral simultaneous stimulation, bilateral marked hyperreflexia or hyporeflexia, coordination defects, disturbance of balance and gait, sensory abnormalities, movement disorders, speech defects, abnormal motor activity, auditory visual integration, choreiform movements on the adventitious motor overflow tests, and cranial nerve abnormalities (such as slight aniscoria, esotropia, eighth nerve deficit proven audiometrically, and mild visual field and retinal defects). Hard signs consisted of localizing findings of CNS abnormality, such as lateralizing cranial nerve findings, pathologic reflexes, unilateral sensory deficits and movement disorders, and unequivocal abnormal electroencephalograms. Rochford et al. noted that neurologic abnormality was found in 36.8 percent of all patients studied, a finding significantly different from that in a control population of normal subjects. Interestingly, they found little neurologic abnormality among patients with affective disorder. The neurologic soft signs were found in a significantly greater number of the schizophrenic patients (65.5 percent). Pollin et al.[5] noted that 72.5 percent of their schizophrenic patients had at least one sign; this percentage compares favorably to the 65.5 percent in the study by Rochford et al.[4]

Davies et al. extended these studies and correlated the occurrence of soft signs with EEG abnormalities.[8] They also postulated that the use of phenothiazines in schizophrenic patients may make evident an underlying EEG abnormality rather than the EEG abnormalities noted with phenothiazine use being primarily due to the drug itself. They cited a 39 percent incidence of abnormal EEGs in schizophrenic patients. Quitkin et al.[11] found a high correlation with neurologic soft signs in schizophrenic patients that they call premorbid asocial and that others might call process schizophrenics. They also noted a high incidence of soft signs in emotionally unstable character disorders.

It is interesting that these studies of soft signs are primarily directed at schizophrenic patients. The major information that we have on the occurrence of soft signs in other diagnostic entities usually relates to these diagnostic categories being used as control populations. With the exception of the study by Quitkin et al.,[11] which used very specific diagnostic criteria for the control groups and studied 350 consecutive admissions, most of the studies either group their subjects into schizophrenic and nonschizophrenic groups or occasionally break out "affective disorders." However, from these studies a higher incidence of soft signs is evident in the character disorder groups and also to some extent in the affective disorder groups, although in all categories to a lesser extent than in schizophrenic patients. Further studies using techniques to evaluate soft signs need to be done with these other diagnostic entities. In the many studies of EEG abnormalities, the incidence of abnormal EEGs in affective diagnostic groups is high, and one would expect that if detailed exams of soft signs were directed at these other diagnostic populations one might find an increased incidence of these signs also.[1,2]

There are some questions that immediately come to mind regarding the presence of soft signs: (1) Are these incidental findings in psychiatric patients? (2) Do these soft signs represent defects specifically related to an illness "process?" (3) Do these soft signs disappear in remission? (4) Do they have some meaning in themselves? To answer some of these questions, let us examine in some detail a study of soft signs and a followup of these same patients 3 years after the original study.

One hundred nine consecutive patients admitted to a psychiatric unit were tested in 1972 with the following standardized tests from the Halstead-Reitan battery:[12,13] (1) a test for finger agnosia, (2) fingertip number writing, (3) the tactile

**Table 9-2**
Neurologic Impairment

|  | Normal | Possible Mild | Mild | Moderate |
|---|---|---|---|---|
| Nonschizophrenic ($n=71$) | 38 | 10 | 14 | 9 |
| Schizophrenic ($n=38$) | 9 | 7 | 10 | 12 |

$\chi^2 = 10.49$, 3 df, $p = 0.0148$.

form recognition test, and (4) the tactile performance test.[14] Of the 109 patients, 45 (41.3 percent) showed *mild to moderate* neurologic impairment; if those with *possible* mild neurologic impairment (the area where the scores are not in the "certain" abnormal range and not in the "normal" range) were included, the total incidence for these neurologic impairments went to 57 percent of the patients admitted. Although schizophrenic patients comprised only 34 percent of the total sample, they comprised *50 percent* of those with neurologic impairments. Of the schizophrenics, 57.8 percent had mild to moderate neurologic impairments (Table 9-2).

While some of these soft neurologic findings may be due to drug effects, aging processes, inattention, anxiety, or noncooperation on the part of the patients, many of these findings have also been reported in other studies where these factors were controlled; the results in terms of incidence remained similar.[4,5]

In 1975, 3 years after the original study, the above 109 patients were restudied.[15] At the time of followup the neurologic tests were readministered, historical data as to treatment and rehospitalization were gathered, and the Katz social adjustment scales,[16] the New Haven schizophrenia index,[17] and the Schneider first rank symptom scale[18] were administered. Overall estimates of patient functioning were also gained from the interviewers and the patients themselves. In this manner 47 of the 109 patients were retested (43 percent), and an additional 37 were contacted by telephone (33 percent), for a total followup of 84 (77 percent) of the original sample.

Of the 47 subjects retested, 47 (44 percent) had neurologic impairment in 1972 and 14 had neurologic impairment in 1975 (29 percent). Although the relative total amount of neurologic impairment decreased somewhat (in terms of the neurologic index—a compilation of the various neurologic test scores), the percentages of those with neurologic impairment remained relatively stable. The decrease in neurologic impairments was most marked in the *nonschizophrenic* group (Table 9-3). Of 18 schizophrenics, 11 had neurologic impairments in 1972 and 8 had neurologic impairments in 1975. Of 29 nonschizophrenics, 9 had neurologic impairments in 1972 and 6 had neurologic impairments in 1975. The *relative amounts* of neurologic impairment decreased most markedly in the nonschizophrenic group; however, it seems that the neurologic impairments persist in *both* groups.

**Table 9-3**
Neurologic Index

|                          | n  | 1972      | n  | 1975        |
|--------------------------|----|-----------|----|-------------|
| Schizophrenic            |    |           |    |             |
| (*both* NHSI and FRS)    | 24 | 9.8 (54%) | 9  | 7.1  (44%)  |
| (*either* NHSI or FRS)   | 46 | 9.2 (61%) | 18 | 7.5  (44%)  |
| Nonschizophrenic         | 63 | 7.2 (31%) | 30 | 4.9* (20%)  |

* $p = 0.03$ (one-way analysis of variance).

## PROGNOSIS

The persistence of the soft signs in most diagnostic categories suggests their being a reflection of a longstanding characteristic. Lilliston showed that process schizophrenics had more organicity.[7] Tutko and Spence[19] showed that process schizophrenics perform closer to results indicating brain damage on various psychological tests but found no significant difference in process versus reactive schizophrenics and organics (however, all of these groups differed from normals). Parsons and Klein[20] showed that the process schizophrenics and the brain-damaged patients could not be differentiated on the category test of the Halstead-Reitan battery but that the reactive schizophrenics and the controls could be differentiated from the others. Quitkin et al.[11] noted that the neurologic signs correlated significantly in those patients with premorbid asociality or what we would call process schizophrenia. In the specific studies cited above we found little distinction in the presence of neurologic soft signs and the process-reactive dimension;[14,15] this may relate in part to the relatively small number of patients that could be called process schizophrenics in the sample studied—most of the patients would be classified as acute or reactive schizophrenics. Also, at followup none of the original schizophrenic group would have met the diagnostic criteria for either the New Haven schizophrenia index or Schneider first rank symptom criteria. While the neurologic findings may not in themselves have prognostic or predictive significance, they certainly are associated with conditions that are longstanding and as such may have prognostic significance by delineating a specific group of patients that have long-term poor prognosis.

## NEUROLOGIC IMPAIRMENTS AND SYMPTOMS

There has been some attempt to correlate specific symptoms with neurologic impairments. Kennard noted that there were more EEG ab-

**Table 9-4**
Prognosis: Diagnostic Measures

|  | n | Symptoms (Katz S-1) | Interviewer Ratings |
|---|---|---|---|
| Nonschizophrenic | 29 | 81.0 | 2.0 |
| Schizophrenic |  |  |  |
| (either NHSI or FRS) | 18 | 84.0 | 2.7* |
| (both NHSI and FRS) | 9 | 76.9 | 2.8* |
| (both NHSI and FRS, and positive neuroimpairment) | 4 | 99.4* | 2.5 |

* $p = 0.0006$ (one-way analysis of variance).

normalities in those patients with thought disorder;[9] Lilliston noted that of three groups of schizophrenics with varying degrees of organic dysfunction those with greater degrees of organic dysfunction also had more emotional symptoms.[21] In our studies it was apparent that in the patients with more neurologic impairment there were also more symptoms, especially thought disorder; more specifically it was found that those patients with neurologic impairments (Table 9-4) also had a greater number of other symptoms. If one examines Table 9-4 in terms of those who had no neurologic impairment in 1972 and those who had neurologic impairment in both 1972 and 1975, there were significantly more symptoms in this latter group as manifested by the Katz S-1 scale (this is basically the Johns Hopkins symptom distress checklist and is weighted heavily towards psychophysiologic symptoms). Consequently, if one adds as a diagnostic criteria the presence of neurologic impairments, then the presence of other types of psychiatric symptoms also rises (Table 9-5). Thus by using both standardized behavioral diagnostic criteria and standardized neurologic criteria, we have distinguished a group that has many more persistent psychiatric symptoms.

**Table 9-5**
Neurologic Impairment Changes

| 1972 | 1975 | n | Symptoms (Katz S-1) | Interviewer Rating |
|---|---|---|---|---|
| None | None | 27 | 78.5 | 1.9 |
| Present | None | 8 | 75.6 | 1.8 |
| Present | Present | 12 | 96.7* | 2.7* |

* $p = 0.06$ (one-way analysis of variance).

Reitan, in a specific study of the implications of sensorimotor deficits in organic patients, noted a strong relationship between increased sensorimotor impairments and increased deficits in cognitive and intellectual functions, as well as pathology, as manifested on the MMPI.[22]

## IMPLICATIONS

While many of the neurologic soft signs may represent normal aging processes, these findings do occur in various psychopathologic entities in a significantly increased incidence unrelated to age.[14] As such they represent intriguing, possibly replicable findings that correlate with a higher incidence of other psychopathologic symptoms in general. As the above studies have shown, they seem to represent rather persistent processes that in themselves may be indicative of genetic or other longstanding conditions. However, they do reflect diffuse CNS dysfunction. These dysfunctions, as noted previously, are more evident in the dynamic state, when the person is functioning. As sensory integrative deficits, they may be indicative of a nonspecific neuropsychologic condition representative of difficulties in integrating sensory data as well as in processing information. It seems logical that they would occur more frequently in those conditions that clinically seem to manifest more integrative deficits, at least in terms of cognitive function. These would be conditions such as schizophrenia, various organic states, and even depressive disorders wherein there are cognitive changes and some characterologic disorders where repetitive patterns are pursued with little ability to change these patterns or see their implications. If these soft signs are a biologic representation of a common cognitive or psychopathologic condition representing various dimensions of the ability to process information or integrate sensory data, they may be reflected in deficits in reasoning and perception, thus leading to symptoms that cut across diagnostic categories rather than those that are exclusive to any diagnostic category.

It is still unclear what the exact implications of these sensorimotor impairments are for the etiology of any psychopathologic process; at present we have correlational evidence that these findings occur with greater frequency in certain diagnostic categories. Certainly they also seem related to long-term persistent psychopathologic processes and greater numbers of symptoms. In this alone they represent findings worth pursuing.

In terms of the etiology of these neurologic impairments, it is possible that they represent either a genetic variation or occur at the pre- or perinatal period, or possibly later in life. If the soft signs represent a genetic variation, they they would seem to be part of a generalized pathologic process; however, if they are acquired, then these impairments (probably traumatically induced) would then interact with specific genetic predispositions to produce a specific psychopathologic entity. For example, if there was the proper genetic predisposition to schizophrenia one might expect the stress that causes these impairments to combine and lead to the occurrence of the illness process; if there was no genetic predisposition to schizophrenia, then we might see evidence of hyperkinesis, learning disability, character disorder, etc. However, the difficulty in integrating sensory and perceptual inputs connoted by these impairments would manifest itself in the symptomatic picture regardless of the etiology and be similar regardless of the specific diagnostic category.

**REFERENCES**

1. Tucker GJ: Psychosomatic studies of psychiatric disorders: Schizophrenia. Int J Psychiatry Med 6:113–121, 1975.
2. Pincus J, Tucker G: Behavioral Neurology. New York, Oxford Univ, 1974.
3. Campion E, Tucker G: A note on twin studies, schizophrenia and neurological impairment. Arch Gen Psychiatry 29:460–464, 1973.
4. Rochford J, Detre T, Tucker GJ, et al: Neuropsychological impairments in functional psychiatric disease. Arch Gen Psychiatry 26:64–67, 1972.
5. Pollin W, Stabenau J, Mosher L, et al: Life history differences in identical twins discordant for schizophrenia. Am J Orthopsychiatry 36:492–509, 1966.
6. Hertzig MA, Birch HG: Neurologic organization in psychiatrically disturbed adolescent girls. Arch Gen Psychiatry 15:509–599, 1966.
7. Lilliston L: Tests of cerebral damage and the process-reactive dimension. J Clin Psychol 26(2):180–181, 1970.
8. Davies RK, Neil JF, Himmelhoch JM: Cerebral dysrhythmias in schizophrenics receiving phenothiazines: Clinical correlates. Clin Electroencephalogr 6(3):103–115, 1975.
9. Kennard M: Value of equivocal signs in neurologic diagnosis. Neurology 10:753–764, 1960.
10. Larson V: Physical characteristics of disturbed adolescents. Arch Gen Psychiatry 10:55–64, 1964.
11. Quitkin F, Rifkin A, Klein DF: Neurologic soft signs in schizophrenia and character disorders. Arch Gen Psychiatry 33:845–853, 1976.
12. Halstead W, Wepman J: The Halstead-Wepman aphasia screening test. J Hearing Speech Disorders 14:9–15, 1949.
13. Reitan R: A research program on psychological effects of brain lesions in human beings. In Ellis NR (ed): International Review of Research in Mental Retardation. New York, Academic, 1966, pp 153–218.
14. Tucker G, Campion E, Silberfarb PM: Sensorimotor functions and cognitive disturbance in psychiatric patients. Am J Psychiatry 132:17–21, 1975.
15. Tucker GJ, Silberfarb PM: Neurologic dysfunction in schizophrenia: Sig-

nificance for diagnostic practice. In Akiskal H, Webb W (eds): Psychiatric Diagnosis: Exploration of Biological Predictors. New York, Spectrum, 1977.

16. Katz M, Lycrly S: Methods for measuring adjustment and social behavior in the community. Psychol Rep 13:503–535, 1963.

17. Astrachan B, Harrow M, Adler P, et al: A checklist for the diagnosis of schizophrenia. Br J Psychiatry 121:529–539, 1972.

18. Mellor CS: First rank symptoms of schizophrenia. Br J Psychiatry 117:15–23, 1970.

19. Tutko TA, Spence JT: The performance of process and reactive schizophrenics and brain-injured subjects on a conceptual task. J. Abnorm Social Psychol 65:381–394, 1962.

20. Parsons OA, Klein HP: Concept identification and practice in brain-damaged and process-reactive schizophrenic groups. J Consult Clin Psychol 35:317–323, 1970.

21. Lilliston L: Schizophrenic symptomatology as a function of probability of cerebral damage. J Abnorm Psychol 82:377–381, 1973.

22. Reitan RM: Sensorimotor functions, intelligence and cognition, and emotional status in subjects with cerebral lesions. Percep Mot Skills 31:275–284, 1970.

## DISCUSSION

*Dr. Gallant:* Were the three schizophrenic patients that had no neurologic impairment on medication also?

*Dr. Tucker:* Yes. Almost all the schizophrenic patients were on medication, similar doses. We found no differences between the two. The incidence of neurologic impairment was similar to that found in Rochford's study of people who were unmedicated. They were only unmedicated for two days. Tardive dyskinesias, the various sensory motor impairments, haven't been studied before and after medication to my knowledge. They may have an important variable.

*Dr. Tucker:* We've had a very large experience, maybe a thousand psychiatric patients, using the Halstead-Reitan battery, and our data have been put on computer, although they haven't yet been published. We really can discriminate patients who have neurologic impairments, using the whole battery, whether they're on medication or not. The differences are apparent. You can see neurologic impairments in the nonschizophrenics as well. But with the diagnosis of schizophrenia, the number of patients with neurologic impairments goes up.

*Dr. Huessy:* Do you know of any studies that have tried to look at the stability of these soft neurologic signs?

*Dr. Tucker:* Yes, there is one study in chronic schizophrenics by Klonoff, I think, over a 10-year period.

*Dr. Huessy:* We have an illness that leads to disordered thinking and some neurologic impairment. When you get over the illness, might they both go away?

*Dr. Tucker:* Well, from the brief data I presented, in a very small number of patients it does seem to go away. The impairment decreases in the nonschizophrenics much more than in the schizophrenics. The longer it persists, the more symptoms they seem to have, so that whether it relates to general severity or not, I'm not sure.

*Chairman Bellak:* How long was the average hospitalization of your patients?

*Dr. Tucker:* I don't recall, but probably about 21 to 30 days.

*Chairman Bellak:* I doubt if that hospitalization period would be responsible for very much. We have seen much iatrogenic effect in long hospitalization. Once upon a time we thought it was a special microbacillus tuberculosis that caused schizophrenia! I myself somatotyped 100 patients with a control group and found that in essence ectomorphy related to length of hospitalization more than anything else. I would wonder, among other things, whether hospitalization and the sensory deprivation that's involved could account for some of the "neurologic" deficit in chronic patients.

*Dr. Tucker:* You know, it's interesting. I was involved in a unit that admitted all Yale University students for about 7 or 8 years, and it was very rare to have a varsity athlete admitted for psychiatric reasons. We had all kinds of other students admitted, but few athletes entered the hospital. Whether they don't think much or they don't have many emotional problems, I don't know, but I think it may relate to the sensorimotor performance.

*Chairman Bellak:* If I go by my experience with West Point cadets, I would say they mostly develop psychosomatic disorders and end up in the medical ward rather than the psychiatric ward.

*Dr. Monroe:* I think one of the things we neglect to look at when considering soft neurologic signs in schizophrenia is sensorium. It is one of the most neglected areas in any of our current rating scales. The International Study neglected this completely. Those schizophrenics that have some kind of clouding of sensorium, whether you call it oneirophrenia or whatever, are much more likely to show neurologic signs. The trouble is that we don't collect data on the sensorium, and I think this is a bad oversight.

*Dr. Gallant:* I would like to say one thing about tests–retests. There were some very confusing findings by Weiss on the EEG for a 5-year followup in hyperactive children, where about 40 percent of the children initially had abnormal EEGs, and also at the end of 5 years; however, after the test–retest it was only 25 percent. That really is something that I don't think anyone can adequately explain. If the EEG is that unstable, the soft signs might also be somewhat unstable over a long period of time.

*Dr. Cole:* How reliable are EEGs in general? I wonder. You keep getting repeat EEGs in patients you suspect something in, and you run three EEGs and one of them will come up abnormal.

*Chairman Bellak:* As to oneirophrenia, Meduna, who coined the term, considered that a particularly benign disorder. I wonder how that would tie in with neurologic findings?

Robert K. Davies
John F. Neil

# 10

# Cerebral Dysrhythmias in Schizophrenics: Clinical Correlates

Despite a body of literature describing the effects of antipsychotic medication on the electroencephalograms (EEG) of schizophrenic patients,[1-8] there have been few systematic studies relating those EEG patterns to the clinical picture that the patients present. Moreover, a controversy over the significance of these EEG abnormalities remains. While some investigators maintain that the EEG changes seen represent artifactual abnormalities or "drug effects,"[9,10] others have demonstrated individual variability in the EEG response to neuroleptics[11-14] and an association between certain drug-related EEG patterns and atypical symptomatology[15] or signs of brain damage.[14,16] It has also been suggested that neuroleptics may facilitate EEG recordings in patient populations by activating dysrhythmias.[17,18]

In an attempt to delineate the pre- and posttreatment developmental, neurologic, and behavioral correlates of drug-related EEG abnormalities in schizophrenics, three studies were carried out. The first was a retrospective study of 114 unselected schizophrenic patients who were admitted to the Psychiatric Inpatient Unit of Yale–New Haven Hospital between 1968 and 1972.[19] The diagnosis of schizophrenia was made by two psychiatrists in accordance with DSM II criteria. All patients were receiving phenothiazine medication. Waking EEGs were routinely obtained on all patients shortly after admission and classified as normal, abnormal-

139

nonparoxysmal (diffuse slow waves) and abnormal-paroxysmal (nonpatterned sharp waves or spikes, patterned spike and wave complexes). For each subject clinical data were obtained for six major areas: (1) type and dosage of drug administered; (2) presenting clinical picture; (3) developmental history; (4) signs of current neurologic dysfunction; (5) family history of psychiatric and neurologic disorders; and (6) course of illness and response to treatment.

In this population 44 percent had EEGs that were interpreted as normal; 27 percent had generalized slow wave abnormalities; and 29 percent had paroxysmal abnormalities (with or without associated slow wave abnormalities). When these EEG findings were correlated with the clinical data, the most striking differences were those between the normal and paroxysmal groups. While the EEG patterns did not correlate with the age of the patient, there was a significant majority of female patients in the paroxysmal group (73 percent) and a preponderance of males in the normal group (66 percent). There were also significant correlations with diagnostic subtypes, with the paroxysmal group being more heterogeneous and diagnosed more frequently as latent, catatonic, and schizoaffective and less frequently as paranoid schizophrenic.

In regard to the clinical presentation of the patients (Table 10-1) there were no differences among the groups on measures of such "core" schizophrenic symptoms as social withdrawal, delusions, bizarre behavior, and blocking. The paroxysmal group, however, did show less flattened affect and greater emotional lability. In addition, patients in this group demonstrated greater irritability and loss of impulse control, more signs of confusion and clouding of consciousness, more nonauditory hallucinations, greater evidence for depersonalization and derealization, and more episodic symptoms.

Importantly, the patients with a paroxysmal pattern to their EEGs also gave evidence for clinical and historical factors often associated with minimal brain dysfunction (MBD). Thus patients in this group reported a higher incidence of multiple adverse events (perinatal complications, high fevers with delirium, severe childhood illnesses) frequently seen in the histories of MBD children and also reported more childhood symptoms (clumsiness, tantrums, phobias) associated with MBD and a greater incidence of clusters of these MBD symptoms. Significantly, the physical examinations of these patients yielded greater evidence for both "soft" and "hard" neurologic signs.

In this study it was difficult to assess the differential efficacy of phenothiazine treatment in the EEG groups, since the length of hospitalization was the same for all; however, more medication changes were made on patients in the paroxysmal group ($p < 0.05$). Since frequent drug changes are not the rule on the unit studied, patient charts were reviewed

**Table 10-1**

Items Showing Differences Between the Normal and Paroxysmal Groups

| Clinical Presentation | Developmental History | Neurologic Impairment |
|---|---|---|
| Irritability‡ | Three or more adverse medical conditions during development‡ | No. with soft signs§ |
| Impulse disorder‡ | Clumsiness† | No. with hard signs‡ |
| Disorientation† | Tantrums‡ | No. with one hard or two soft signs§ |
| Confusion§ | Phobias‡ | No. with at least one sign (any type)§ |
| Clouded consciousness‡ | Three or more childhood symptoms‡ | |
| Difficulty concentrating* | | |
| Nonauditory hallucinations† | | |
| Depersonalization† | | |
| Derealization† | | |
| Less flattened affect* | | |
| Mood lability† | | |
| Fewer loose associations* | | |
| Episodic symptoms§ | | |

* $p < 0.1$.
† $p < 0.05$.
‡ $p < 0.01$.
§ $p < 0.001$.

141

in an attempt to determine the reason. The records suggested that in some cases the phenothiazines seemed to aggravate symptoms, while in others they failed to relieve some of the atypical features of the psychosis.

The second study,[20] done at the Western Psychiatric Institute and Clinic, attempted to replicate and extend the original data. Eighty-three schizophrenic patients admitted to the Neuropsychiatric Assessment Unit were studied. All met the Research Diagnostic Criteria for schizophrenia or schizoaffective psychosis[21] (patients with latent schizophrenia were excluded from this study), and none had evidence for adult onset brain disease or a clearcut seizure disorder.

It was possible on all patients to obtain EEGs, both before and 10–14 days after the initiation of therapy with antipsychotic medication. Of the 83 patients, 45 percent (group I) had EEGs that were normal both before and during drug treatment; 22 percent (group II) had normal pretreatment EEGs and diffusely slow EEGs during treatment; 14 percent (group III) had normal pretreatment EEGs and paroxysmal EEGs during treatment; and 19 percent (group IV) had paroxysmal EEGs, both before and during treatment. This last group showed an accentuation of the pretreatment paroxysmal abnormality during drug administration. As in the first study, there were no correlations among the groups in regard to type or dosage of antipsychotic medication. Also, individual patients showed consistent EEG responses during trials of neuroleptics from different chemical classes.

Again, the greatest differences in clinical symptoms occurred between the normal group and the two with paroxysmal EEGs. Analysis of the presenting clinical picture revealed similar patterns to the first study. Both paroxysmal groups showed greater disorientation and confusion, depersonalization and derealization, and affective lability than the normal group. Group IV alone showed greater irritability, impulse disorder, episodic symptoms, and nonauditory hallucinations and less flattened affect and loose associations. Group III alone showed similar trends for these last items, although they did not reach statistical significance, and also showed significantly more concrete thinking and depression than the normal group.

When the data in groups III and IV were combined and compared to the normal group, items such as increased irritability, mood lability, impulsivity, disorientation, confusion, depersonalization, derealization, and episodic symptoms and less flattened affect showed strengthened correlations, while correlations were reduced on such items as concrete thinking, depression, and nonauditory hallucinations. These data support the notion that the clinical presentation of patients with both normal and paroxysmal pretreatment EEGs is similar, provided that the EEG during neuroleptic treatment shows paroxysmal activity.

Analysis of the developmental histories of these patients again revealed that the paroxysmal groups had significantly more symptoms suggestive of MBD (perinatal difficulties, clumsiness, hyperkinesis, and especially the presence of three or more symptoms of MBD). The data also suggested that the paroxysmal groups showed a poorer response of episodic symptoms and mood difficulties to antipsychotic treatment alone.

The third study[22] looked at psychological test results on 30 (18 with normal and 12 with paroxysmal EEGs) of the original 114 patients who had been administered the Rorschach test, MMPI, Maudsley Personality Inventory, and a Perceptual Experiences Inventory as part of a separate study. The tests were scored without knowledge of either the clinical diagnosis or EEG results. On the Rorschach test patients with normal EEGs tended to give more responses with primitive unsocialized drive content than patients with paroxysmal EEGs ($p = 0.055$), the difference being largely due to a higher incidence of sexual responses. On the other hand, patients in the paroxysmal EEG group showed a nonsignificant trend for more socialized aggressive content to their responses. Color-dominated responses, interpreted by some as a sign of affective lability, were more prominent in the paroxysmal group. Rorschach signs of disordered thinking did not differentiate the two groups.

On the MMPI the paroxysmal group showed significant or trend differences from the normal EEG group on measures of lower ego strength ($p = 0.055$), higher dependency, lower dominance, lower social responsibility, higher psychesthenia, and higher social introversion. Consistent with the last finding, the paroxysmal group scored higher on the Maudsley Introversion Scale.

Of interest is that both groups reported similar experiences of stimulus overinclusion on testing shortly after admission. However, the experience of being flooded by stimuli persisted in patients with paroxysmal EEGs but subsided in the others after 7 weeks of hospitalization.

## DISCUSSION

In two studies of schizophrenic populations an association between a paroxysmal EEG pattern (whether spontaneous or activated) and a clinical picture that includes irritability, impulse dyscontrol, dissociative states, labile and not flattened affect, and episodic symptoms has been demonstrated. The clinical findings are similar in patients with both spontaneous and drug-induced EEG abnormalities and would appear to reflect individual patient factors and not effects specific to the drug itself. The association of the EEG abnormality with the behavioral clusters may reflect a common etiology, namely, cerebral dysfunction, and the presence of soft neurologic signs in these patients lends support to this hypothesis. Thus it would appear that in the populations studied the significance of a paroxysmal EEG is the same whether the dysrhythmia appeared spontaneously or only after neuroleptic treatment. The neuroleptics simply are activating latent abnormalities already reflected in certain psychopathologic behaviors.

The results of the psychological tests (although admittedly done only on a small subsample) point to the possibility that patients in the paroxysmal group are experiencing greater affect. The differences in the experience of drive, as reflected in the Rorschach responses, are harder to understand; nevertheless, the presence of greater socialized aggressive drive in the paroxysmal group is consistent with the clinical findings of irritability and loss of control of aggressive impulses in these patients. The signs of sustained stimulus flooding in this group confirms similar findings by Bellak that he relates to "some soft neurologic disorder."[23] It is possible that the persistent stimulus overinclusion in the paroxysmal group represents a "trait" function related to MBD; alternatively, it may simply reflect slower resolution of the psychosis. The self-report questionnaires show consistent results indicating greater disturbances in social relations in the group with paroxysmal EEGs. Possibly the reported greater introversion and dependency and lower social responsibility of these patients reflect difficulties with drive, affect, and stimulus control.

The developmental data from the "paroxysmal" groups suggest that some of the psychopathologic symptoms begin early in life and resemble difficulties seen in children with MBD. In fact, the behavioral clusters seen in the adolescent and adult schizophrenics in this study are not unlike such "adult MBD" symptoms as emotional overreactivity, short temper, and impulsivity.[24] It is possible that the early symptoms reflect the same cerebral dysfunction responsible for the later abnormal EEG and behavioral clusters. In at least one study of MBD children[25] paroxysmal EEG changes (not including 14 and 6 spiking) were seen in 23 percent of children presenting at a mental health center. The severity of these EEG abnormalities correlated positively with the severity of both brain dysfunction and psychiatric impairment.

It is not clear from the data presented how cerebral dysfunction and schizophrenia relate. It is possible that the MBD factors may lead to the development of schizophrenia in some direct way. This may occur by interfering with language and cognitive development, causing perceptual distortions, interfering with sequencing ability, etc. It is also possible that the perceptual motor impairments and EEG dysrhythmia may simply provide additive factors or modify the form in which the illness is expressed. If schizophrenia is a heterogeneous disorder,[23,26-28] then it is plausible that subtle cerebral dysfunctions appear only in certain sub-groups and that the neurologic findings (including the EEG dysrhythmias) can be used to define these subgroups. It also seems likely that the group of schizophrenics with "organicity" or "MBD" also needs to be sub-divided.

The kinds of behavioral manifestations in schizophrenics that have been thought to be associated with neurologic impairment vary from asociality[28] to impulse dyscontrol[19,23,27] to oneiroid symptoms.[19,26] The differences may be explained by assuming that discrete clusters of be-havior are related to different types of neurologic difficulties or different sites of malfunction.

For instance, the behavioral clusters described in this report closely resemble those in other, nonschizophrenic groups with similar EEG findings. Other investigators have pointed out the association of these symptoms with epileptiform EEG discharges in both nonpsychotic psychiatric patients and prisoners.[27,29] A recent study of patients meeting criteria for the diagnosis of borderline syndrome[30] again revealed a strong association between a paroxysmal EEG abnormality and symptoms of impulsivity, mood lability, depersonalization, and dyscontrol. It would thus appear that the EEG correlates better with such clusters of behavior than with global diagnostic categories. One might assume the same for other neurologic findings in schizophrenics.

It is tempting to postulate that the dysfunction evidenced in the EEG abnormality reflects subcortical temporal lobe–limbic dysfunction. These structures are sensitive to hypoxic and other traumatic events and mediate such functions as modulation of affect and impulsivity,[27] sense of identity (and therefore depersonalization),[31] control over the stimulus barrier,[32,33] and selection of appropriate behavioral patterns.[33] It is also possible that cortical impairments release subcortical processes in addi-tion to causing cognitive difficulties on their own. MBD is most likely a multifocal disorder leading to a variable expression of neurologic and behavioral difficulties depending on the specific locations of disturbance.

The present findings are in agreement with those of Bellak[23] and Monroe[27] that schizophrenics with evidence for neurologic dysfunction have a poorer response to neuroleptic treatment. It would appear that in the above patient groups this was in part due to a worsening of, or failure to ameliorate, the episodic and affective symptoms. The persistence in the paroxysmal group of test signs of stimulus overinclusion and stimulus flooding even 7 weeks after admission corroborates the slower response to treatment. The addition of anticonvulsant medication along with the use of lower neuroleptic dosages led to significant further improvement in a majority of, although by no means all, patients in whom it was used. Currently anticonvulsants tend to be given to those patients with signs of schizophrenia and cerebral dysrhythmia whose episodic impulsive, perceptual, or affective symptoms worsen or fail to respond to neuroleptic treatment alone. It is assumed that the anticonvulsants are reducing subcortical, ictal, or subictal events responsible for the episodic and impulsive behaviors. Prospective studies are underway to predict phenothiazine response in schizophrenics with and without EEG and neuropsychologic abnormalities and also to test the efficacy of anticonvulsants in a double-blind fashion.

In conclusion, one must be aware that paroxysmally abnormal EEGs in schizophrenic patients may be the first indications that they are suffering from a variant of the disorder involving neurologic dysfunction. This dysfunction predisposes the patient to certain episodic impulsive behaviors and perceptual distortions. Optimal treatment may include lower than usual doses of neuroleptics combined with anticonvulsant medication.

**REFERENCES**

1.  Jorgensen R, Wulff M: The effect of orally administered chlorpromazine on the electroencephalogram of man. Electroencephalogr Clin Neurophysiol 10:325–329, 1958.
2.  Hollister L, Barthel C: Changes in the electroencephalogram during chronic administration of tranquilizing drugs. Electroencephalogr Clin Neurophysiol 11:792–795, 1959.
3.  Kooi K, Bennett J: The effects of phenothiazine derivatives on the electroencephalogram. Electroencephalogr Clin Neurophysiol 12:755–756, 1960.
4.  Fink M: Quantitative EEG in human psychopharmacology: II. Drug patterns. In Glaser GH (ed): EEG and Behavior. New York, Basic Books, 1973, pp 177–197.
5.  Fink M: Quantitative EEG and psychopharmacology: III. Changes on acute and chronic administration of chlorpromazine, imipramine, and placebo. In Wilson WP (ed): Applications of Electroencephalography in Psychiatry. Durham, Duke Univ, 1965, pp 226–240.
6.  Goldstein L, et al: Electro-cerebral activity in schizophrenics and non-psychotic subjects: Quantitative EEG amplitude analysis. Electroencephalogr Clin Neurophysiol 19:350–361, 1965.
7.  Borenstein P, Cujo P: Effects of major tranquilizers on the resting EEG. In Itil TM (ed): Psychotropic Drugs and the Human EEG. Basel, Karger, 1974, pp 1–21.
8.  Itil T, et al: Differentiation of psychotropic drugs by quantitative EEG analysis. Agressologie 9:267–280, 1968.
9.  Müller H, Müller A: Effects of some psychotropic drugs upon brain electrical activity. Int J Neuropsychiatry 1:224–232, 1965.

10. Steiner W, Pollack S: Limited usefulness of EEG as a diagnostic aid in psychiatric cases receiving tranquilizing drug therapy. Prog Brain Res 16:97–105, 1965.

11. Liberson W: Individual differences in the EEG effects of chlorpromazine. Electroencephalogr Clin Neurophysiol 9:159, 1957.

12. Ulett G, et al: The effect of psychotropic drugs on the EEG of the chronic psychotic patient. In Wilson WP (ed): Applications of Electroencephalography in Psychiatry. Durham, Duke Univ, 1965, pp 241–257.

13. Helmchen H, Künkel H: The EEG in psychiatric pharmacology. Electroencephalogr Clin Neurophysiol 20:276, 1966.

14. Itil T: Electroencephalography and pharmacopsychiatry. In Freyhan F, et al. (ed): Modern Problems of Pharmacopsychiatry, vol 1. Basel, Karger, 1968, pp 163–194.

15. Bente D: Elektroencephalographie und psychiatrische Pharmakotherapie. In Achelis JD, von Ditfurth H (eds): Anthropologische und Naturwissenschaftliche-klinische Grundlagenprobleme der Pharmakopsychiatrie. Stuttgart, Thieme, 1963, pp 75–97.

16. Winfield D, Aivazian G: EEG changes associated with intensive promazine therapy. Am Practitioner 10:1182–1188, 1959.

17. Bente D, Itil T: Chlorpromazine sleep as an electroencephalographic activation method. Electroencephalogr Clin Neurophysiol 9:355, 1957.

18. Stewart L: Chlorpromazine: Use to activate electroencephalographic seizure patterns. Electroencephalogr Clin Neurophysiol 9:427–440, 1957.

19. Davies RK, Neil JF, Himmelhoch JM: Cerebral dysrhythmias in schizophrenics receiving phenothiazines. Clin Electroencephalogr 6:103–115, 1973.

20. Neil JF, Merikangas JR, Davies RK, et al.: Validity and clinical utility of neuroleptic facilitated electroencephalography in psychotic patients. Clin Electroencephalogr (in press).

21. Spitzer RL, Endicott J, Robins E: Research Diagnostic Criteria (RDC) for a Selected Group of Functional Disorders. New York, Biometric Research, New York State Psychiatric Institute, 1975.

22. Quinlan DM, Davies RK, Neil JF, et al: Unpublished data.

23. Bellak L: A possible subgroup of the schizophrenic syndrome and implications for treatment. Am J Psychother 30:194–205, 1976.

24. Wood DR, Reimherr FW, Wender PH, et al: Diagnosis and treatment of minimal brain dysfunction in adults. Arch Gen Psychiatry 33:1453–1460, 1976.

25. Gross MB, Wilson WC: Minimal Brain Dysfunction. New York, Brunner/Mazel, 1974.

26. Yamada T: Heterogeneity of schizophrenia as demonstrable in electroencephalography. In Mitsuda H (ed): Clinical Genetics in Psychiatry. Tokyo, Igaku Shoin, 1967, pp 197–208.

27. Monroe R: Episodic Behavioral Disorders: A Psychodynamic and Neurophysiologic Analysis. Cambridge, Mass., Harvard Univ, 1970, p 517.

28. Quitkin F, Rifkin A, Klein DF: Neurologic soft signs in schizophrenia and

character disorders: Organicity in schizophrenia with premorbid asociality and emotionally unstable character disorders. Arch Gen Psychiatry 33:845–853, 1976.

29.  Hill D: EEG in episodic psychotic and psychopathic behavior: A classification of data. Electroencephalogr Clin Neurophysiol 4:419–442, 1952.

30.  Davies RK, Pickar D: Unpublished data.

31.  Williams D: Man's temporal lobe. Brain 91:639–654, 1968.

32.  Stevens JR: An anatomy of schizophrenia? Arch Gen Psychiatry 29:177–189, 1973.

33.  Gloor P: Discussion of paper by B. Kaada. In Clemente CD, Lindsley DB (eds): Aggression and Defense. Berkeley, Univ California, 1967, pp 116–124.

## DISCUSSION

*Dr. Gallant:*    Did the paroxysmal group have a better history of remission?

*Dr. Davies:*    No. I can't tell you over the long course, but I can tell you that the resolution of their illness was slower.

*Dr. Gallant:*    What anticonvulsant medications are you using?

*Dr. Davies:*    We've used mostly Dilantin. Lately we've been using much more Tegretol than before. An interesting thing is that our incidence of Dilantin rashes and lymphadenopathy and fever is four times the incidence on the neurology service at Yale–New Haven Hospital.

*Dr. Gallant:*    Is that with patients already receiving phenothiazines?

*Dr. Davies:*    These are both with patients receiving phenothiazines and not receiving phenothiazines but receiving only anticonvulsants. In fact, we have a much larger group on Dilantin of borderlines who have had no recent phenothiazine treatment.

*Dr. Klein:*    Is it your impression that Dilantin plays a beneficial role in the borderline?

*Dr. Davies:*    Yes. We're getting a clearly observed decrease in anger and irritability. They also report that their thinking is clearer and they have an inner feeling of less pressure behind their feelings. They'll say, for instance, that they get angry and would like to explode, but just can't. They also report fewer separation difficulties and a great sense of interpersonal relatedness. We have seen that not so much in the schizophrenics, but in the borderlines.

*Dr. Monroe:*    I'm enthusiastic about what you're saying. I just want to point out another concept that may be valid here. That is the idea of the third psychosis, espoused by Mitsuta and the group in Japan. I think this is a very viable concept that we have to explore. We should explore it genetically, too. I wish some of the family and genetic studies would look for not only affective and schizophrenic disorders but epileptoid disorders or a different group in the family history. I do think it's quite likely that we may have a third psychosis here.

*Dr. Davies:* We did a little bit of investigation, namely, just asking patients about family history and a little bit from the family. The normal EEG sample more often gave a negative history for psychiatrically ill relatives, but that was not significant. Subjects in the abnormal group reported a greater number of family members receiving outpatient treatment. That was significant.

*Dr. Klein:* Just one more thing about that Dilantin response—Was it very quick? Did it take a while to develop?

*Dr. Davies:* It really occurs when the blood level ranges become adequate. It is frequently associated with their levels going up, frequently associated with several days of worsening of symptoms. If somebody is getting worse, our nurses get happier because they think it's going to predict a better response.

*Dr. Klein:* Is that a maintained response?

*Dr. Davies:* For several months anyway. We've had a few patients on as long as a year.

*Dr. Cole:* By taking a while, do you mean 3 weeks or 2 months?

*Dr. Davies:* I mean 10 days.

*Dr. Huessy:* Of course, I don't think that if you use Dilantin for MBD disorder, in that small percentage that get an excitatory response to stimulants, the effective blood level necessarily has to be as high as when the drug is used as an antiepileptic. We have a lot of patients who responded to 200 mg a day.

*Dr. Davies:* Some early studies on Dilantin in irritable outpatients showed it had no more effect than placebo. Those were using 200 mg a day, and I suspect that they were not achieving adequate blood levels. In the studies that used 300 mg a day, the results are stronger, if you're looking at irritability.

*Dr. Gallant:* When you're looking at blood levels, what blood levels are you looking for with the Dilantin in relation to this?

*Dr. Davies:* Ten to twenty $\mu$g/ml.

*Dr. Tucker:* The results of some studies correlating symptoms with blood level of Dilantin showed that the higher the blood level, the fewer the behavioral symptoms associated with the condition.

*Dr. Wender:* Is there any effect on mood in these borderlines, besides anger?

*Dr. Davies:* Oh, yes. We compared the borderlines to 20 unipolars, and the borderlines have brief depressions, they don't report longstanding depression, and those brief depressions tend to smooth out, with much less mood lability. The unipolars do not report brief depressions.

*Dr. Wender:*   That's what we find with our adult MBDs. One of the major symptoms is mood lability, appearing in about half of them, with highs as well as lows. And interestingly, the highs tend to go away with stimulants as well as the lows.

*Dr. Davies:*   I think what we're seeing is lability; I don't know what the relationship is, but I think there are probably two groups of border-lines.

*Dr. Neal:*   In respect to the use of anticonvulsant medication, since going to Pittsburgh I've used much more carbamazapine than Dilantin in the group of schizophrenics and have found that I don't even depend on blood levels. I go by clinical response; usually the dose range I'm using is 600 to 800 mg a day, in addition to lower doses of phenothiazines. The symptoms that seem to respond best are the affective lability and irritabil-ity. I have had relatively few side effects, far fewer than with Dilantin in the past. It raises interesting questions with respect to what other people have said about the use of imipramine in adult minimal brain dysfunction patients because of the structural similarity of Tegretol to imipramine as well as its anticonvulsant properties.

# 11

# General Discussion

*Dr. Klein:* I should like to present a set of more or less random thoughts to respond to the variety of issues that have come up in these very heterogeneous papers, which, I think, reflect the heterogeneity of MBD.

Dr. Wender said that there are lumpers and splitters. I'm clearly a splitter. It's been my idea to try to derive smaller groups from the groups of schizophrenias, character disorders, and affective disorders, primarily using the technique I've been calling "pharmacologic dissection," that is, trying to determine which subgroups respond in a similar fashion to medication. That's not logically coercive, since patients don't necessarily have the same thing wrong with them because they respond the same way to medication, but I think it is useful nonetheless. Dr. Bellak might say that my propensity for splitting is due to a chronic failure of the synthetic function.

The two groups that I consider show some evidence for brain dysfunction, over and above their developmental history, in terms of psychological testing and more recently in terms of neurologic examination, are two groups that are really very different from each other. One group is the type that I've been calling schizophrenics with childhood asociality; these are simply those who from their early life don't relate very well. They don't have friends; they are made scapegoats of by the other children; they seem to lack sending ability.

In the studies that Fred Quitkin, Art Rifkin and I have done over the years, we have also found people who aren't frankly schizophrenic but have asocial histories and are often called schizoid character disorders, although they may never have been outright psychotic.

The other group of people are those whom I've been referring to as impulsive destructive people. These are more likely to be people with histories that go along with very marked hyperkinesis and conduct disorder as children. In their later life they are primarily character disorders, rather than psychotics or schizophrenics, although they frequently will pick up the label of schizophrenia because they are often drug abusers and do irrational things.

There is some overlap in these groups, but not a great deal. A few people as children are friendless and isolated as well as hyperactive, impulsive, destructive people. In general, their course is much closer to the terrible parasitic course of the asocial type, whereas the impulsive, destructive ones do not necessarily have that chronic downhill course.

In a double-blind controlled study where schizophrenic patients were randomly assigned to imipramine or placebo regardless of diagnosis, one group of schizophrenics showed a very sharp psychotic exacerbation on imipramine. They were practically all childhood asocial schizophrenics, whereas the schizoaffectives, given imipramine, for example, were frequently improved by it. These were not taking phenothiazine at the time, just imipramine, 300 mg a day. That was a fixed-dosage study; everyone got 300 mg.

*Chairman Bellak:*    You feel that was too high a dose for patients with MBD, is that right?

*Dr. Huessy:*    I would expect that effect from that dosage.

*Dr. Klein:*    The bad effects that we got were very narrowly limited to the schizophrenics with childhood asociality. It was a biphasic effect that occurred quite regularly. In the initial stage, within the first week or two of the imipramine, the schizophrenics frequently brightened up, appeared more cheerful, more outgoing, and less catatonic, and then a week later they became psychotic.

That's of some clinical utility, because not infrequently I'll see this sort of thing when I'm called in for a consultation. I'll be told about a schizophrenic who is refractory to phenothiazines. When I have the patient in my office or see him on the ward, I find that the he is quite crazy on phenothiazine but is also receiving imipramine, which had not been mentioned. Typically you find that the patient had been chronically withdrawn, perplexed, peculiar, and on phenothiazines; somebody had added imipramine to it, the patient had brightened up, become cheerful, more outgoing, more friendly, and that marked imipramine as being a "good" drug for that patient. Then when he really got psychotically exacerbated 2 weeks later, nobody related that exacerbation to the imipramine, which had by then been labeled a good drug for that patient. All you had to do was to discontinue the imipramine and the phenothiazine-refractory patient was no longer a phenothiazine-refractory patient.

*Chairman Bellak:* Why was he phenothiazine-refractory to start with?

*Dr. Klein:* He wasn't phenothiazine-refractory; the kind of asocial schizophrenics I'm referring to are awkward, withdrawn people. On phenothiazines their delusions and hallucinations go away, but they develop a mode that I've been calling schizoid compliance. They are awkward, withdrawn, fringe-of-the-crowd people with a lot of akinesia, so that it is understandable that the doctor would try to add some imipramine in the hope of livening the patient up.

*Dr. Arnold:* What would happen if you just reduced the imipramine dose to the place where you had the same blood level as that first week when they looked so good with it?

*Dr. Klein:* That's a good question. We've tried that, and it turns out to be an extremely precarious matter. It's very hard, almost impossible, to find a level at which the person stays stabilized. Most of them will be either crazy or withdrawn. We did have a few patients where we could do that and get some decent long-term effects, but it's very precarious.

*Dr. Huessy:* A paper in the APA journal implied that biochemically the immediate effect of imipramine is different from the antidepressant one, and so you're getting a result from the immediate effect. Then when the antidepressant effect comes into being, they get. . . .

*Dr. Klein:* It took 10 days, a couple weeks, for the biphasic effect, so that it does seem a little faster than the usual antidepressant. But the mood improvement is not exactly immediate, it's not like the first day or anything of that sort, as you see with MBD children, for instance.

*Dr. Gallant:* Would you relate this patient population in the asocial group at all to the process chronic schizophrenic?

*Dr. Klein:* I would say that they are one subgroup of the process patients. There are a lot of other patients also called process, who, for instance, will have a fairly normal childhood development, nothing particularly wrong with them. Then they reach adolescence and start becoming more and more peculiar; they, too, are called process.

*Dr. Gallant:* We found the same results with imipramine in what we call our true homogeneous schizophrenic population.

*Dr. Klein:* Perhaps, if you have the histories, you might find out that those true homogeneous ones had a very asocial development, but it's hard to get that history from the patient.

*Dr. Gallant:* They're also more likely to have a family history of schizophrenia.

*Dr. Klein:* It's my impression that they're less likely to have a family history of schizophrenia.

My colleagues, Dr. Rifkin and Dr. Quitkin, reviewed George Winokur's cases, the Iowa 500, all the schizophrenics that he has family histories on, and they selected 12 patients whom they thought clearly met the criteria for developmental asociality. Not one of those patients had any schizophrenia anywhere in his family. So it's a little odd.

We have been collecting a variety of psychological tests on these patients, and recently showed them to a neuropsychologist, Rita Rudel, who works at Columbia. She reviewed them and said, "Clearly right-sided damage." That's interesting because there is a current theory that Flor-Henry and a few other people endorse that if schizophrenics have lateralized deficit, it is left-sided, but that's apparently not what we're finding in our psychological tests.

Let me just make a few other points. We have a controlled study that shows that lithium is a useful drug for adolescents with extremely marked mood lability who frequently have a history of childhood hyperkinesis. Nobody, however, claims that lithium is terribly good for hyperkinetic children. That lithium is good for the adolescent and adult mood-labile person with a history of childhood hyperkinesis strikes me as peculiar.

One other thing that was curious about it. Between 20 and 40 percent of the schizophrenic patients at Hillside have histories of childhood asociality. When we went over the Iowa 500 the percentage of schizophrenics with childhood asociality was much, much less (and they had very good histories).

They may have used the Feighner criteria to diagnose their schizophrenics. They had a lot of other patients who were called schizophrenics at the Iowa Psychopathic but who they did not feel met their criteria for schizophrenia. We took a quick look at some of them and there was a higher incidence of asociality there. One of the reasons for that may be that when asocial schizophrenics "get crazy" it's largely on a communicative, disorganized, can't-make-sense sort of basis. They don't have the flagrant delusions or hallucinations that are called schizophrenic by the Feighner criteria.

I've been interested in this whole business about minimal brain dysfunction for 20 years now. A few years ago Fred Quitkin in my department suggested doing blind neurologic examinations on patients who were off drugs and for whom I would do a diagnosis. From our past work we would expect that we would have more neurologic defect in the asocial schizophrenics and in the extremely labile character disorders.

The results were literally too good to believe. We found that there was indeed a higher incidence of neurologic soft signs in the schizophrenics, but only in the asocial group. That is, in the nonasocial schizophrenics we had no higher incidence of neurologic soft signs than we had in, say, our depressives, where we had practically none.

Where we had a variety of character disorders, passive-aggressive, hysterical, emotionally unstable character disorders, again it was in the emotionally unstable character disorder that we had the excess of neurologic soft signs.

One unexpected finding was that when we simply correlated the number of neurologic soft signs with IQ, we found substantial correlation, as reported in our article in *The Archives [of General Psychiatry]*. You might say that is so because the two groups, the asocials and the emotionally unstables, were both "stupid" and had a lot of neurologic soft signs, which is simply an artifact of level. But in fact when we took the other psychiatric groups that did not seem to have very many neurologic soft signs, the hysterics or the schizophrenics with nonasocial characteristics, there too we got substantial correlations of IQ and soft signs. That would seem to indicate that perhaps soft signs represent a burden on the central nervous system that can have a pathoplastic effect upon a variety of psychiatric illnesses but that they have a sort of nonspecific interaction as well as a perhaps more specific one. That was a nice finding because it indicated that the neurologic soft signs that we were measuring in a sense had to be reliable or they just couldn't have correlated with something as objective as IQ.

Dr. Monroe mentioned the Porteus maze and Dilantin. Porteus maze is a test that we've used quite extensively in our work with learning disability and hyperkinetic children. You can get fantastic effects with Ritalin on the Porteus maze. The children who were constantly getting lost in the Porteus maze all of a sudden just zip right through it.

We then related that to the behavioral effects of the drug. A lot of people say that the attentional deficit in MBD is what leads to the so-called hyperkinesis, that these children aren't really overly active; it's just that they can't stay focused, so that they're all over the place. One might assume then that those children who improve the most on the Porteus maze will also be those who improve the most behaviorally. In fact, we found no relationship whatsoever. As a matter of fact, we did a very elaborate analysis of the changes on all of our psychological tests with a large variety of behavioral changes, and there just wasn't any relationship.

*Chairman Bellak:* Could I go back a moment to your finding of a high correlation between intelligence and soft signs—What kind of testing did you do for intelligence?

*Dr. Klein:* The WAIS.

*Chairman Bellak:* Since the whole performance part of the WAIS is one of the best indicators we have for soft signs, I think you may have largely found that soft signs correlate with soft signs.

*Dr. Klein:* Maybe so, but we also found some variable correlations, too.

*Dr. Arnold:*   Could you tell us what particular subtests did correlate most?

*Dr. Klein:*   I'd have to go back and check, but it is in our article.

In regard to Dr. Monroe's presentation, I think it's true that impulsiveness goes along with paroxysmal activity. Dr. Struve's group at Hillside has done a number of studies in which he's related impulsiveness to things like suicidal ideation and attempts. Again, the paroxysmal activity related most clearly to that.

With regard to Dr. Tucker's paper, I think you mentioned that results on your object sorting test correlated to impairment on the various neurologic perceptual motivations. We haven't published our data yet, but Alan Wilner, who works with us and has developed a lot of cognitive tests, also found that his cognitive test correlated very nicely with the amount of neurologic impairment on the soft signs.

In our own study, when the patients were on drugs, it did confuse the data considerably for us.

In regard to Dr. Davies' work with Dilantin, all I have to say is, "Good luck." At one time we had a real interest in the use of anticonvulsants in both severe character disorders and schizophrenics, but it didn't work out.

I am interested in the remark about Tegretol. I have practically no personal experience with Tegretol, except one lady who really did have temporal lobe epilepsy and on Tegretol calmed down very nicely. That's an interesting drug. There is also evidence that imipramine itself is an anticonvulsant.

*Dr. Neil:*   There is a great deal of literature from Europe to attest to the psychotropic properties of Tegretol in epileptics and how it improves such symptoms as lability, irritability, and social withdrawal in epileptics with behavior disturbances.

*Dr. Klein:*   In regard to Dr. Bellak's paper, I'm frankly a little surprised that you say your scale demonstrates high reliability. It is a scale that seems to me to require a great deal of continued contact with a patient before you can come to a firm judgment about a number of those issues. I'm reminded somewhat of the attempts of the Menninger psychotherapy study to develop scales along quite similar constructs. As I remember, it ended up with all the scales sort of collapsing together, they really couldn't be kept separate.

It's a difficult psychometric problem to determine when scales really are one scale and when they're separate scales. One of the difficulties, of course, is that if the scales are unreliable enough, they look more separate than they really are, and that has to be corrected for.

About the rod-and-frame test—In our early studies we did the rod-and-frame test, as well as the embedded figure test, IQ, and so forth, on several hundred patients. At the time I really knew very little about statistics, factor analysis, anything of that sort. At any rate we had all these data including measures of the EEG and of critical flicker fusion, about 40 different items. We consulted Jack Cohen, an eminent statistician in New York City, who suggested doing a factor analysis.

He did a correlation matrix on all the data. Then we did three analyses, based on there being four, five, or six factors. Each analysis showed different loadings, and we never did publish the data from that study.

*Chairman Bellak:*   With regard to the reliability and validity of the ego-function scales, you will have to look at the data in our book *Ego Functions in Schizophrenics, Neurotics, and Normals* (John Wiley & Sons, 1973). Incidentally, Jack Cohen was the statistical consultant on that study.

*Dr. Wender:*   In testing our 64 adults for neurologic soft signs, the question arose of what neurologic exam to use. As an inept pediatric neurologist I have found that no tests are good because you need different norms at different ages. I decided to give the Lincoln-Oseretsky test, which at least goes up to age 15. By the Lincoln-Oseretsky criteria our adults are all very clumsy. Perhaps psychomotor ability declines after the age of 14, but our adult MBD patients seem to be incredibly inept!

# Therapeutic Aspects

Stanley I. Greenspan

# 12

# Principles of Intensive Psychotherapy of Neurotic Adults with Minimal Brain Dysfunction

I will discuss aspects of psychotherapy for patients who suffer from a syndrome that has been referred to as MBD (minimal brain dysfunction) in adults, or ABD (adult brain dysfunction).[1] The discussion will focus on a number of issues:

1. MBD in adults (ABD) can manifest itself in a variety of ways and with a variety of symptom complexes from neurotic to borderline or psychotic psychopathology, but there is a central perceptual integrative impairment of neurophysiologic regulation that is related to individual constitutional and developmental differences.
2. Certain unique features in psychotherapy of adults with this particular type of neurophysiologic pattern can be understood better by looking at what the patients' infancy and early childhood experiences might have been like.
3. Intensive long-term psychotherapy, even psychoanalysis, is possible with such individuals, although the primary impairment is often thought to be associated with an organic etiology. The major determining factor of the appropriateness of intensive psychotherapy or psychoanalysis is the detailed assessment of the total personality and a specific assessment of how this primary difficulty has affected the development of basic ego functions and the capacity for stable and long-term interpersonal relationships.

161

4.  There are a number of precise issues on which we should focus in the psychotherapy of such individuals, including a specific type of transference configuration that is often associated with special kinds of countertransference problems.

Adult patients with MBD have compromises in a variety of ego functions related to individual differences and developmental level of CNS integration. A common difficulty is focusing attention and processing and integrating their stimulus worlds. During childhood this impairment may show itself as a variety of manifest difficulties, including learning problems related to perceptual motor integration and regulation and organization of attention, activity, impulses, and thoughts. In some very bright youngsters, however, impairment may be compensated for by a variety of coping mechanisms and may not show itself during childhood. In adulthood this basic impairment may be manifested quite differently because of further but incomplete development (in both CNS integration and consolidation and differentiation of certain ego functions). Depression, anxiety, and their derivatives as well as compromises in ego structure—from psychotic and borderline to characterologic and neurotic proportions—are frequently diagnosed in adults, sometimes without regard for the underlying CNS integrational impairment, because a careful mental status examination is not done or early history not taken.

In considering a psychotherapeutic approach for children and adults either with or without medication, most attention is usually directed at the secondary effects of the central impairment—the effect of either a sense of "defect," or a depressive awareness of impulse or learning problems on one's self-image (feelings about oneself), and various defenses against these painful feelings toward oneself, e.g., denial, counterphobic behavior, grandiosity, anger, projection, etc. In such approaches, together with either medication or remedial educational procedures to improve social functioning and generate more positive feedback and self-regard, the person is helped to become aware of maladaptive defenses against aggressive and negative feelings about self and objects, to tolerate these feelings, and to learn adaptive styles of coping.

While the above is important therapy, the adult particularly needs to direct attention at the "primary impairment" at both the level of CNS integration and, most importantly, at the level of psychological structure and the self-object representations (with their drive affect dispositions) that form the basis of their character and organization.

In this context it is important to emphasize that an individual exists in relationship to an internal as well as external stimulus world and to consider how difficulties in focusing attention and processing and integrating experience from all the stimulus worlds encountered (internal and external, animate and inanimate) manifest themselves and play a role in the individual's overall functioning. From the perspective of an individual's development (prenatally, first year of life, to adulthood), patterns of individual differences in CNS maturation (and capacity to focus attention and process and integrate experience) interact with the early and later environments (intrauterine, mother-infant dyad, etc.) to influence the development of biologic and psychological structure. Such developing psychological structure often has unique defects and characteristics that are intertwined. Specific wishes and feeling states organized around early identifications may, together with particular defects, form a central core from which certain compensating, defensive, and/or coping patterns emerge. The core issues as well as the secondary defensive and adaptive patterns must be dealt with in treatment. Because the core issues often involve very painful and frightening feeling states and often stimulate certain defensive counterreactions in the therapist, they are ignored, and secondary patterns of defense and adaptation are the only focus of treatment. Feelings of defectiveness and loss of control are relatively easy to deal with in comparison to primitive yearnings and aggressive and sexual feelings that may exist in undifferentiated forms and frighten both the patient and the therapist. I will try to delineate aspects of the relationship between CNS maturation and this "core" affective state and then discuss strategies for psychological treatment (both with and without pharmacologic approaches) that take into account maturational factors, affective factors, and cognitive and emotional structural factors.

## EARLY DEVELOPMENT

Let us first consider the relationship between individual differences in neurophysiologic regulation and the way in which infants relate to their environments. The integrity and character of early psychological structures are determined by these early interactions that have certain implications for later psychotherapy. For example, individuals with MBD may as infants have trouble habituating to stimuli. As a visual or auditory stimulus is presented, the infant becomes stimulated but then finds it difficult to calm down. The habituation pattern will vary with maturation of the central nervous system. Another difficulty related to MBD in children and adults may be in an infant's orienting response (e.g., looking at mother). The integrity and organization of the infant's perceptual motor system may be immature. More complex evaluations of the way in which infants transfer habituation patterns across sensory modalities or across stimuli and establish patterns and rhythmic cycles in the first month of life (e.g., sleepwake patterns, eating patterns) may also demonstrate individual differences between those who develop the MBD syndrome and those who do not.

There are a number of parameters that make it possible to observe individual differences in a baby's constitutional style[2-4] that may be related to patterns of adaptation as a youngster grows and develops. Not only does the infant in a general sense contribute to the early mother-infant interaction[5,6] but the quality of that interaction can be determined in part by the infant's constitutional differences.[2] Some infants are much harder to nurture than others. For example, an infant who is hyperalert, hyperactive, hard to control, orients and habituates poorly, and does not permit mother to have a "mutual gaze" experience, while putting great demands on her, may compromise the early mother-infant relationship. In observing such a mother-infant dyad, one often observes a great deal of pain and frustration. Rather than a "rhythmic, peaceful dance" that might characterize an optimal mother-infant dyad, this dyad is characterized by discomfort and irritability. The optimal dyad would be based on attachment experiences that are mutually pleasurable. Mutual interaction would lead to gradual differentiation as the infant's capacities differentiate throughout the first year of life. In contrast, a great deal of early pain and frustration may compromise attachment and differentiation. The structure and character of developing psychological structure, beginning with the internalizing events in the latter part of the first year through the phases of separation-individuation[7] and the experience and resolution of the triangular oedipal phase, will be affected by these early patterns and their derivatives.

While the patterns of neurophysiologic regulation influences, as suggested, the dyadic relationships during infancy and early childhood and thereby the structure and character of early personality formation, a specific dynamic pattern should be emphasized. As described above, the early dyadic relationship is full of pain and frustration, in part related to the infant's individual constitutional differences. As development continues, the infant-child, because of further maturation of the central nervous system, becomes capable of a better "fit" with the dyadic partner. Dynamic patterns that have been set in motion, however, often prevent this potential "better fit" from occurring. Specifically, the early intense levels of frustration, irritation, and rage lead, later, when an improved relationship is possible, to immense fears of destroying the object. In addition, the object, through the mechanism of projection, becomes perceived as having the rage and lack of control that the individual originally had early in life. Therefore the dyadic partner is dealt with quite carefully. A great deal of anxiety (fear of destroying the object) and fear (fear of being destroyed and later abandoned) permeate all important relationships. To the degree neurophysiologic regulation is still relatively vulnerable to regression, the cycles of fear and anxiety compromise optimal functioning at the CNS level. More importantly, the cycles of fear and anxiety compromise the integrity of evolving ego functions and the opportunities for "better relationships" that would facilitate more optimal development. As will be discussed later, through the development of a transference situation psychotherapy should attempt to provide an opportunity to rework and work through these early experiences.

We have observed two reaction patterns in parents of an infant who orients poorly and is hypersensitive to stimulation. One reaction in "concerned parents" is to become overprotective and overcontrolling in a very dominating, manipulative manner while trying to calm the infant. These parents are not sensitive to the infant's individual temperamental style, and they often feel guilty, repeating over and over that they are at fault and that they don't have a good relationship with their baby. A second reaction is one of helplessness, passivity, and withdrawal; parents with this reaction become discouraged and shift their attention elsewhere.

If environmental circumstances are optimal, even with the above constitutional patterns, development may proceed so that there are no basic ego defects (e.g., a youngster who has achieved basic differentiation of self-from-nonself, age-appropriate reality testing, age-appropriate organization and integration of affect and thought, and the development of language). While basic ego functions may be intact in such youngsters, they may still have special patterns stemming from their early differences in CNS regulation that originally affected the way they handled their internal and external stimulus worlds as infants.

The structure of psychological life and the meanings that a person gives to it will be altered by early individual neurophysiologic differences. If the individual is assessed as neurotic, then that individual has in fact reached a high level of integration and has moved into the oedipal phase of development. A neurotic personality organization condenses earlier developmental issues into a cohesive structure with a great deal of economy. A person at this level of development is not fragmented; there is a central core of meaning to the way of experiencing both internal and external worlds. Meanings become elaborated in relationships and influence various affects of the subject's life. In this sense a neurosis is a developmental step, a milestone, not just a type of psychopathology.

How do some of the early CNS differences referred to affect the formation of the neurotic structure? They certainly might affect the types of defenses selected in that structure, the types of adaptive and coping styles used, and, more importantly, the degree of flexibility of that structure. Beginning early in life with certain individual CNS differences that cannot deal flexibly with stimulation may lead to a structure that is integrated but very rigid. There is little flexibility to deal with upheaval from the internal stimulus world (stimulation coming from within the organism—feelings, thoughts, derivatives of the drives and affects) or external stimulus configurations, such as complex interpersonal events, and aspects of the inanimate world. Regressive patterns that are likely to emerge under stress may also be affected. Consider a youngster between ages 4 and 6 years who has a tendency to become hyperalert, has difficulty in focusing attention, and is a poor habituator. That youngster may find it very easy to become hyperstimulated by feelings of the oedipal phase of development, such as sexual and rivalrous feelings, growing awareness of the body, and curiosity about sexual differences. The aggressive component of the child's rivalrous feelings may be felt intensely and with a sense of "I can't control myself."

The phase of development that usually occurs between ages 4 and 6 years may be the richest time in a youngster's psychological life. People who work with children and have the opportunity to conduct evaluations have observed that the fantasy life of the oedipal child is extraordinarily rich and varied. For a youngster who doesn't have appropriate regulation and control, however, this rich varied internal experience may be quite frightening rather than pleasurable. Curiosity, while always a "little scary" to children, can also be experienced as "out of control."

We might hypothesize that certain defenses may have a direct relationship to early neurophysiologic constitutional individual differences. For example, a tendency to shift attention may play a role in the way one deals with being overwhelmed by the internal stimulus world. The mechanism of displacement may be used extensively as a particular psychological defense. There may also be a tendency to use the motor system to deal with discharging tension (impulsivity, etc.). A tendency may exist to alter the configuration of stimulus input, to turn it around, just as we observe in the approach of children with perceptual motor immaturity to writing or reading letters.

There may be a tendency to rotate internal feeling states, to turn them into their opposites. In this context there may also be a tendency to take certain kinds of feelings, such as those of "longing" and wishes for closeness, and turn them completely around. We see adults and children with this syndrome who have turned libidinal longings into aggressive feelings. For example, "It is not that I want to be close to mother, it is that I am angry at mother." The wish therefore becomes enacted in a compromised manner, since the aggressive piece of behavior does bring the person close to the loved object. While this can be a defense that is learned, it may also be a mechanism that is very closely related to the original neurophysiologic propensity to alter stimulus configurations, akin to rotating letters. The tendency to shift passive into active seen in such individuals may also be related to early constitutional individual differences. There may be, for example, a tendency to shift internal feelings into external ones (the use of externalization and projection). The infant who cannot control internal stimulation may tend to externalize aspects of the "self."

In addition, the adult with MBD who has remained at a neurotic level probably has used the successful internalization of objects to maintain control. The internalized objects, however, are likely of a very severe and harsh nature because of the level of aggression mobilized in early frustrating relationships. One may therefore see a very rigid neurotic structure with many reaction formations. At the same time one may see the tendency to lose the focus of attention intermittently and lose control of impulses, which in turn serve to reinforce harsh self-punitive tendencies.

## ISSUES IN TREATMENT OF NEUROTIC ADULTS WITH MBD

Individuals with the MBD syndrome are capable of intensive psychoanalytic psychotherapy and even psychoanalysis, depending on their personality structure. Individuals who have attained a neurotic level of organization despite their CNS-processing difficulty have moved through dyadic relationship patterns and into triangular oedipal patterns. They have been able to organize a neurosis although affected by specific types of experiences and defensive alignments that would in part be determined by their unique ways of processing experience. In such cases, a complete assessment of personality functioning is necessary to determine the individual's availability for intensive psychotherapy or psychoanalysis.[8-10] In particular, the ability to maintain reality testing even in the face of stress, to experience intense affects, including sadness and longing, and to maintain empathic interpersonal relationships over reasonably long periods of time should be assessed. Regardless of the variety of symptomatology, if these abilities are present the prognosis for being able to benefit from long-term psychotherapy may be excellent.

### Principles of Intensive Psychotherapy

Described below are some principles for conducting long-term psychoanalytically oriented psychotherapy or psychoanalysis with MBD patients.

CNS STYLE OF PROCESSING STIMULATION

There should be a general acknowledgment of the particular central nervous system style of processing stimulation. For example, if a person is hyperreactive to stimulation and has always been that way, or if the individual has difficulty in focusing attention, the possibility of an individual difference in style related to the maturation of the central nervous system should be acknowledged by a confirmatory response from the therapist. If the patient makes a statement such as, "I have always had trouble focusing attention even on such things as reading," the therapist might respond with, "Yes, that sounds like it has been a lifelong difficulty." In other words, once this diagnosis is made, there should not be an attempt to search for psychodynamic causes of the basic processing difficulty. Such attempts will only entangle the patient further in what are already guilty self-recriminations.

The patient's unique processing style should first be clarified and elucidated in the context of the inanimate or impersonal stimulus world. Where possible, these trends should be highlighted in terms of the person's inability to read a book or listen to a lecture without becoming distracted. As much as possible, these difficulties should be pointed out in nonconflictual domains; e.g., if the person is listening to a lecture and feels competitive with the lecturer, it would not be useful to point out the difficulty in focusing attention. When the patient is reading a book and has no particular feelings toward the author, however, it may be beneficial to help the patient document something about his or her particular processing style. This helps such patients to recognize something about their basic constitutions that has influenced their subsequent development.

After a particular processing style has been documented in terms of the impersonal world, there should be an attempt to show how some of these same tendencies exist in terms of the person's internal emotional world and affect-laden interpersonal world. For example, persons may notice difficulty in staying with a certain feeling; if they are uncomfortable with anger, they are easily distracted to another feeling state. While some of this certainly has dynamic significance, the tendency to displace from one feeling to another may also be related to the basic CNS style. Here, then, is an excellent opportunity to point out how a particular style of processing internal and external experience can be caught up with dynamic issues and relate not only to the impersonal external world but also to the way experience and stimulation are processed in the affect-laden emotional internal and interpersonal worlds. A person may come to recognize certain typical styles of defense, such as displacement, externalization, and turning passive to active. Such analysis does not suggest to the patient an inability to change these basic styles. In fact, the awareness of how the styles are used in the context of the affect-laden internal and interpersonal worlds permits the patient to use the adult, mature ego, which has alternatives available to it that probably were not available in early childhood, to develop new styles of processing internal experience. The analyst's position is therefore to recognize the constitutional basis for the selection of particular defenses and coping mechanisms and at the same time, together with the patient, to be aware that as an adult there now are new potentials available.

## DELINEATING DERIVATIVES OF DEFENSE AND/OR ADAPTIVE COPING STYLES

The third principle involves delineating derivatives of defense and/or adaptive coping styles that the patient may have developed from the foundation of that patient's unique individual constitutional differences. For example, some adults who as children experienced difficulty in focusing attention and in regulating their activity levels may decide that they don't really have a problem. Using denial, they decide that it is good to be inattentive and active. They then develop a counterphobic way of handling feelings. On the other hand, a person with a similar difficulty in focusing attention and regulating activity and behavior may recognize that this *is* a difficulty and institute rather severe and harsh inhibitions in order to maintain regulation and control. Such a person may develop an overly rigid obsessive-compulsive system of defenses to deal with the "fear of going out of control."

The above are just two examples of how, by building on a primary difficulty, individuals may develop their own specific derivative defense and adaptive styles based on unique life experiences and the way in which they perceive and react to their individual differences. It is important early in treatment, after delineating the unique individual differences in the impersonal and in the affective and personal realms, to look at the derivative styles that have emerged; this will involve exploration not only of current issues in the person's life but also their historical antecedents.

## THE THERAPEUTIC ALLIANCE

Another basic principle relates to the therapeutic alliance one develops with such patients. It is important to establish a responsive but not overcontrolling style of relatedness. Patients who have difficulty in focusing attention and maintaining internal regulation often covertly invite an overcontrolling or rejecting style in others and often attempt to involve the therapist in one of these two reactions. The therapist seeks to control what patients feel they cannot or loses interest in such patients because the work is frustrating. As stated earlier, during the infancy and early childhood of such individuals it may have been very hard for their parents to develop a mutually rewarding, self-esteem–producing "fit" with them. As babies these patients tended to be hyperreactive to stimulation and unable to reach a state of equilibrium. Their parents became discouraged quickly and developed either styles of guilt and overcontrol or depression and withdrawal. It therefore is important for the therapist to develop a "fit" that is respectful of the patient's individual differences. The nature of the working relationship calls for therapists to be very sensitive to their own reaction patterns. In a general sense a very empathetic, respectful, but not overly controlling posture on the part of the therapist is appropriate. Being empathetic to the patient's feelings of "being out of control" without subtly becoming controlling is not an easy task.

TRANSFERENCE

The type of transference patients with this syndrome tend to develop is unique. If the above steps can be carried out and the patient can be maintained in an intensive psychoanalytically oriented therapeutic relationship, or in psychoanalysis for a significant period of time, eventually a transference configuration will begin to organize itself. It is most important to emphasize that the transferences that are developed by patients with this syndrome have their roots in various developmental levels of childhood. The oedipal and preoedipal transference issues may be dealt with no differently than they would be in any other psychoanalytic situation (interpretation of defense leading to transference interpretations and reconstructions and ideally to recollections).

What deserves special focus is a particular transference configuration that exists at a preverbal level derived from the first 1½ years of life and that manifests itself in such patients and is particularly difficult for the therapist to handle. As was stated earlier, as babies patients with this syndrome often were hyperreactive to stimuli, had difficulty in focusing attention, and were frequently in a state of panic. They had a hard time developing a good or homeostatic-producing dyadic relationship with the primary caretaker(s). Because it is difficult to achieve a peaceful homeostatic experience early in infancy, there is a great deal of frustration and therefore, together with the state of being out of control, a great deal of irritability and, later, rage. Together with the irritability and rage, which is related to frustration, there is also a deep-seated longing for the type of relationship that perhaps was never present or if present was present only for brief periods of time. There is a longing for a homeostatic, peace-producing dyadic equilibrium that was at best attained only intermittently. Thus together with irritability, rage, and fears of being out of control there is a tremendous amount of dependent and passive longing. Because this transference configuration emanates from the very earliest time of life, feelings experienced in the transference tend to be of a very primitive nature. The rage tends to be global and undifferentiated and almost defies verbal representation. Similarly the passive longings defy verbal representation, as do the concerns about being out of control. In the transference situation these feeling states need to be reconstructed largely through the therapist's empathetic responses to the patient's feeling state. Words should approximate feeling states that under ideal circumstances become reexperienced in the transference. Both the therapist and the patient may not find just the right words to describe these states. If both can have an empathic feel and sense of conviction about the feeling tone that exists in the transference, however, this kind of confirmation will prove very useful.

In order for this very early transference configuration to manifest itself, however, the therapist must not prematurely interpret the patient's rage, irritability, passive longing, concerns with feeling out of control, or compensatory defenses arising from these feeling states. Maintaining a respectful, noncontrolling posture, the therapist, through facilitating the associative process, must allow these feelings to become experienced. When the patient talks about feeling out of control the therapist should empathetically inquire further about what feelings are related to this rather than attempt closure in this area with premature interpretations or reassuring comments. Because both the rage and the longing are of a primitive, undifferentiated, preverbal nature, they tend to frighten both patient and therapist. Early dependent longings may take on sexual coloring from later developmental stages or may come out as bizarre, primitive fantasies. Similarly, the rage may take on highly frightening characteristics (bloody, gory images, etc.). It is quite important for the therapist to tolerate and facilitate the full development of these very primitive feeling states and their verbal approximations without jumping to the conclusion that the patient is psychotic and therefore in need of new medication or support.

As these feeling states become organized, quite often the patient becomes extremely frightened of destroying the therapist (the love object), either because of the intensity of the longings that will literally swallow up the therapist or because of the intensity of the rage that the patient feels towards the much-needed but frustrating object. Not unusually at this juncture, the patient will attempt either to flee treatment or to find some other means to deal with these painful feeling states.

Specific attention must be focused on the patient's anxiety around destroying the object (the therapist) and being damaged and/or left by the therapist. As indicated earlier, individuals with this syndrome are capable of better functioning at both CNS and emotional levels, but the cycles of fear and anxiety around early states of need and aggression lead to a degree of cautiousness in later potentially developmentally facilitating relationships (at a time when CNS maturation would have permitted better functioning). Experiencing and working through in the treatment relationship both the primitive feelings and the accompanying fears and anxiety permits CNS functioning and the capacity for human relationships, even if less than optimal, to reach their original potential.

In contrast to the borderline patient, adult neurotic patients with MBD have differentiated self from object and can deal with intense feeling states. Such patients give an appearance of disorganization in thinking that is quite different from the borderline patient's disorganization. Self–object differentiation is maintained. The concerns around themes of destruction are organized, differentiated, stable fantasies rather than regressive states of dedifferentiation. The degree of primitive preoedipal material that must be dealt with is not a sign of arrested development but may be related to the unique, individually different constitutional patterns of patients with MBD. The role of certain developmentally early patterns are therefore accentuated, even though major areas of development may continue quite appropriately.

These points are illustrated by the case of a young man with childhood history of MBD who had been in analysis for several years and wanted to leave analytic treatment and take medication for his "minimal brain dysfunction of adulthood." In talking with him (as a consultant) it became clear that he was experiencing passive longings and intense rage toward his therapist. Some of his longings had a homosexual tinge, and at the same time he was very frightened of "losing control." His wish to change therapists and receive medication was a request in essence to put a lid on frightening feeling states that he mistakenly felt he could not deal with. Perhaps this image of himself may have been true as an infant and child, but it was no longer true as an adult (he had developed some quite mature coping mechanisms that could help him work through these issues). Consultation enabled him to return to his analysis, and followup a year later indicated that he had resolved a number of these issues and had made significant gains not only in his overall functioning as a young man but also in his ability to focus his attention and organize his activity. He had been able to work through very early transference material.

It is crucial that the primary impairment be dealt with in psychotherapy if the patient is to have an opportunity to reach his optimal potential in human functioning. Even a constitutionally based individual style of CNS processing and regulation can be altered through the process of working through transference configurations that stem from the period of life when adaptation to unique individual CNS styles was first organized. For example, an infant whose mother provides an appropriate environment can often be helped to develop compensatory mechanisms to help focus attention and regulate activity in the first year of life.

It is rare, though, that the environment provides such unique care. That there is a relationship between structure and function, however, cannot be ignored. Early in life the type of environmental response to particular individual patterns of CNS regulation will help to determine, in part, how further development occurs. Thus a hyperactive infant with poor capacity to focus attention and organize internal experience can be helped to use multiple sensory modalities to focus on environmental cues and thereby focus attention. This requires a patient and sensitive maternal environment that can respond to the infant's disorganization with security and support and help the infant use available sensory and motor integrative response patterns to deal with frightening panic states. In treatment the transference permits the reexperience of some of these early frightening states. It is not a corrective emotional experience that then occurs however; rather as an adult the individual has already developed certain auxiliary ego functions that can permit that person to carry on at a more effective level if the early feeling states can be brought into awareness and, in a sense, made accessible to the full capacity of adult personality functioning. As long as these early feeling states are walled off in conflict and fear, they continue to exert an undue effect on behavior. When they are more fully brought into awareness and experienced through the transference, the full extent of adult personality functioning can be brought to bear on them. To the degree that working through some of these early transferences occur, there is also the type of learning occurring that involves the relationship between structure and function that would ordinarily happen in the developmental phases of early childhood.

There are a few "don'ts" that are worth repeating. It is important to try not to be overly supportive with such patients. If they have some areas of solid ego functioning, a therapist giving advice assuming an overcontrolling style permits the patient to maintain a pseudohelpless posture. It is also important to avoid becoming authoritarian even if the patient demonstrates intense manipulative and sociopathic trends at various times (as such patients often will). It is important to set limits and interpret acting-out but to not be seduced into an authoritarian posture that will close off intense affect expressions and disguise early infantile longings and/or oedipal longings with an emotional but more comfortable sadomasochistic pattern.

It is worth repeating that the transferences that these patients develop differ from those of more typical borderline patients who are seen in intensive analytic psychotherapy. Many of the ABD patients (if they have achieved a neurotic level of integration) have reached the triangular oedipal level of development in terms of object relationships as well as psychosexual development. They have a capacity for continuing and intimate relationships. Self–object differentiation is stabilized. Their concerns tend to be not with fusion with the object but with the intensity of developmentally early preverbal wishes and affects and the fear of destroying the object. Often their adult levels of integration are better than they appear because cycles of fear and anxiety around their often not-dealt-with early wish and affect states give an appearance of disorganization.

## CONCLUSIONS

We have focused on a number of issues—the syndrome of MBD in adults, or ABD; the nature of early experience of such individuals; and how the nature of the early experience leads to certain principles of conducting psychoanalytically oriented psychotherapy or psychoanalysis. The same principles also hold in more supportive therapies, where transference issues may not be dealt with to the same degree or with the same intensity. It is important to emphasize that such individuals, whether or not on medication, can be helped to a high level of psychological integration through long-term psychotherapy. It is only in rare circumstances that such an approach would be inappropriate. Once a person does embark on a long-term therapeutic relationship, the wish to drop treatment or the wish to be put on medication or have medication increased is often related to a fear of certain transference states rather than realistic concerns about functioning.

Through considering possible early developmental experiences,[11,12] this paper has reviewed principles of psychotherapy and psychoanalysis with adult neurotic individuals with MBD. It was seen that the relationship between constitutional individual differences in CNS regulation and specific early environmental experiences set in motion characteristic patterns that have implications for the selection of defensive constellations, the type of transference formed in treatment, and certain core issues that should be worked through for treatment to be successful.

It should be emphasized that while this discussion focused on a specific syndrome, it attempted to delineate principles that would apply more generally to the relationship between individual constitutional differences, early experience, personality development, and treatment. Most individuals are born with individually different constitutional tendencies that will determine aspects of their earliest experiences. Close attention to the parameters of these earliest experiences will facilitate a fuller understanding of the treatment relationship.

## REFERENCES

1.   Mann H B, Greenspan S I: The identification and treatment of adult brain dysfunction. Am J Psychiatr 133: 1013–1017, 1976.

2. Brazelton T B: Neonatal Behavioral Assessment Scale. Philadelphia, J.B. Lippincott, 1973.
3. Emde R, Gaensbauer T, Harmon R: Emotional expression in infancy: A biobehavioral study. Psychol Issues, Monograph No. 37. New York: International Universities Press, 1976.
4. Sander L: Issues in early mother-child interaction. Am Acad Child Psychiatry 1:141–166, 1962.
5. Gewirtz J L: A learning analysis of the effects of normal stimulation, privation and deprivation on the acquisition of social motivation and attachment. In Foss B M (ed): Determinants of Infant Behavior, vol 1. London, Methuen, 1961.
6. Stern D: Mother and infant at play: The dyadic interaction involving facial, vocal and gaze behaviors. In Lewis M, Rosenblum L (eds): The Effects of the Infant on Its Caregiver. New York, John Wiley & Sons, 1974.
7. Mahler M S, Pine F, Bergman A: The Psychological Birth of the Human Infant, Symbiosis and Individuation. New York, Basic Books, 1975.
8. Greenspan S I: The oedipal-preoedipal dilemma: A reformulation according to object relations theory. Int Rev Psychoanal 4:381–391, 1977.
9. Greenspan S I, Cullander C C H: A systematic metapsychological assessment of the course of an analysis. J Psychoanal Assoc 23:(1):107–138, 1975.
10. Bellak L, Hurvich M, Gidiron H, et al.: Ego Functions in Schizophrenics, Neurotics, and Normals. New York, John Wiley & Sons, 1973.
11. Brazelton T B: Personal communication, 1970. [Cited by Korner A F: Early stimulation and maternal care as related to infant capabilities and individual differences. Early Child Dev Care 2:307–327, 1973.]
12. Gewirtz J L: Levels of conceptual analysis in environment-infant interaction research. Merrill-Palmer Q 15:(1):9–47, 1969.

L. Eugene Arnold

# 13

# Philosophy and Strategy of Medicating Adults With Minimal Brain Dysfunction

The philosophy and strategy of medicating adults with minimal brain dysfunction (MBD) depend on an understanding of the complexity of possible etiologies and possible interventions or treatments. Figure 13-1 illustrates in a hydraulic parfait model how various degrees of different etiologies can sum in different individuals to produce similar-appearing symptoms. It is conceivable that at times two or more different causes may act in synergy rather than mere summation. Not all individuals showing the MBD syndrome have the same relative importance of the various possible causes.

## TREATMENT LEVERAGES

Similar considerations can apply to the potential effectiveness of various treatments. Figure 13-2 shows a leverage model of treatment. We can conceptualize the weight of symptoms at one end of a beam lifted by the counterbalancing weight of various amounts and combinations of interventions on the other side of a fulcrum. For each patient there is a specific leverage point for each intervention. For example, patient A may have the leverage point for psychotherapy near the fulcrum, the leverage point for skill remediation near the end of the lever, and that for medica-

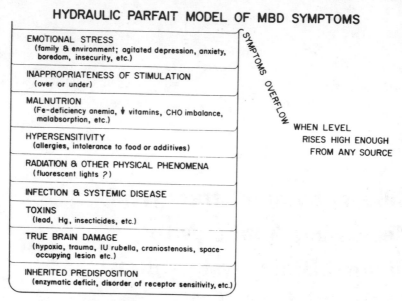

Fig. 13-1. Hydraulic parfait model of minimal brain dysfunction. When level of total pathology rises high enough from any combination of layers, behavior and learning disorder symptoms spill. [Reproduced by permission from Diseases of the Nervous System (37:172, 1976).]

tion midway between. Patient *B* may have medication and family therapy leverage points at the end of the lever, skill remediation leverage near the fulcrum, and psychotherapy between. Patient *C* may have change of job near the end of the lever and all other interventions near the fulcrum. An intervention whose leverage point is near the fulcrum can sometimes be increased in quantity to compensate somewhat for poor leverage, but this is not as efficient as using an intervention with more leverage.

Sometimes an intervention with poor leverage can be potentiated— have its leverage increased—by simultaneous use of a potentiating intervention. For example, the leverage of psychotherapy might be increased by simultaneous medication. In such a case the results would be greater than might be expected from a mere summation of the moments of force anticipated from applying the interventions at their original leverage points. A factor that can potentiate the effectiveness of any intervention is the motivation of the patient attempting to throw off symptoms.

## ADULTS VERSUS CHILDREN

As with MBD children, medication should be used in MBD adults only as part of a comprehensive multimodal treatment plan—in conjunc-

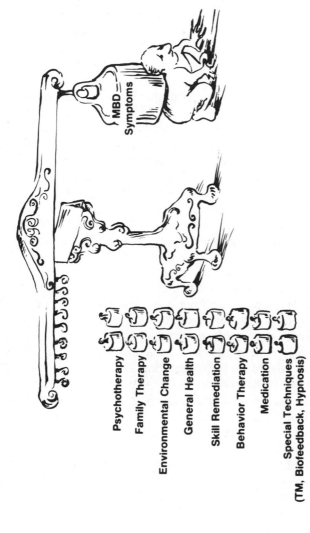

Psychotherapy

Family Therapy

Environmental Change

General Health

Skill Remediation

Behavior Therapy

Medication

Special Techniques
(TM, Biofeedback, Hypnosis)

Fig. 13-2. Leverage model of treatment of minimal brain dysfunction. For each patient there are specific leverage points for each possible treatment or intervention, making some treatments more efficient than others. Efficiency (leverage) of each treatment varies from patient to patient.

179

tion with other interventions, not as a substitute for them. Nevertheless, there are several differences from the situation with children. Most of these tend to make drug treatment more acceptable for MBD in adults than in children:

1.  While children are usually treated by someone else's decision, adults ordinarily seek treatment of their own volition and in most cases are unquestionably competent to give their own informed consent for such treatment, including use of drugs. There is more assurance than in the case of children that the potential risks, side effects, and expenses are understood and appreciated and that the decision to accept drug treatment is made on the basis of enlightened self-interest.

2.  The most favored drugs, stimulants, seem by and large more useful for enhancing performance and behavior than enhancing learning. It might be argued that the main task of children is to learn rather than to perform. What they learn in school is more important than the quality of work that they hand in. By contrast, adults' main requirements on the job are to perform, to produce, rather than to learn. Therefore assuming the same degree of impairment from MBD it seems more appropriate for performing, producing adults to take such drugs than for children to do so.

3.  The more worrisome and common side effects of stimulants include such things as appetite loss, possible growth retardation, and possible effects on the developing cardiovascular system. All of these would be of less concern in a healthy young adult, particularly in a healthy young adult who is being closely monitored.

4.  There is one difference in situation between children and adults that constitutes a disadvantage for medicating adults with stimulants. We feel rather secure in the knowledge, or at least the strong belief, that there is no increased risk of addiction in children treated with stimulants for minimal brain dysfunction; however, we do not yet have an adequate data base to make firm conclusions about the addiction risk in adults thus treated. My prediction is that this will not be a serious problem for the MBD adults themselves; however, as the practice of medicating adults in this way becomes more widespread we may expect to see "speed freaks" faking minimal brain dysfunction in order to obtain a stimulant supply, analogous to narcotic addicts faking kidney stones. This risk can be minimized by careful collection of history, including school and work records, and by insisting that medication be used only as part of a comprehensive treatment plan. Eventually, physiologic tests such as evoked EEG response, galvanic skin response, and electropupillogram may be developed as objective tests of medication advisability.

## CULTIVATING PLACEBO BENEFIT

One similarity between medicating children and medicating adults is the importance of enhancing placebo benefit. Figure 13-3 illustrates a psychosocial vicious cycle initiated by MBD in childhood. Without adequate intervention, it can persist into adulthood, with self-perpetuating discouragement, decreased motivation, failure to gain practice, decreased skill development, failure self-image, low self-esteem, frustration, poor impulse control, poor relations with peers and authorities, and possibly even a paranoid view of the world as an unfair place. Much of the vicious cycle is maintained by negative expectations that grease the skids of negative self-fulfilling prophecy. One of the therapeutic qualities that medication shares with other interventions is that of the placebo effect—changing negative expectations to positive expectations. The adroit clinician, for the good of the patient, expertly cultivates positive expectations and placebo benefit by specific, concrete, honest descriptions of the expected benefits.

Honestly cultivating positive expectations for the unpredictable stimulants requires a little thought, planning, and practice. One method begins by stating that there are many different medicines that are helpful in this kind of problem, that one of these medicines may be better for one person and another better for another person, but that there is no sure way of telling ahead of time which is best for a given person. Furthermore, the dose required may vary from one person to another. Therefore the patient need not get discouraged if the dosage or even the type of medicine has to be changed several times in order to find the best dosage of the best medicine. This allows for the possibility that the first medicine tried may not be satisfactory but couches it in terms of the optimistic assurance that another might be better. Most people, on hearing this, will tend to pick up the optimistic, confident note rather than the implication of uncertainty.

Having established these disclaimers, the clinician should explain in detail the expected benefits: The patients will probably find it easier to concentrate, to control themselves (including their tempers), to ignore distractions, and to do what they want to do when they want to do it. Medication may make it possible for them to behave and perform in the way that they have always wanted to but have had difficulty doing until the present. They should also expect temporarily to lose appetite, possibly become irritable and depressed for a while, and possibly have trouble sleeping. Coupling the mention of side effects with the description of anticipated benefits tends to make them more acceptable; it also tends to make them reinforcers of the positive expectations. When the predicted side effects occur, they confirm the credibility of the doctor who also

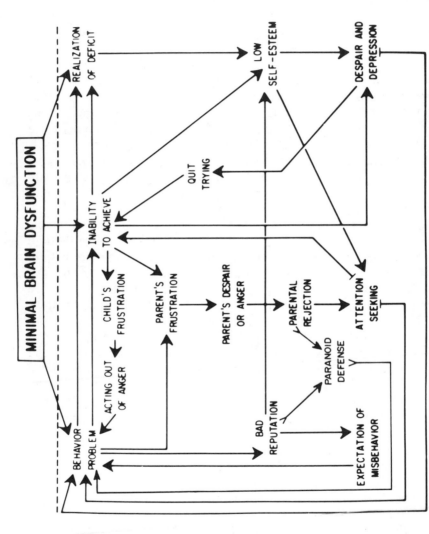

Fig. 13-3. Psychosocial vicious cycles initiated by minimal brain dysfunction. Destructive feedback loops can perpetuate cycle even after MBD is "outgrown," as depicted by the dotted line. [Reproduced by permission from Clinical Pediatrics (12:35–41, 1973).]

predicted the benefits: "The medicine is working just like the doctor said it would."

With the patient's permission, important others (such as spouse) can be enlisted in the placebo effort by sharing with them specific predictions of improvement. Occasionally, even a sympathetic boss could be included. One way to handle this could be to tell the patient, "I would like to explain to your spouse (parent, boss, etc.) what I just told you about the medicine so she (he) can help us monitor the effect as we adjust dosage. Would you have him (her) call me?" When the call comes, one could say, "*X* has probably told you about the medicine he (she) is starting and that we would like your observations to help decide the best dose. The effects you'll need to look for are more even temper, better attention span, better learning from experience, better organization. . . ."

## TIMING OF DRUG THERAPY

Ordinarily, medication would not be prescribed at the first visit unless the situation seemed urgent, analogous to a child who is on the verge of being expelled from school. Such emergencies might include the threat of job loss or danger of a marriage breaking up because of the patient's symptoms. In cases that do not seem so urgent, a trial of other appropriate interventions usually makes sense. In some cases, the MBD itself has "burned out" and the patient is actually suffering from residual vicious cycle symptoms as described above. Perhaps the vicious cycle can be disrupted without medication. If it becomes obvious after a month or so that such nonmedical interventions will not be effective, medication should then be added to these interventions without discontinuing them. The combination of drugs with the other interventions may be effective where either alone would not have been.

In most cases the period of drug therapy should not be considered indefinite. It should ordinarily be considered a temporary facilitation of the individual's ability to make use of other resources in adapting and compensating. This is particularly true if some of the patients' main problems concern skill development. Many skills that require intensive attention in the learning process can, once learned, be practiced or executed with far less attention. A good example is driving a car. Even some social skills, such as holding one's temper, stopping to think how things would sound to another, or checking how the other person feels, are also much harder to learn initially than to maintain once they have become habitual.

Furthermore, anxiety and depression tend to exacerbate MBD symptoms. The intensity of symptoms manifested prior to medication by a patient who is distressed by current poor adjustment and poor functioning reflects aggravation by anxiety or depression. With medication patients may discover that they are able to help themselves, to improve, and to function better. This improved adjustment and success can allay their anxieties and/or depressions, allowing the medication to be withdrawn without recrudescence of the symptoms. Of course, the symptoms may reappear when such a patient is subjected to anxiety or depression from life events. At such a time it may be necessary to reinstitute the medication temporarily to tide the patient over that particular crisis.

**CONCLUSION**

MBD is a chronic disorder that the patient needs to adjust to and compensate for. The patient needs a long-term supportive relationship with a clinician to whom he can return at times of crisis. The objective is not cure but to help the patient find a way of lowering the level of hydraulic parfait far enough to keep symptoms from spilling out. In doing this, the clinician can choose various interventions, among them medication. The clinician needs to consider how much leverage can be exerted by each intervention in the case of a given patient and needs to capitalize on the additive or synergistic effects of several treatments in combination. If medication is used, it must be as an adjunct to other interventions in a comprehensive, multimodal treatment plan, and the potential of placebo benefit needs to be exploited. Finally, the clinician needs to be available occasionally to deflate the hydraulic parfait of symptom causation when circumstances again flood the patient with anxiety, depression, or other distress.

Donald M. Gallant, Moderator

# 14

# General Discussion

*Dr. Gallant:*   First I'd like to make a few comments on the background and neurophysiologic aspects of this possible syndrome of MBD.

As mentioned by Dr. Wender and others, the dopaminergic theory is an attractive one, and Satterfield's findings of low skin conductance, possibly associated with lower walls of threshold, can be correlated with a relative dopaminergic deficiency.

As I was listening to Dr. Wender, I was reminded of our work at Tulane in the late 1960s in evaluating the neurophysiologic differences between antipsychotic and antidepressant agents in cats with implanted cortical and subcortical electrodes and tried to relate it to the theoretical concepts concerning the beneficial effects of imipramine on some of these patients. One consistent effect that we found was that in our electrode-evoked potential responses in animals the neuroleptic agents always facilitated the electrode-evoked responses in the hippocampus, intellect complex, cordate, and cortex but inhibited the MRF and posterior hypothalamus. On the other hand, the antidepressants, no matter what their chemical structure, consistently facilitated the MRF and posterior hypothalamus while inhibiting the areas above, as far as the electrode-evoked potential responses were concerned. Perhaps in some patients that have a lower wall of threshold, facilitation of the MRF and posterior hypothalamus might be of neurophysiologic benefit.

As has been noted by others, in von Economo encephalitis there is a depletion of dopamine stores in the substantia negri.

*Dr. Wender:*   The same thing that produces Parkinson disease in adults produces postencephalitic behavior disorder in children.

*Dr. Gallant:* John Werry reported in *The Archives* [*of General Psychiatry*] in 1974 on a study comparing methylphenidate and haloperidol that showed that high doses of haloperidol, which is probably one of the more potent dopaminergic-blocking antipsychotic agents, can exacerbate the symptoms of some hyperkinetic behavior syndromes. Thus relatively dopaminergic agents, such as L-dopa (provided methyl-dopahydroxylates are used in combination with amantadine), would be better drugs to use in controlled studies, since they are somewhat purer in their dopaminergic properties. Although they would not provide full confirmation of some of the concepts concerning dopamine deficiency, they surely would substantiate some of the theory in this area.

The development of dopamine denervation hypersensitivity, as may be seen in postencephalitic Parkinsonism, may also exist in MBD. Dr. Wender's observations concerning adults not requiring any greater dosage of methylphenidate than children might be associated with this type of hypersensitivity that develops from chronic denervation.

*Dr. Wender:* Or just chronic low dopamine levels and the kind of compensatory mechanism that CNS is trying to make up for, by increasing receptor sensitivity.

*Dr. Gallant:* Relatively speaking, on a milligram per kilogram basis, you're using a lower dosage in the adult as compared to the child.

*Dr. Wender:* The same or lower.

*Dr. Gallant:* It may be that we should think of another subgroup of MBD, those nonresponders to the dopamenergic agents, and possibly try the opposite side of the coin.

*Dr. Wender:* Something was recently published about people who started to abuse anticholinergic agents because they made them euphoric.

*Dr. Gallant:* We've had lots of patients that do that, by the way. Artane is one of the biggest sellers right now in our methadone clinics.

An interesting thought would be to try deanol, an acetylcholine precursor, or more powerful acetylcholine precursors in those patients who do not respond to stimulants but are definitely thought to have MBD.

Concerning the term "minimal brain dysfunction," I find it to be quite repelling to many of my adult patients. In fact, I find it a very ugly term, to be quite blunt about it. We do use some of the techniques that Dr. Bellak referred to, in addition to drug therapy, in our group of patients. The term we use is "paroxysmal behavior dyscontrol." The adult patients find this much more acceptable to listen to, understand, and accept, without feeling that we're calling them brain damaged. I think MBD is a terrible label and a nontherapeutic one. I can think of many other labels more therapeutic in their connotation that would not confuse the issue any more than MBD does.

Dr. Arnold's "hydraulic parfait model," which I thought was a dessert when I first heard about it, offers us a very practical guideline for explaining the variety of symptoms that can occur as a result of underlying CNS disturbances by a chemical cause, or causes, of MBD. In addition, it could be an excellent teaching instrument for showing the clinician, as well as the patient, that treatment approaches have to be varied in relation to the predominating influences, genetic and environmental, that result in a disabled symptomatology. The same model can be used for almost any psychiatric syndrome, such as schizophrenia, alcoholism, drug addiction, and even severe personality disorders and depression. I like the way you can sort of push down a lever and have an overflow and then start cutting off some of the causative agents involved, whether they be environmental or genetic.

Dr. Arnold has detailed some of the reasons drugs are more acceptable to the adult MBD. However, Safer found that adolescents were less compliant than children, and we've had the same problem in our adults. Despite the fact that on a theoretical basis it seems that adults should take the medication more, on a practical basis some of my patients will only take it when they feel like it. When they feel like they want to explode and enjoy it, they'll stop their medication. I really don't find a compliant medication situation to be significantly better in the adult population.

Dr. Arnold also raised the question about not having sufficient data in adults to make firm conclusions about the risk of addiction. This is an important question. Just within the last 4 weeks I've seen two clinical patients with adult MBD who showed symptoms of the recent onset of alcoholism preceded by an early history of definite amphetamine abuse. A comment by one of the patients was, "Speed calmed me down and made me feel so cool I thought another pill or two would make me feel even more smooth. After a week or two I needed a larger dose to get the same feeling."

It's generally agreed that the hyperactive child syndrome of MBD is likely to result in the development of alcoholism and sociopathy in men and hysteria in women. This makes me think of Antabuse, which is an interesting compound because it not only inhibits beta-substituted acetic aldehydes but it is also a dopamine betahydroxylase inhibitor and a mild inhibitor of monoaminooxiclase. Theoretically, a double-blind study with Antabuse in alcoholics diagnosed as having MBD as well would be of interest from two perspectives, both beta-substituted acetic aldehyde and dopamine betahydroxylase inhibition.

*Dr. Wender:*    One problem is that you would have to use very large doses.

*Dr. Gallant:*    Another problem is misdiagnosis. Some patients might have underlying schizophrenia, and they would become really psychotic. In fact, if you treat enough patients, you're going to make the misdiagnosis sooner or later and have a psychotic break on the Antabuse situation, probably because of the excessive dopamine stimulation. Also, with a dose of 500 mg or more, we start getting a lot of sedation in some patients, particularly those patients who seem to be low in peripheral dopamine betahydroxylase. A recent paper correlated the incidence of side effects that occur with the administration of Antabuse to the plasma dopamine betahydroxylase levels. Dr. Greenspan suggested, as have Dr. Bellak and Dr. Wender, that depression, anxiety, and their derivatives, as well as psychotic and borderline diagnoses, in some patients may be secondary manifestations of a similar underlying central nervous system physiologic impairment. He emphasizes the core causes of painful and frightening feeling states and the need to treat the causing symptoms rather than concentrate on their secondary manifestation. His focus on the causative symptoms should produce more rewarding therapeutic results.

As to the studies being done in adult MBD, I was encouraged by the direction toward well-designed controlled studies evident in some of the presentations here, especially since I was discouraged by the lack of such studies when I reviewed the literature before this meeting.

Prospective studies are usually of more value and validity than retrospective studies. These prospective studies should include use of Waldrop's list of congenital anomalies. She lists 16 key items that I feel should be a part of every controlled evaluation, whether it is an EEG evaluation, laboratory data evaluation, or clinical evaluation. These anomalies are very easy to measure, and I find her correlation of them with the appearance of the minimal brain dysfunction problem quite impressive.

*Dr. Wender:* One problem is that some anomalies in childhood change with age. For example, the cathedral palate flattens out.

*Dr. Gallant:* Also, I don't think we really know enough yet about the incidence in normals. At what point they become statistically significant, as far as correlation with MBD, is an area in which a lot of work remains to be done. Still, I don't see any reason why these items should not be used routinely, since they're so easy to measure and evaluate.

We should also remind ourselves that there can be an association between the development of depression and the appearance of hyperactive behavior. Connors has noted that depressed children show a high incidence of hyperactivity, school phobias, and so forth. He believes that these complaints can be differentiated from those found in hyperkinetic children or other neurotic disturbances because the symptoms tend to appear only when the children are depressed. Thus primary affective disorders associated with hyperactivity in children may be confused with the hyperkinetic behavior syndrome if the appearance of depression is not correlated with the secondary acting-out symptomatology. The confusion of diagnostic categories in children is further demonstrated by the observation that even gross organic brain syndromes can have a labile presentation and also by the fact that hyperkinetic children often give the appearance of cyclic patterns that can be confused with early bipolar illness because of their tendency to overreact to different types of environmental stimuli. Thus clinical criteria alone should not be used for making a definitive diagnosis of MBD in adults; objective criteria such as neurologic evaluation or EEG findings, or at least neurophysiologic testing, are necessary. Millichap reported in the *Annals of the New York Academy of Sciences*, 1973, in the issue entitled "Minimal Brain Dysfunction," a correlation between the number of soft signs and the degree of response to methylphenidate. There are children without soft signs who also respond to methylphenidate, and there are normals, of course, who respond to methylphenidate, but the controlled observations by Millichap do indicate that we should look for evidence of soft signs in adults who supposedly have the diagnosis of MBD.

Since a higher psychopharmacologic response rate has been reported in those hyperkinetic children who have had either one hard or two soft neurologic signs, similar types of criteria for evaluation of efficacy of various types of medications for the treatment of MBD in adults should be part of future protocol designs. I believe that the diagnosis of MBD without utilization of objective clinical findings, such as hard and soft neurologic signs and laboratory aids (such as EEG abnormalities), will result in an overdiagnosis of this condition in adults, as was suggested by Dr. Bellak in relation to the possible overdiagnosis of this condition in some children. In other words, up until recently it appears that the condition has been underdiagnosed, but if we allow the clinical symptomatology to be used as the main feature in diagnosis, since the clinical signs are so diverse in quality and quantity, the clinician may resort to this syndrome as a wastepaper-basket diagnosis after a while.

I should say that the use of drug response as a basis for splitting MBD into subgroups is an intelligent approach. However, I would strongly urge all investigators who are interested in this important but confusing CNS dysfunction to also focus on correlating the possible objective clinical and laboratory findings with the clinical symptomatology and not merely assume the diagnosis and then use the treatment modality for confirmation.

*Chairman Bellak:* Thank you for a well-balanced presentation. None of us likes, for labeling purposes, the term MBD, and I wish that one of the things that would come out of this meeting would be a generally more acceptable term for use with patients. That's one of the many

problems that MBD shares with schizophrenia. There are many concerned, from Karl Menninger to Loren Mosher and lots in between, with
labeling people as "schizophrenics" with all the social consequences and
the bad aura that it has acquired over the decades.

I want to press the claim once more for neuropsychological signs,
since I believe that they are probably much more sensitive indicators than
neurologic soft signs.

# 15

# Closing Remarks

*Dr. Cole:* I have a question. The world of dyskinesia, which overlaps with this one, has been confounded lately by the idea that there are presynaptic dopamine receptors that have different effects from post-synaptic dopamine receptors. We have a little evidence with tardive dyskinesia that a low dose of Sinemet will improve the dyskinesia and a high dose will make it worse. Is there any evidence that very low doses of stimulants have a different effect from high doses in MBD.

*Dr. Wender:* Recently, people have found inhibitory and excitatory dopamine pathways. Low doses of morphine decrease motor activity, whereas higher doses will increase activity. I think the same has been shown for amphetamines, but I'm not certain.

*Dr. Gallant:* With methylphenidate in high dosages there have been reported cases of tics, twitches, and involuntary movements.

*Dr. Cole:* Is there any evidence that deanol is, in fact, useful for hyperkinetic children?

*Dr. Cantwell:* In one study with higher doses than had been used before, it was effective. That study was done after Connors' review of the literature on the use of deanol in hyperkinetic children, which did not show it to be effective. He himself suggested in the review that a higher-dose study be done, and when it was done it seemed to be effective.

*Dr. Klein:* I'd like to make a point about reliance on neurologic soft signs for diagnosis. There are several studies in which they've tried to correlate the presence of neurologic soft signs with response to drugs. Some indicate a correlation; others don't. Millichap's work is one of the stronger supports for such a correlation, but I think that there's a reason for that. You can understand his findings as an artifact and misdiagnosis. There's a substantial percentage of misdiagnosis when children are called hyperkinetic, depending on the variety of information sources used. If, for instance, it's true that hyperkinetic children on the average have more soft signs than normal ones (and that seems to be well established) and the hyperkinetic children respond to Ritalin and normal ones don't. . . .

*Dr. Gallant:*   Normal children do apparently respond to it.

*Dr. Klein:*   We did a study in which we gave 60 mg of Ritalin a day to nonhyperkinetic learning-disabled children, and we got very minor, apparently no, behavioral effects at all. It was a placebo control study.

*Dr. Gallant:*   John Werry would tell you your dosage was too high and theoretically you might have interfered with their learning ability.

*Dr. Klein:*   I'm not talking about learning ability but about the behavioral effects. The other point I wanted to make is that correlation between neurologic soft signs and response to Ritalin can very well be confounded by how much misdiagnosis you have in your sample. We found that the more the data indicating the child is hyperkinetic, the higher the drug effect. It's not 70 percent at all. If you have enough data, you can get it well over 90 percent.

What we did was this: First of all, many of the studies depend upon one source of information, like the teacher's report. When we first started our studies, we insisted upon what we call "transsituational" hyperactivity. There had to be at least two different people in two different situations who said the child was hyperactive. That could be the teacher and the parent, or the teacher and the doctor, because frequently hyperkinetic children will be reported as hyperkinetic by a teacher but on a one-to-one basis with a doctor they won't act that way.

In another study the children had to be transsituationally hyperactive on the testimony of either the teacher, using scales, or the mother, and of a blind observer in the classroom. The observers were truly blind; they didn't even know why they were there. They were given two children in a classroom to observe, using a variant of O'Leary's scale that he developed for classroom observation. These children were entered into a drug-placebo comparison, and showed well over 90 percent, almost 100 percent, responses.

*Dr. Tucker:*   How many of the ones that were reported by the two observers as being hyperkinetic were not rated hyperkinetic?

*Dr. Klein:*   Less than half of them.

*Dr. Tucker:*   There's a lot of difference in subjective reporting.

*Dr. Klein:*   One of the things that's not recognized is that if you do time sampling observations on them in a classroom, it's very easy to miss the hyperkinetic behavior. The teachers are often right and the observers wrong, because the teachers see them over a period of a month during which at various times the child's been acting up, whereas the observers just see them once. In fact, we also did a double-blind study of the children who were reported as hyperkinetic by two different sources, but not seen as hyperkinetic in the classroom by the observer, and we got substantial drug-placebo differences there, too.

*Dr. Gallant:* What criteria or what symptomatology was predominant in this tremendously high drug respondent group?

*Dr. Klein:* The primary thing was time-off-target. These children either didn't have the attention span or they were distractible in the sense that they were on the prowl, other things were very interesting to them.

Let me make just one further point. With this very high response rate to drug, trying to predict nonresponsiveness becomes almost impossible. That is, you're really trying to predict a very rare event. A lot of the predictor studies, I would think, are best understood as misdiagnosis. The same thing applies to Satterfield's work. I think that what he has is a mixture of truly hyperactive, probably underaroused, children and children who are behavior problems in various ways who got the label hyperactive. But, if you take, as we did, the children who you are quite certain are hyperactive, at that point you can't find any predictors at all, certainly not neurologic soft signs or EEGs.

*Dr. Greenspan:* Freud used the way the patient responded to psychoanalytic treatment as his major means of making a diagnosis. It was what the patient did on the couch that established whether he was neurotic, borderline, psychotic, and so forth. Is it reasonable to use response to medication as a clue to the etiology and the biologic makeup of the disorder? Is it reasonable to use it, as we are, to subsume a clinical entity, with all the other obvious things that can go into determining drug response? There is also the fact that drug response may involve something like a final common pathway to everlasting different types of things.

*Dr. Klein:* I don't think anyone is claiming that homogeneous drug response asserts cohesively homogeneous etiology.

*Dr. Greenspan:* Or even disorder.

*Dr. Gallant:* What was the dosage of Ritalin you were using?

*Dr. Klein:* In that particular study it ran around 35 mg a day.

*Dr. Gallant:* Where are the results reported on this high a dosage interfering with learning?

*Dr. Klein:* The evidence is pretty shaky. I've been through that literature very carefully and it concerns primarily not learning from the point of view of school achievers but rather learning tested by the specific laboratory tests.

*Dr. Cantwell:* It's also not consistent with what Swanson and

Kinsbourne reported in *Science*. They also reported a state-dependent effect, and Werry does not report a state-dependent effect. If you read enough, you can always find one study to dispute another.

*Dr. Greenspan:*   Rapoport's study seems to refute the use of response to medication as a diagnostic criterion, and I think we're dealing with somewhat the same as her sample of children of very bright upper-middle-class parents—bright, interested children, some of whom come across as hyperactive to certain school teachers. You know, they all had a very positive effect in terms of maintaining stability of focus of attention. You may not agree with some of the methodologies she used, but her findings do question the use of the pharmacologic response somewhat.

*Dr. Cantwell:*   If you look at Weiss and Laddis's old review of the effect of amphetamines on adults, there are certain tests in which normal adults on amphetamines seem to improve and others in which they do worse. All the tests that Rapoport used on those children were those that, at least according to the Weiss and Laddis review, the children would do better on. There are certain tests that hyperactive children do better on, that normal adults, according to the Weiss and Laddis review, do worse on with stimulants, and those are the tests that Swanson and Kinsbourne have used and showed a positive effect. So I would like to have seen some of those tests included.

*Dr. Gallant:*   What are the main focuses of these tests that they do better on that they normally would do the worse on?

*Dr. Cantwell:*   Usually it's in maintenance of attention, vigilance, or other kinds of selective attention. Barbara Keogh at UCLA has criticized greatly the use of "attention" as an all-inclusive term, noting that in fact the process of attention involves many things, the coming to attention, maintaining attention, selective attention. It may very well be that hyperactive children have a defect in one of these specific areas and not in others. If you use a global measure, like a continuous performance test or a test that measures many other things besides attention, you may get a positive effect that is obscured in terms of hyperactive children.

The second thing is that the written report doesn't include the results after the children came off the Dexedrine. In general, when hyperactive children get off the medication, they return to their baseline state, whatever that happens to be. These children apparently "crashed," because Rapoport got calls from the parents saying, "Oh, my God, the kid is really depressed," or something. I don't know why she didn't mention it in the article. She did present it in Hawaii. These children were all those of friends and some of her own, so that they distinctly had a different coming-off effect than the true-blue hyperactive children had.

*Dr. Wender:*   In the early days, when it wasn't known if learning-disabled children improved on stimulants, I tried a lot of them on it because nothing else seemed to work, and what I got was irritable learning-disabled children. Since 10 mg a day didn't do any good, I gradually went up to 20 mg. They didn't go through a good period, there wasn't a U-shaped curve with an optimal dosage, none of the dosages did any good, and the more I gave them, the worse they felt.

*Dr. Arnold:*    What little experience I have had suggests to me that if the child has mainly a learning problem, and not much in the way of a behavior problem, he will respond to the very smallest dose or not at all. I've treated several children who had a good response to a very low dose, such as 5 mg of Ritalin a day.

*Dr. Klein:*    When we gave those children what might be questionably high doses of Ritalin, we got a very marked effect on psychological tests, such as the Porteus maze, but on achievement tests they showed no improvement and on school performance we got nothing over a 3-month, placebo control, double-blind trial.

By the way, we've since done another study that might interest you. One of the things that occurred to us was that since these children might have suffered from attention deficit all their lives, when you give them a drug that helps them with their attention deficit it's rather like giving somebody who's had one leg all his life a false leg and saying "Okay, now ride a bicycle." He hasn't learned the skills necessary to make use of the ability to attend. So we followed the study in which we gave Ritalin versus placebo with another study in which we used a lower dose of Ritalin and a three-group design. One group got specific remediation of a kind developed by some woman in New York plus placebo, another group received specific remediation plus Ritalin, and the third group got an attention control plus placebo. When we compared the specific remediation plus placebo against the attention control plus placebo groups, we found a specific remediation effect, so that we were able to demonstrate that the specific remediation was effective. But a comparison of the specific remediation plus placebo versus the specific remediation plus Ritalin groups showed no differences at all. The Ritalin didn't help the children any better. So that, in our hands at any rate, with children who are learning-disabled, normal in IQ, and specifically screened out for hyperkinesis, the drugs just weren't of help.

*Dr. Gallant:*    Why don't you keep on using methylphenidate instead of dextroamphetamine? Because it's more dopaminergic specifically?

*Dr. Klein:*    I don't think we have any good reasons for it.

*Dr. Arnold:*    I want to comment on that issue. In our comparison of levo- and dextroamphetamine, we found that on the Bender-Gestalt there was no difference between levoamphetamine performance and placebo but there was a significant difference between dextroamphetamine performance versus either levoamphetamine or placebo. Now, if levoamphetamine is dopaminergic, as Sol Snyder hypothesizes, and dextroamphetamine is both norepinephrinergic and dopaminergic, then that might suggest that a dopaminergic drug is not helpful for the kind of tasks that would be reflected in Bender-Gestalt performance, and if methylphenidate is indeed mainly dopaminergic you might get better results with dextroamphetamine than with Ritalin.

*Dr. Klein:* One of the things that Dr. Gallant recommended was a study of Pirebidil as being possibly pure dopaminergic drug, and that has been done by Rapoport. She found that Pirebidil was relatively ineffective with hyperkinetic children, so that's another fly in the dopaminergic ointment.

*Dr. Gallant:* Another problem is that Vince Siegal, in a comparison of levodopa versus dextrodopa, found no difference in learning disability at all.

*Dr. Monroe:* There has been very little comment here about lithium as a treatment. Dr. Klein, in terms of that study that you, Quitkin, and Rifkin did on your emotionally unstable disorder [EUD] group and their good response to lithium, it strikes me that your EUD sounds very much like some of the syndromes that were presented here. I was struck by your finding of the effectiveness of lithium. There is a tendency in the literature to decide that a patient who is a lithium responder has been misdiagnosed and is not schizophrenic or whatever, but really a cyclothymic. If you look in those articles that present any clinical data, they don't sound like bipolar at all, but like emotionally unstable disorder. I think this is a very interesting trend, and I was wondering whether anybody else has any experience.

*Dr. Wender:* I've got experience but I don't have any data. One of our residents began treating a group of people we now think of as adult hyperactives with lithium, and the same thing happened with them as happened with the children we treated at the NIMH; mainly, they got "stupid" and slowed down and thought this was a bad drug. Dr. Klein and I can't resolve our different results because his patients also had childhood histories of hyperactivity.

*Dr. Klein:* I would say the majority of them did. We found no correlation between history of childhood hyperactivity and drug effect. Also, there's a different sex ratio with the emotionally unstable characters, at least in our experience. They are mostly women, whereas the hyperkinetic children are mostly boys, so that it can't be a coterminus thing.

*Chairman Bellak:* I wonder if many of the psychotropic drugs aren't symptom specific rather than disorder specific, and whether in that case it isn't the antiaggressive action of lithium, for instance, that is effective in these particular patients. I think that many of the phenothiazines, for example, have nothing to do with schizophrenia but with some of the symptoms that they happen to alleviate. That would be my favorite explanation, that sometimes lithium is effective in people who suffer from a lack of impulse control, regardless of what the label may be.

*Dr. Arnold:* Just to confound the confusing number of options further, I'd like to throw out an idea. Harold Goldman has the hypothesis that the problem with MBD is not really minimal brain dysfunction but minimal peripheral nervous dysfunction in that the problem is not in the central nervous system but rather with catecholaminergic feedback loops in the sensory end organs, which because of insufficient inhibition run rampant and overdamp the peripheral stimulation. One of the interesting things about this idea is that the inhibition in the feedback loop for the cochlea is, I think, norepinephrinergic and for the retina is dopaminergic, or vice versa. One of my fantasies has been to take a look and see, when there's a difference in auditory and visual perception, if it's among the children who respond better to a dopaminergic or norepinephrinergic drug.

*Dr. Wender:* You're saying that they're understimulated?

*Dr. Arnold:* The hypothesis is that they're understimulated.

*(Unidentified):* That, of course, is contrary to all clinical experiences. These children get overexcited in stimulating environments.

*Dr. Greenspan:* Infant studies show that it takes a while before the peripheral sensory system becomes developed. Initially, in the first 3 months of life, it seems that regulation of behavior comes from more central areas of the central nervous system, and as myelinization proceeds, and also a certain kind of social and emotional behavior proceeds, you get a movement toward the periphery. Behavioral and neurophysiologic observations have shown that people are more sensitive to interpersonal clues in determining behavior after 3 months than, say, at 1½ months when the internal state is regulating. It just throws another observation into the pot of speculation, I suppose, but it's an interesting one in that it would mean that your suggestion is not inconsistent with your observations.

*Dr. Arnold:* Well, it's easy enough to test. There must be a drug that would have peripheral dopaminergic or norepinephrinergic effect that doesn't cross the blood-brain barrier.

*Dr. Wender:* Just administer epinephrine or norepinephrine—neither will pass the blood-brain barrier.

*Dr. Cole:* That gets us back to Dr. Schattner and his people, who found that nonlearning psychopaths learn with epinephrine.

*Dr. Arnold:* I'd like to mention one other thing. On doing soft sign exams I'm impressed with how many of these children have jerky eye movements. I get the uneasy feeling that the optometrists may really have something with their little swinging ball exercises and things and that maybe some of their accusations against the medical profession may have a little bit of basis in fact. In other words, that we're ignoring an important area.

One thing that's made me even more uneasy about this possibility is the recent findings by Vinod Bhatara and David Clark on vestibular stimulation. They found significant results on the parent and teacher behavior questionnaires, comparing sham treatment with systematic spinning in a chair under controlled conditions for two sessions a week for a month. One of the things that they found in looking at the postrotatory nystagmus is that the hyperkinetic children are different in their adaptation time constants for return of the eye movements to normal. They have a significantly longer latency period, a longer intersaccadic interval, than normal children, and after they've been subjected to the spinning treatment this tends to normalize, as well as their behavior. Of course, the vestibular system is closely tied in with eye movements.

*Dr. Cole:* Did they show that duration of response was about the same as with normals? Is this one of the things Hossain at Worcester State, who's working with schizophrenics, is concerned with?

*(Unidentified):* Hossain's observation was that when two things didn't go both ways in schizophrenics, an underreactive vestibular apparatus was consistently found. They all showed less response to being spun around or at least having cold water put in their ears than normal people did.

*Dr. Arnold:* Another thing is that these children did not get nauseated up to the age of 10 years. A normal 8- or 9-year-old will get nauseated like an adult, but these hyperkinetic children at that age did not. The four over 10 years old were not helped, and one of them did get nauseated.

*Chairman Bellak:* Any other comments?

*Dr. Monroe:* I wanted to bring up one other thing that probably reflects the heterogeneity of what we're talking about here today. In our dyscontrol symptom, or episodic psychosis, at one time or another, more frequently than not, imipramine seemed to make patients worse and actually precipitated seizures in several of them very quickly. They had been taking it for a day or two at relatively modest doses. Thus I was struck by the fact that imipramine is reported as being effective by so many of this group, when we found it's almost contraindicated in our group.

*Chairman Bellak:* Could your group have been more disturbed than the people we have been generally discussing? I mean neurologically speaking?

*Dr. Monroe:* These were, by and large, patients that were committed to the hospital and completely identified as having endogenous depression without a really good history being taken to show that they'd frequently had in their life very transient, but very intense, depressions, the kind that would last sometimes only for a few hours, even for a few minutes. They were now in one that was more prolonged and they were immediately put on the antidepressant, and then within 1 or 2 days they had a grand mal convulsion, the first they'd ever had in their lives. Then when you went back and got their history, you found many more characteristics of the dyscontrol syndrome. Two that had convulsions were put on anticonvulsants. One of them was on Mysoline and one was on Dilantin-phenobarb combination for 7 years and 5 years, respectively, with no recurrence of their depression.

*Chairman Bellak:* In effect, you're telling me that the neurologic problems were not so marked that they were hospitalized or referred for them. Is that correct?

*Dr. Monroe:* They were referred for their affective disorders, but they did have abnormal EEGs.

*Chairman Bellak:* Which would not be true for the majority of the patients we have been discussing, so that in that sense it was a sicker group, which might help explain that particular aspect.

*Dr. Greenspan:* I just wanted to shift the focus a little bit. I wonder if we don't need to look for better models to help generate some of the kinds of hypotheses that have been discussed. One model I'd like to suggest that has to do with understanding early development is to consider where the medication works, whether it's at the symptom level or some primary integrational level, to look at various levels of organization when we study, for example, nonresponders and responders. Let's say hyperkinetic children respond better than the nonhyperkinetic children with learning difficulties and consider a model that would explain that. For example, one might be that the children who are not hyperkinetic may have received certain kinds of early care whereby they learned to shift more from central CNS control to peripheral control. That is, they could attune to the environment better and receive feedback, and very early in life this may have made a change not only in their behavior but also in the way they organize the stimulus world at a CNS level. We've had, for example, very hyperreactive infants where a mother who tunes in rather well and is able to provide a rather nuturing rhythmical experience is able to help that infant establish basic cycles and rhythm. At 3 or 4 months that infant is better able to use social cues to organize his or her behavior. When the mother can't help the hyperactive infant in this way, he or she is still somewhat controlled from within and can't use social cues, can't tune in, can't organize as well at 3 or 4 months. You can see basic differences in the first year of life with people with similar constitutional styles, depending on environment. This leads to secondary and tertiary elaborations of these neurophysiologic behavioral organizations that may, in part, help explain individual differences among groups.

I wanted to comment briefly on some therapeutic principles that I have personally found helpful, which I want to elaborate in five quick steps. I think that by focusing only on the medication aspect, we miss how helpful we can be with appropriate psychotherapy. Often these individuals are difficult to treat with psychotherapy, either with or without medication, but we can help them to further develop and mature in terms of their overall psychosocial development.

First, establish a responsive fit, but not an overcontrolling one, and be respectful of their neurophysiologic patterns and individual differences.

Secondly, recognize unique individual differences in the CNS level of integration and help the patient clearly delineate these. For example, in the inanimate world we work by helping clarify that they have trouble reading for a long period of time, that they quickly lost track; there is nothing complex, like fights with their spouse or difficulties with their children. But in just sitting down with a book they can recognize some of their individual differences that are not related to difficult affective experience. Or some of them have a hard time listening to certain musical sounds—that's an auditory sensitivity. There are various other ways that they can get clues as to their own unique differences in terms of how they process stimulation in the inanimate world. Then you can delineate through clarifications how the same style may apply to their internal world of emotions and affects. They also have similar difficulties in processing and organizing experience in terms of interrelationships with their spouse, with their children, or over issues at work, or just feeling states that may occur to them. Then, delineate for them and with them arrive at defenses and coping styles and the way the person has elaborated this to his or her current point of development. Then, if one can tolerate a long enough engagement in a psychotherapy relationship to permit a transference, help these people deal with some core transferring states that frequently, I think, frighten the therapist. These have to do with the patient's passive longings, unmet early dependency needs, and fear of loss of control around early feelings of frustration, because it's so difficult for mothers, parents, families in general to establish a good nurturing environment for these kinds of children.

There's a lot of primitive rage. Now the patient often handles this primitive rage by wanting to protect the therapist; he or she has fear of destroying the therapist. You could trace back a lot of fear of destroying and losing the parents. Often the patient wants to leave therapy or have the medication increased if there's concomitant medication at this time. At this particular juncture it's very important not to jump to increasing the medication, shifting the therapeutic regimen, or changing the sequence of sessions, but rather to help work through this fear of losing control and the derivative affect states that are behind the fear.

I've done a number of consultations with people in psychotherapy who have been referred to me because I wrote an article about using medications and they want to get medication and get away from their therapist, and there are two kinds of countertransference tendencies that are stopping the therapists working with these patients. One is that the therapist became authoritarian and somewhat controlling of the patient, which is very similar to one style of parenting of these kinds of children. In other words, the parents overcontrol the child who can't control himself, which makes him very frustrated. The other is that the therapist became frightened of these primitive affect states, which involve not only aggressive but sexual feelings and passive sexual longings, and withdrew from the therapeutic relationship. The therapist actually, covertly, supports the patient's wish to get higher doses of medication or leave and form an alliance with another therapist.

It's very important to interpret acting-out at these particular junctures but to also maintain the therapeutic relationship, continually pointing out that there are certain intense feeling states that frighten the patient and showing willingness to be there in the room with the patient while these feeling states are experienced.

It's important to differentiate these kinds of individuals in treatment from the borderline individuals. Some differentiating characteristics are that these individuals do not generally have difficulty with self-object differentiation, do not fear fusing with the therapist. They're often fearful of something about their impulses and feeling states having some harmful effect on the therapist, and usually their hold on reality testing can be maintained if the therapist is willing to have a kind of holding environment for them.

*Chairman Bellak:*    Thank you very much. We still have a few minutes. I have one suggestion for what we might do with the next five minutes and that is to handle this problem that advertising agencies usually handle, namely, "What is the best name for the product?" Since none of us is happy with the labeling that's involved in MBD, do any of you have ideas for a more appropriate and less harmful label? My one suggestion is that we call it a syndrome, whatever else we call it. What else can anybody come up with?

*Dr. Gallant:*    I don't have any suggestions for what you call a syndrome. I do suggest using behavioral terms with a patient, such as "paroxysmal episodic dyscontrol." This is much more acceptable and less threatening to a patient. That's just a clinical point of view and obviously it's not meant to cover this very complex syndrome.

*Chairman Bellak:* Any other offers for something that would be a little easier to pronounce?

*Dr. Wender:* Hoffman syndrome.

*Chairman Bellak:* Hoffman syndrome runs counter to the trend of not using proper names, but all right.

*Dr. Cole:* Did I hear correctly?

*Dr. Cantwell:* Heinrich Hoffman. He was a German pediatrician who wrote a book in which there is not only fidgety Phil, but an anorexic, a firesetter, an enuretic, a number of others. I'm convinced that what he did was to write nursery rhymes about his patients.

*Chairman Bellak:* No child in the German culture grew up without learning about der Struwelpeter. So far we have two labels. Any more?

*Dr. Greenspan:* Perceptual integration dysfunction?

*Dr. Arnold:* Could I raise a question? Would people really object to using the term "adult minimal brain dysfunction" for the purpose of the monograph, since that seems to be the name commonly used to refer to the syndrome in children, even though we all realize that that will never be in DSM III? It seems to me that we're talking about two different things. One is a diagnostic category for the statistical manual, and another is a title of a monograph that will convey to other professional people what it's about.

*Chairman Bellak:* I think we're pretty well committed to that as a matter of communication, but it wouldn't be bad to come up with a better label for it.

*Dr. Monroe:* I have one objection to "paroxysmal episodic dyscontrol"—it's a little redundant with the paroxysmal in there. I've used just "episodic," but I'm not sure that's the same thing we're talking about today.

*Dr. Tucker:* I think that if we changed the name it really might not convey to the patient what we're talking about. It's a pretty well-established term, even though it doesn't mean anything.

*Chairman Bellak:* Thank you all very much for your contribution in papers and discussion. I will attempt to see if a subcommittee of members of this group might want to concern themselves with the coining of a more acceptable term for what, in view of the currently most widely accepted usage, we have called MBD or minimal brain dysfunction in arranging this conference.

# Index